Asbestos Litigation

Stephen J. Carroll, Deborah Hensler, Jennifer Gross,
Elizabeth M. Sloss, Matthias Schonlau, Allan Abrahamse,
J. Scott Ashwood

RAND INSTITUTE FOR CIVIL JUSTICE

The research described in this report was conducted by the RAND Institute for Civil Justice, a unit of the RAND Corporation.

Library of Congress Cataloging-in-Publication Data

Asbestos litigation / Stephen J. Carroll ... [et al.].
    p. cm.
    "MG-162."
    Includes bibliographical references.
    ISBN 0-8330-3078-7 (pbk.)
    1. Products liability—Asbestos—United States. 2. Asbestos industry—Law and legislation—United States. 3. Actions and defenses—United States. I. Carroll, Stephen J., 1940–

KF1297.A73A82 2005
344.7304'6335—dc22

2005012235

The RAND Corporation is a nonprofit research organization providing objective analysis and effective solutions that address the challenges facing the public and private sectors around the world. RAND's publications do not necessarily reflect the opinions of its research clients and sponsors.

RAND® is a registered trademark.

Published 2005 by the RAND Corporation
1776 Main Street, P.O. Box 2138, Santa Monica, CA 90407-2138
1200 South Hayes Street, Arlington, VA 22202-5050
201 North Craig Street, Suite 202, Pittsburgh, PA 15213-1516
RAND URL: http://www.rand.org/
To order RAND documents or to obtain additional information, contact
Distribution Services: Telephone: (310) 451-7002;
Fax: (310) 451-6915; Email: order@rand.org

RAND Institute for Civil Justice

The mission of the RAND Institute for Civil Justice (ICJ), a division of the RAND Corporation, is to improve private and public decisionmaking on civil legal issues by supplying policymakers and the public with the results of objective, empirically based, analytic research. The ICJ facilitates change in the civil justice system by analyzing trends and outcomes, identifying and evaluating policy options, and bringing together representatives of different interests to debate alternative solutions to policy problems. The Institute builds on a long tradition of RAND research characterized by an interdisciplinary, empirical approach to public policy issues and rigorous standards of quality, objectivity, and independence.

ICJ research is supported by pooled grants from corporations, trade and professional associations, and individuals; by government grants and contracts; and by private foundations. The Institute disseminates its work widely to the legal, business, and research communities, and to the general public. In accordance with RAND policy, all Institute research products are subject to peer review before publication. ICJ publications do not necessarily reflect the opinions or policies of the research sponsors or of the ICJ Board of Overseers. For additional information about the RAND Institute for Civil Justice, contact:

Robert T. Reville, Director
RAND Institute for Civil Justice
1776 Main Street, P.O. Box 2138
Santa Monica, CA 90407-2138
Phone: (310) 393-0411 x6786; Fax: (310) 451-6979
E-mail: Robert_Reville@rand.org
Web: www.rand.org/icj/

ICJ Board of Overseers

Preface

The RAND Institute for Civil Justice began analyzing asbestos litigation with an initial study in the early 1980s. That study was the first to examine the costs of and compensation for asbestos personal injury claims. It was followed by other research that addressed the courts' responses to asbestos litigation and a number of studies of mass tort litigation in general.

In spring 2001, the ICJ initiated a new study that would provide the most comprehensive description of what is now the longest-running mass tort litigation in U.S. history. In this study, we revisited the issues raised in the initial ICJ studies: How many claims have been filed and for what injuries? How are the cases litigated, and what are the consequences of court management strategies and lawyers' practices? How much is being spent on the litigation, and what is the balance between the compensation paid to claimants and the costs to deliver it? What are the economic effects of the litigation? Are there alternative strategies for resolving asbestos injury claims that would deliver adequate and fair compensation more efficiently?

We provided preliminary answers to these questions to the staff of the Senate Judiciary Committee and the House Judiciary Committee of the U.S. Congress in briefings on August 13 and 14, 2001. That briefing was documented in *Asbestos Litigation in the U.S.: A New Look at an Old Issue* (RAND Corporation, DB-362.0-ICJ, August 2001). We subsequently conducted extensive analyses of data, including confidential data provided by various participants in the litigation as well as published data and information gathered from interviews with plaintiff and defense attorneys, insurance-company claims managers, financial analysts, and court-appointed neutrals. We presented the preliminary results in a briefing to numerous audiences. That briefing was documented in *Asbestos Litigation Costs and Compensation: An Interim Report* (RAND Corporation, DB-397-ICJ, September 2002).

This monograph is the final report on the project. It builds on the previous briefings, includes results of more detailed analyses, and updates some of the data and results to summer 2004.

This monograph should be of interest to state and federal policymakers concerned with asbestos litigation. It should also be of interest to those involved in that litigation.

This research was funded by the RAND Institute for Civil Justice.

Contents

Figures

Tables

Summary

Asbestos litigation is the longest-running mass tort litigation in the United States. The litigation arose as a result of individuals' long-term and widespread exposure to asbestos, which can cause serious and sometimes fatal injuries, and as a result of many asbestos product manufacturers' failure to protect workers against exposure and failure to warn their workers to take adequate precautions against exposure. Over time, the history of the litigation has been shaped by changes in substantive and procedural law, the rise of a sophisticated and well-capitalized plaintiff bar, heightened media attention to litigation in general and toxic tort litigation in particular, and the information science revolution. In turn, asbestos litigation has made a significant contribution to the evolution of mass civil litigation.

Within the past few years, there have been sharp and unanticipated increases in the number of asbestos claims filed annually and the number and types of firms named as defendants. Some plaintiff attorneys have expressed concern about whether compensation is being divided fairly among claimants with varying degrees of injury severity, and many defendants claim that responsibility for paying compensation is not being allocated among defendants in proportion to culpability. Moreover, there are growing concerns on all sides that the cost of settling masses of claims filed in recent years will deplete funds needed to compensate claimants whose symptoms have not yet surfaced but who will eventually become seriously ill.

Study Purpose and Approach

This monograph describes asbestos litigation up through summer 2004. It addresses the following questions: What have been the patterns of past exposure to asbestos, and what are the current best epidemiological estimates of future asbestos disease? How has asbestos litigation progressed over time? How many claims were filed through 2002? What were the injuries and diseases asserted in those claims? How many defendants have been named in the litigation and how are they distributed among industries? How much have defendants spent on asbestos litigation? How much of the funds spent on asbestos litigation has been consumed by transaction costs and how much has gone to claimants? How many defendants have filed for bankruptcy? How has the current litigation system performed to date and are there alternative strategies that might deliver adequate and fair compensation more efficiently?

The key to addressing the study questions was gaining access to information that is widely dispersed and often highly confidential. There is no national registry of asbestos claimants. Federal courts collect data on asbestos cases, but most claims are not filed in federal courts but rather in state courts, which do not report such information. Most of the data on asbestos litigation are gathered by individual defendants and insurers with a stake in the litigation. RAND researchers gained access to a good deal of these data, as well as to some proprietary studies, from participants on both sides of the litigation—access that was granted under conditions of utmost confidentiality. The study team also conducted more than 60 interviews with key participants in the litigation, including plaintiff attorneys, corporate counsel, outside defense counsel, insurance company claims managers, investment analysts, and court-appointed "neutrals." Drawing upon RAND's previous research on asbestos litigation and other analyses that are publicly available, we synthesized information from all these sources, while acknowledging that we are providing only best estimates because the data are still far from complete.

Scope of Study

Our research focused on how the litigation system has been performing in resolving asbestos claims. Tens of millions of Americans were exposed to asbestos in the workplace over the past several decades. Given the available resources for this study, we could not examine the circumstances of those who were injured by asbestos or what employers, product manufacturers, and others did or failed to do to protect worker health and safety. Of those exposed to asbestos in the United States, more than 700,000 had brought claims through 2002 and almost as many more are likely to bring claims in the future. We focus on what happened to those who claimed injury from asbestos, what happened to the defendants in those cases, and how lawyers and judges have managed the cases.

Asbestos-Related Injuries

Millions of American workers have been exposed to asbestos. Although the dangers of asbestos were known well before World War II, many asbestos product manufacturers did not warn their employees of the risks of exposure or provide adequate protection for them. It was these failures that precipitated what has been called the worst occupational health disaster in U.S. history.

The injuries caused by asbestos exposure are mesothelioma, other cancers, asbestosis, and pleural abnormalities. Mesothelioma is a deadly cancer of the lining of the chest or abdomen for which asbestos is the only known cause. Lung cancer is the other frequently claimed malignant disease that can be caused by asbestos, although many other forms of cancer have been related to asbestos exposure, including leukemia, and cancers of the bladder, breast, colon, pancreas, and prostate. Of course, lung cancer has other causes as well. Asbestosis, a chronic lung disease resulting from inhalation of asbestos fibers, can be debilitating and even fatal. Pleural plaques, pleural thickening, and pleural effusion are abnormalities of the pleura, the membrane that lines the inside of the chest wall and covers the outside of the lung.

Estimating the incidence of these injuries is very difficult because so few data on them exist. Mesothelioma, for example, was not recorded as a cause of death on death certificates until 1999. Since that date, it is reported as a cause of death in only nine geographic areas (five states and four metropolitan areas) that may not be representative of the rest of the country. Lung cancer, on the other hand, is recorded on death certificates across the country, but we have no way of knowing how many of those deaths were caused by asbestos exposure. As for asbestosis, the National Institute for Occupational Safety and Health publishes limited data on deaths from this disease, but there is no record of the prevalence of nonfatal cases, which are far more common.

It is very difficult to estimate the number of asbestos-related injuries in the future because there is such a scant record of injuries that have already occurred. The long latency period before any symptoms are manifested—about 40 years, according to the Manville Personal Injury Settlement Trust (2001)—further complicates projections. It is therefore not surprising that published accounts of asbestos injuries make vastly different predictions of the numbers of people who will manifest asbestos injuries in the future. Litigators rely heavily on a study by Nicholson et al. (1982), which claimed that 228,795 deaths would occur from 1985 to 2009 as a result of cancer caused by extensive asbestos exposure from 1940 through 1979. But other studies have predicted far fewer cancer cases (one study estimates 39,385 to 41,985 during the same period).

Because Nicholson et al. (1982) and other studies used complicated models and required voluminous input—such as extensive labor-force data to estimate the number of asbestos workers—replication of their studies would be time-consuming and expensive. We did, however, conduct a limited test of Nicholson et al.'s projections as part of this study. Our approach was to compare Nicholson et al.'s mesothelioma predictions to the actual incidence rates for mesothelioma in the five years between 1977 and 1997 for which data exist from both the Nicholson et al. study and the National Cancer Institute's Surveillance, Epidemiology, and End Results (SEER)

Program. We found that Nicholson et al.'s projections are very close to the actual rates observed during those years. One implication of this finding is that the unanticipated increases in claims filings in recent years are more likely to be a result of changes in claiming behavior than differences between projected and actual rates of asbestos-related illness.

Litigation Dynamics

In most mass torts, once the dimensions of claimed injuries are understood, the parties in the litigation (with the courts' assistance) negotiate a settlement that resolves all or most claims, usually using some type of administrative scheme. The profile of asbestos litigation contrasts sharply with this conventional pattern. To date, notwithstanding extensive efforts over time, neither the parties nor the courts have arrived at a comprehensive settlement of asbestos claims. The litigation has not only persisted over a long period of time but also continually reshaped itself, in the process presenting new challenges to parties and courts. Law firms that played leading roles in the litigation in the 1980s have left the field and been replaced by new firms with new litigation strategies and business models. Trial judges developed innovative procedures in the 1980s to manage large asbestos caseloads. Some other judges subsequently emulated those procedures; others have substituted different procedures of their own. The focus of the litigation has shifted from federal to state courts, and now, increasingly, to bankruptcy courts. Corporations that initially were perceived to have little or no exposure to asbestos-related liability now find themselves at the center of the litigation. We analyzed the key dimensions of these litigation dynamics so that policymakers seeking to understand how best to address asbestos-related injuries could understand why the litigation has evolved as it has and its key features today.

In the past several years, the most significant developments in asbestos case processing have been the failure of global class action settlements, the reemergence of deferred dockets as a popular court management tool, the increased frequency and scale of consolidated trials, and the increased use of bankruptcy reorganization to develop administrative processes for resolving current and future claims.

The Failure of Global Settlement Efforts

When federal asbestos cases were transferred to Judge Charles Weiner by the Judicial Panel on Multidistrict Litigation (JPMDL) in 1991, many asbestos lawyers anticipated that Judge Weiner would help parties negotiate a global settlement of all federal cases against all defendants that would in turn provide a model for resolving state cases. Ultimately, the search for a single overarching settlement failed. Instead, a consortium of about 20 major asbestos defendants negotiated two settlements with leading asbestos plaintiff attorneys under the aegis of the transferee court, one a "private" (not judicially supervised) settlement of all claims those attorneys then had pending against the defense consortium and the second, a class action settlement of *all claims that might be brought in the future by any plaintiff (and plaintiff attorney)* against the consortium. The class action settlement provoked sharp attack from lawyers who were not part of the negotiated agreements, public interest attorneys, and legal ethicists. When the settlement was rejected by the U.S. Supreme Court in *Amchem Products v. Windsor* (521 U.S. 591 [1997]), and when the Court subsequently rejected a similar class settlement of asbestos claims against another major defendant in *Ortiz v. Fibreboard Corp.* (527 U.S. 815 [1999]), efforts to achieve a global resolution of asbestos litigation through class action litigation collapsed.

After the failure of the *Amchem* and *Ortiz* settlements, the landscape of asbestos litigation began to change. Filings surged, and many of the asbestos product manufacturers that plaintiff attorneys had traditionally targeted as lead defendants filed for bankruptcy. Plaintiff attorneys sought out new defendants and pressed defendants that they had heretofore treated as peripheral to the litigation for more money. With new firms engaged in litigating on the plaintiffs' behalf, and new corporations drawn into the litigation or assuming a more central role, old understandings about how to deal with asbestos cases began to unravel.

Deferred and Expedited Dockets

Courts are faced with large asbestos caseloads that include a large fraction of cases involving claimants who are not currently functionally impaired but who do have a legally cognizable injury and, hence, face a statute of limitations bar in many jurisdictions if they fail to file a claim within a specified time period. In response to this situation, some courts have established deferred dockets (sometimes called "inactive dockets" or "pleural registries"), which enable unimpaired asbestos plaintiffs to satisfy statutes of limitation by filing their lawsuits but delay processing and resolving those lawsuits until the plaintiffs' injuries have progressed further. Nonmalignant claims are removable from the deferred docket only if they meet prespecified clinical criteria (e.g., diagnosis of malignancy, certain radiological exam results, and certain pulmonary function test ratings) or if a claimant's lawyer is otherwise able to persuade the court that a claim should be activated. State courts in Massachusetts, Cook County, Illinois, and Baltimore established deferred dockets in the late 1980s and early 1990s. Courts that have established inactive dockets in recent years include New York City, Seattle, and Madison County, Illinois, all of which now have substantial numbers of asbestos cases on their inactive dockets. In a variation on this policy, some courts have established "expedited dockets" that give priority to cancer claims, placing the claims of those without functional impairment at the back of the queue.

Although pleural registries preserve plaintiffs' right to pursue compensation in the future, they do not provide compensation for whatever losses the plaintiffs might already have suffered or for monitoring their health going forward. In courts in which discovery does not begin until a case is transferred from the deferred to the regular (active) docket, attorneys who have agreed to represent plaintiffs who are not currently functionally impaired do not have to invest time and money to investigate the case. But the plaintiff lawyers who represent non-impaired plaintiffs also cannot secure fees immediately, making it harder for them to spread the risks of litigating more serious cases and perhaps making it less financially attractive for them to represent asbestos plaintiffs generally. From the defendants' perspective, pleural registries are attractive because they reduce the number of claims paid out annually by eliminating payments for those who are not functionally impaired. In jurisdictions in which placement on pleural registries is mandated, if nondisabled plaintiffs never develop injuries that meet the criteria necessary to be removed from the registry, defendants will pay fewer claims in total over time and likely less in total compensation to all those who have been exposed to asbestos.

Trial Consolidation

Federal and state courts have struggled to manage asbestos caseloads more efficiently to reduce private and public transaction costs. Over the years, judges have come to believe that the key to managing asbestos litigation is aggregation. Aggregative techniques in asbestos litigation have included informal group settlement processes, multidistrict litigation under 28 U.S.C. §1407, and state multidistrict rules, class actions (which have only rarely been sustained), and consolidation under F.R.C.P. 42 and its state counterparts.

In recent years, mass trial consolidations in asbestos litigation have been the subject of great controversy. According to *Mealey's Litigation Report: Asbestos,* from 1993 to 2001 there were 526 jury trials that reached verdicts on 1,570 plaintiffs' claims. About 60 percent of the trials involved a single claim; most of the remainder involved fewer than ten claims. But the proportion of all *claims* that were tried individually was only about one-quarter; about half were tried in groups of six or more. In comparing claims tried individually with claims tried in small groups, we found little difference in outcomes.

In some instances, judges have consolidated hundreds or thousands of asbestos claims for trial. There is little or no case law regarding the selection of representative parties for nonclass consolidated trials, and judges appear to make the selection on an ad hoc basis. In large-scale consolidations, some judges select a few representative cases for trial of liability and other crosscutting issues. The jury decides those issues and then decides damages (if necessary) in the representative cases. The jury's decisions on the crosscutting issues are applied to *all* cases in the consolidation, and other juries then hear damages issues in the other cases that are part of the consolidation. From 1993 to 2001, we identified 14 large-scale consolidated trials involving 100 claims or more. Each of these large-scale consolidated trials was complex; some were extraordinarily complex.

Trying thousands of cases together raises due process questions for plaintiffs and defendants alike. If, as is common, the liability phase is tried first with representative plaintiffs, and the jury decides in favor of the defendant, all of the plaintiffs lose. Defendants, however, believe that large-scale consolidation tilts the playing field against them. Many judges have also expressed doubts about the appropriateness of mass consolidations. We were able to determine at least some trial outcomes for 13 of the 14 large-scale consolidation trials we identified. Six resulted in a mix of plaintiff and defense verdicts, six resulted in plaintiffs' verdicts in all cases against some or all defendants, and one resulted in defense verdicts.

Bankruptcy Litigation

Since the early 1980s, asbestos litigation in federal and state courts has played out against a background of parallel litigation in the bankruptcy courts, which has influenced the primary litigation against non-bankrupt defendants and, in turn, has been shaped by that litigation. When the Manville Corporation filed for bankruptcy in 1982, it temporarily disrupted asbestos litigation patterns, as plaintiffs and non-bankrupt defendants alike sought to prevent the stay of litigation against Manville, which had until then been the lead defendant in the litigation. The difficulties attendant in estimating Manville's liability exposure highlighted for non-bankrupt defendants the difficulties of estimating their own future liabilities. The Manville bankruptcy reorganization at first provided cautionary lessons on the use of bankruptcy to resolve asbestos claims. But after Congress amended the bankruptcy statute to facilitate the creation of post-bankruptcy trusts to resolve claims, many looked to the Manville Trust as a model for aggregating claims and capping corporate liability exposure due to asbestos even for those corporations that were not at the time facing bankruptcy themselves.

When increasing asbestos claims rates encouraged scores of defendants to file Chapter 11 petitions in the late 1990s, the resulting stays in litigation against those defendants drove plaintiff attorneys to press peripheral non-bankrupt defendants to shoulder a larger share of the value of asbestos claims and to widen their search for other corporations that might be held liable for the costs of asbestos exposure and disease. In turn, the surge of filings for reorganization under Chapter 11 of the bankruptcy code may have provided an additional incentive for some asbestos plaintiff law firms to file large numbers of claims: Under Section 524(g) of the bankruptcy code, a proposed reorganization plan must obtain support from 75 percent of current asbestos claimants to win court approval, meaning that law firms that represent large numbers of claimants will wield the most power over the reorganization negotiations.

As bankruptcy proceedings have expanded to include most of the original lead defendants in asbestos litigation and scores of other companies besides, bankruptcy litigation has come increasingly to mirror the primary litigation in federal and state courts. Borrowing from case management practices in trial courts, district courts have consolidated multiple bankruptcy reorganizations and assigned mass tort "specialist" judges to preside over them. Parties have sought to transfer related claims to bankruptcy courts in the hope of achieving an attractive global resolution of those claims. One judge ordered that claimants with cancer would have their claims processed before claimants with non-cancer claims, essentially establishing an expedited docket. And seemingly borrowing a page from the controversial "futures" settlements that were rejected by the U.S. Supreme Court in *Amchem* and *Ortiz*, lawyers have sought to fashion resolutions of bankruptcy claims against a number of major corporations that offer attractive settlements of current claims in exchange for support for reorganization plans that will determine payments of other claimants far into the future.

Claimants

We used data from a number of sources, with much of the data provided to us on a confidential basis, to estimate the numbers of people who filed asbestos personal injury claims through 2002. Our primary findings are as follows:

- **Approximately 730,000 people had filed an asbestos claim through 2002.**
- **The number of claims filed annually has increased sharply in the past few years.** Annual claims against major defendants have increased sharply over 1990s. For example, defendants who were receiving 10,000 to 20,000 claims per year in the early 1990s were receiving three to five times as many claims per year by the year 2000. Increasing numbers of claimants primarily reflect rising awareness of asbestos-related injury and of the availability of legal remedies, most likely resulting from increasing access to information (e.g., from the Internet) and lawyer advertising.
- **Claimants with nonmalignant injuries account for most of the growth in claims.** Throughout the 1980s, claims of all types grew at approximately the same rate. But beginning in the early 1990s, the number of people asserting a nonmalignant injury, including those with little or no current functional impairment, grew much faster than the annual number of new claimants asserting some form of cancer. Nonmalignant claims accounted for roughly 80 percent of all claims entering the system through the 1980s. The fraction of claims that asserted nonmalignant conditions began to grow in the early 1990s, rising to more than 90 percent of annual claims in the late 1990s and early 2000s.
- **The number of claimants with mesothelioma has been increasing in recent years.** Although the absolute numbers of claims for mesothelioma—a virulent form of cancer for which asbestos exposure is the only known cause—are very small, they have been growing. Since 1994, more of such claims have been filed

each year, resulting in a doubling of mesothelioma claims in the eight-year period to 2002.

- **Some evidence suggests that most nonmalignant claimants are currently unimpaired.** Based on the available data, it appears that a large and growing proportion of the claims entering the system in recent years were submitted by individuals who at the time of filing had not suffered an injury that had as yet affected their ability to perform the activities of daily living, although they had suffered a legally cognizable injury.
- **Claims filed by workers in "nontraditional" industries who were exposed to asbestos are increasing.** Early in asbestos litigation (the decade or so following *Borel v. Fibreboard* [493 F.2d 1076 (5th Cir.)] in 1973), most claims came from workers who were exposed to asbestos in industries such as asbestos mining and manufacturing, shipyards, railroads, and construction, where they worked in enclosed tight quarters in an atmosphere thick with asbestos fibers. Participants in the litigation call these the "traditional" industries. Now many claims come from workers who were exposed to asbestos while working in other industries, such as textiles, paper, glass, and food and beverage, where they typically did not handle asbestos but asbestos was present in the atmosphere.

Defendants

This study produced the following findings regarding asbestos litigation defendants:

- **At least 8,400 entities have been named as asbestos defendants through 2002.** This number is probably an underestimate, because the sources we used to verify the names of defendants do not list firms that did not exist in 2002, even though they may have existed at some prior date. Thus, this number does not include firms that were named as defendants at some time before 2002 but then subsequently ceased doing business under the names they had when they were named as defendants.
- **Defendants are distributed across most U.S. industries.** Using the U.S. Department of Commerce Standard Industrial Classification (SIC) system, we found that 75 out of 83 different industries listed at the 2-digit level in the SIC system included at least one entity that had been named as an asbestos litigation defendant.
- **But the litigation is concentrated in eight industries.** Although asbestos litigation is widespread throughout the U.S. economy, only eight industries individually account for 4 percent or more of the firms that have been named as defendants. Many industries include only a few firms that have been named as

defendants. Each of 49 industries includes fewer than 1 percent of the firms named as defendants.

Costs and Compensation

We estimated the amount of money spent on asbestos litigation from its inception in the 1960s through the end of 2002, including the total amount spent on personal injury claims and the proportion of those costs that ended up in claimants' pockets. The components of those costs are as follows (see Figure S.1).

- **Total Spending.** Total spending on asbestos litigation through 2002 was about $70 billion. This sum is the amount defendants spent after being reimbursed from insurers plus the amount insurers spent after being reimbursed by reinsurers.
- **Defense Transaction Costs.** Total spending is broken down into defense transaction costs and the gross compensation paid to claimants. Defense transaction costs include the costs defendants and insurers incurred in all asbestos-related litigation, including litigation with other defendants and insurers. These costs amounted to more than $21 billion by the end of 2002, or about 31 percent of total spending.
- **Gross Compensation.** Gross compensation equaled about $49 billion, or about 69 percent of total spending. Average compensation for mesothelioma claims has increased sharply since the early 1990s.
- **Claimants' Transaction Costs.** Claimants' transaction costs added up to about $19 billion, or 27 percent of total spending through 2002.
- **Claimants' Net Compensation.** We estimate that claimants' net compensation through 2002 equaled about $30 billion, which is about 42 percent of total spending.

Estimates of the number of people who will file claims in the future—and the costs of those claims—vary widely. However, all accounts agree that, at most, only about three-quarters of the final number of claimants have come forward.

Figure S.1
Components of Asbestos Litigation Cost and Compensation

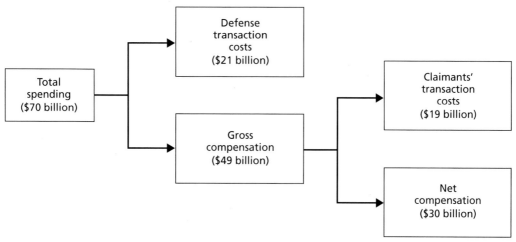

RAND *MG162-S.1*

NOTE: Dollar figures are approximate.

Bankruptcies

The costs of asbestos litigation to date and the prospect of future costs have led many firms to file for bankruptcy. This study produced the following findings regarding asbestos-related bankruptcies:

- **Bankruptcies are becoming more frequent.** Following 1976, the year of the first bankruptcy attributed to asbestos litigation, 19 bankruptcies were filed in the 1980s and 17 in the 1990s. Between 2000 and mid-2004, there were 36 bankruptcy filings, more than in either of the prior two decades. At least 73 firms that had been named on a substantial number of asbestos claims had filed for bankruptcy through mid-2004.
- **Bankruptcy reorganization can be a major drain on defendants' resources.** The academic literature on bankruptcy shows that the cost of reorganization is equal to about 3 percent of the average firm's book value or about 6 percent of a firm's market value.
- **Bankruptcy can impose costs on the filing firm's labor force.** An analysis by Stiglitz et al. (2002) of the effects of asbestos-related bankruptcy filings through September 2002 estimated that the bankruptcy filings resulted in the loss of 52,000 to 60,000 jobs and that the workers displaced by these bankruptcies will lose, on average, an estimated $25,000 to $50,000 over their lifetimes. The

Stiglitz study also estimated that workers at bankrupt firms with 401(k) plans lost, on average, about 25 percent of the value of those plans.

- **The economic effect of asbestos litigation extends well beyond the bankruptcy of a number of firms.** Defendants that have not filed for bankruptcy have nonetheless incurred asbestos litigation costs. As a result, these firms may reduce their investment levels. Reductions in investments, in turn, can lead to reductions in the creation of new jobs.

Is There a Better Way?

Efforts to improve the resolution of asbestos litigation implicate strongly held views about the tort system, which has traditionally been the primary vehicle in the United States for compensating victims of injurious behavior by others and an important tool for regulating corporate behavior. Traditionally, the tort system in the United States has been viewed as having three objectives: compensation, deterrence, and individualized corrective justice.

In theory, the system properly compensates injury victims for their losses, properly calibrates defendants' incentives to avoid injuring others, and provides a sense that "justice has been done" through individualized consideration of each plaintiff's and defendant's situation. Moreover, as a common law (rather than statutory) system, tort liability has proved remarkably adaptable to changing social, cultural, and technological trends. The commitment of tort law to "make victims whole," deter injurious behavior, and provide individuals with their "day in court," as well as its adaptability to change, is generally seen as the justification for the tort system's transaction costs, which are understood to be considerably higher than the costs associated with delivering benefits through administrative systems, such as workers' compensation and social insurance schemes.

How Well Is the Tort System Working for Asbestos Litigation?

Most of the factual data that are reported in this monograph are not disputed by participants in asbestos litigation. The sharp differences between and among plaintiff attorneys, defense counsel, defendant corporations, and insurers derive primarily from differences in assessments of the performance of the tort system among various parties who have stakes in the litigation.

Compensation
Typically, the high costs of tort litigation screen out of the system the majority of claims for minor injuries and modest losses. In asbestos litigation, however, mass liti-

gation strategies have effectively opened the courts to everyone who can prove exposure to asbestos and demonstrate a legally cognizable injury. As asbestos litigation has continued, an increasingly large fraction of those who have come forward and found representation are not currently functionally impaired, although they do meet the legal standard for a compensable injury.

Some participants in asbestos litigation, and some observers also, view asbestos claimants' increased access to the courts (in comparison with other tort victims) as a positive achievement, fulfilling—at least in this instance—the promise of tort law. Others argue that opening the system so widely jeopardizes the ability of the tort system to compensate claimants who will come forward in the future, some of whom will have serious or fatal injuries.

To our knowledge, there is no published research comparing the total compensation received by asbestos plaintiffs with their economic loss, nor were we able to obtain such data for our study. It is certain that many of the asbestos personal injury trusts established as a result of Chapter 11 bankruptcy reorganizations pay only a small fraction of the agreed-upon value of plaintiffs' claims; there is no reason to believe that the reorganizations currently in process will yield vastly different outcomes. However, how these diminished payments resulting from bankruptcy will affect adequacy of compensation is uncertain, as shortfalls in compensation from bankrupt defendants may be compensated by increased compensation from corporations that are newly drawn into the litigation.

Deterrence

It is indisputable that the asbestos manufacturers that were the prime targets of litigation through the 1980s were responsible for widespread asbestos exposure. As the litigation spread to companies outside the asbestos and building products industries, however, the culpability of the defendants called upon to pay asbestos victims is more in dispute. From a deterrence perspective, the issue is not whether asbestos victims should be able to receive compensation from some entity, but rather what entity should fairly be called upon to shoulder the financial burden. Requiring companies that played a relatively small role in exposing workers to asbestos to bear substantial costs of compensating for asbestos injuries not only raises fundamental questions of fairness but undercuts the deterrence objectives of the tort system. If business leaders believe that tort outcomes have little to do with their own behavior, then there is no reason for them to shape their behavior so as to minimize tort exposure.

Individualized Treatment

In asbestos litigation, individualized justice is a myth. Most cases are settled rather than tried, and many are settled according to standardized agreements negotiated by defendants and plaintiff attorneys. (In fact, many plaintiff attorneys conventionally refer to their "inventories" of cases.) Under such agreements, all cases against some defendants may be settled for a flat fee, while cases against other defendants will be sorted into a "matrix" of claims, according to a few distinguishing characteristics, and paid the value associated with that matrix cell. Bankruptcy personal injury trusts, which will pay an increasing share of asbestos compensation in the future, institutionalize this administrative compensation process for asbestos claims.

Among the small numbers of asbestos claims that reach trial, a majority is tried in group form, along with a few or more like or unlike claims. Sometimes, more than a hundred claims may be tried together; sometimes, the trial of a few claims will decide critical outcomes for thousands more. Claims against multiple defendants, in arguably quite different circumstances, may also be tried together. Although consolidated trials are not unique to asbestos litigation, they do appear to be more prevalent, of a larger scale, and more complex in asbestos litigation.

Alternative Strategies

Any effort to devise an alternative to tort for resolving asbestos claims must address the very same questions that have complicated resolution of the claims through tort: How many claims will come forward in the future? What will be the distribution of claims by severity of injury? What are the proper standards for allocating compensation among those with diverse injuries, ranging from nondisabling pleural scarring to fatal mesothelioma? How should the responsibility for paying for these injuries be allocated among those who manufactured or distributed asbestos products or operated workplaces in which asbestos was present?

For the past several years, plaintiff and defense attorneys, defendant corporations and insurers, labor unions, and the allies of all these groups have worked in different combinations and contexts to consider alternative strategies for resolving future asbestos claims. Two competing strategies emerged from these reform efforts, neither of which was able to secure sufficient support for passage in the 108th Congress (2003–2004). Both strategies have been put forward again in the 109th Congress. In lieu of federal reform, critics of current asbestos litigation processes look either to state legislatures and courts or to bankruptcy proceedings and personal injury trusts to improve the resolution of asbestos claims in the future.

Congressional Reforms

Medical Criteria. One reform strategy, supported by the American Bar Association, seeks to limit compensation for asbestos disease to plaintiffs whose injuries met certain specified medical criteria. In essence, this proposal would prevent people who are not currently functionally impaired and do not have an asbestos-related cancer from claiming compensation in the tort liability system, even if they have clinical evidence of asbestos exposure—e.g., pleural scarring—that under current state law in many jurisdictions would allow them to seek compensation. To its supporters, the medical criteria approach has the benefit of making arguably minimal changes in the tort liability system, leaving questions of how to deal with all those claims that meet the medical criteria and remain within the litigation system to state tort doctrine and procedural rules.

Because it would prevent many asbestos-exposed workers who are currently eligible for compensation from claiming compensation in the future unless and until they met the specified criteria, this reform strategy has been opposed by those who represent these workers, including many asbestos plaintiff attorneys and labor union leaders. Some defendant corporations and insurers also are reluctant to support the medical criteria proposal because they fear that the costs of compensating mesothelioma claimants and other seriously injured claimants might be so high in the future as to offset any economic benefits to them that might accrue from eliminating unimpaired claims from the liability system.

Trust Fund. With the success of the medical criteria proposal in doubt, many defendant corporations and insurers began to pursue an alternative strategy that would eliminate tort liability for asbestos claimants entirely and substitute an administrative compensation program, funded by defendant corporations and insurers (i.e., a trust fund). Unlike the medical criteria approach, which would leave each defendant to respond to the suits that remain within the tort system as the defendant sees fit, the administrative compensation program strategy requires that defendant corporations and insurers agree on a funding formula. To achieve consensus, defendant corporations and insurers have had to grapple with the same questions that have challenged designers of asbestos personal injury trusts in Chapter 11 proceedings and those who have sought to negotiate long-term settlements of asbestos litigation outside of bankruptcy: How many claimants will appear in the future? How much should each defendant and potential defendant pay?

With the federal government unwilling to act as guarantor of the compensation program, payors' and claimants' representatives need to consider what might happen if the amount originally negotiated proves to be inadequate. Some defendants also worried that eligibility was too broadly defined. Unlike previous trust fund proposals, the one debated in the 108th Congress did not limit compensation to cancer victims and those with a severe respiratory impairment. As negotiations continued, the price tag for the proposed fund mounted to a level that some were unwilling to support, and the parties were not able to reach agreement on a formula before the time for congressional action expired. Now the 109th Congress has taken up the trust fund proposal again.

State Reforms

With the success of congressional initiatives in doubt, by the end of 2004, asbestos litigation reformers were turning their attention to the states. Medical criteria statutes were introduced into state legislatures in Louisiana, Ohio, and Texas. Legislation limiting successor liability, adopted previously in Pennsylvania, was adopted in Texas as well. Venue rules that had invited large-scale consolidations in Mississippi were amended, and stricter venue rules were also adopted in Texas. Together, these changes may temper the rise in frequency of claiming for asbestos diseases. But such efforts are likely to leave in place a patchwork of tort doctrine and mass litigation procedural rules that promises continuing variation in asbestos outcomes for plaintiffs and defendants and would do little to mitigate the high transaction costs of asbestos litigation.

Bankruptcy Proceedings and Personal Injury Trusts

With an increasing number of corporations in Chapter 11 bankruptcy proceedings, some observers have suggested that the personal injury trusts that usually result from reorganization offer the most promising means of resolving asbestos claims quickly and with lower transaction costs, particularly if the debtors and tort creditors negotiate "prepackaged bankruptcies" before a formal petition for Chapter 11 is filed. "Prepacks" have the potential to substantially shorten the Chapter 11 process, which historically has averaged about six years for asbestos defendants. But some plans that have emerged from pre-pack processes have proved to be controversial, resulting in lengthy appellate processes and ancillary litigation. Moreover, some of these plans have been challenged on grounds of unfairness to certain classes of asbestos plaintiffs. Whether bankruptcy proceedings and personal injury trusts will significantly improve the resolution of asbestos claims is uncertain.

Acknowledgments

We owe thanks to many people for an enormous amount of help. We are particularly indebted to RAND colleagues John Adams and David Kanouse, who reviewed drafts of both this report and our earlier studies and provided numerous helpful comments. We also benefited from comments and suggestions offered by the members of the ICJ Board of Overseers and by many participants in asbestos litigation who reviewed this report and our earlier studies.

We also received valuable advice at various stages of the research from experts and analysts who have studied asbestos litigation. We particularly thank David Austern of the Manville Personal Injury Settlement Trust, Jennifer Biggs and Michael Angelina of Tillinghast-Towers Perrin, Raji Bhagavatula of Milliman USA, and Frederick Dunbar of NERA for their help.

A great many people have contributed to our understanding of the workings of asbestos litigation. We cannot name every person who spent time with us; the list would be very long, and several of our conversations were on a non-attribution basis. We thank the many plaintiff and defense attorneys and representatives of public and private organizations who shared their perspectives and concerns with us. And we thank the people involved in the day-to-day activities of asbestos litigation who devoted many hours of their time to helping us understand how asbestos litigation works in practice.

For some analyses, we used confidential data provided to us by participants in the litigation. Because we agreed not to disclose the identities of those who provided data to us, we cannot explicitly acknowledge their assistance here. But we could not have conducted this analysis without the data they provided.

Finally, at RAND, we thank Laura Zakaras for helping us with the structure and clarity of this report, Christopher Dirks for his technical help on earlier versions of this document, and Nancy DelFavero, whose editorial expertise greatly improved the overall quality of this report.

Acronyms

ABA	American Bar Association
AMA	American Medical Association
ATSDR	Agency for Toxic Substances and Disease Registry
CCR	Center for Claims Resolution
EPA	Environmental Protection Agency
JNOV	judgment notwithstanding the verdict
JPMDL	Judicial Panel on Multidistrict Litigation
KBR	Kellogg, Brown & Root
MDL	multidistrict litigation
NIOSH	National Institute for Occupational Safety and Health
NSP	National Settlement Program
NYSE	New York Stock Exchange
OSHA	Occupational Safety and Health Administration; Occupational Safety and Health Act
SEC	Securities and Exchange Commission
SEER	Surveillance, Epidemiology, and End Results Program (National Cancer Institute)
SIC	Standard Industrial Classification (U.S. Department of Commerce)
UNR	Union Asbestos and Rubber
USG	U.S. Gypsum Company

CHAPTER ONE

Introduction

In 1973, asbestos manufacturers were found strictly liable to workers injured as a result of exposure to their products (*Borel v. Fibreboard*, Fifth Circuit, U.S. Court of Appeals, 1973). Following that decision, increasing numbers of product liability claims against asbestos manufacturers flowed into the courts. By the early 1980s, more than 20,000 claimants had initiated lawsuits alleging injuries from exposure to asbestos. The growing volume of this type of litigation began to attract the attention of public policymakers.

Many of those involved in asbestos litigation devised procedures to streamline the litigation process and reduce the burdens and costs they faced. Courts developed formal and informal approaches to managing asbestos litigation. A series of court decisions resolved most of the coverage disputes between defendants and insurers. Many defendants chose not to aggressively contest liability and instead negotiated settlements of large numbers of cases with leading plaintiff attorney firms. These agreements typically called for settling hundreds or thousands of cases per year at amounts specified in administrative "schedules" that reflected differences in injury severity and other characteristics deemed to affect the value of cases. Asbestos litigation continued to be a critical concern for the firms frequently named as defendants, but at the time there were only a few dozen firms in this position. Most observers tended to view asbestos litigation as "manageable" in the sense that the effects of the litigation were largely limited to those few dozen or so defendants. Asbestos litigation became a lower priority on the national political agenda.

In the past decade, however, and particularly in the past few years, the situation has changed dramatically. Sharp increases in the number of asbestos claims filed annually, the number and types of firms named as defendants, the costs of the litigation to these defendants and their insurers, and the number of firms filing for bankruptcy have reawakened policy concerns. In particular, there are growing concerns that these trends put at risk the compensation of future claimants who suffer from serious injuries. Asbestos litigation poses challenges for asbestos-injury victims seeking compensation, plaintiff attorneys representing those claimants, defendants who must respond to the litigation while protecting shareholders' interests, insurers who must cover the losses, and financial institutions attempting to accurately assess the magnitude of current losses and future liabilities. Because of the number of people exposed to asbestos in the United States, the injuries those people have incurred, the financial losses attendant to those injuries and the ensuing litigation, and the potential economic impact of that litigation, asbestos litigation also poses unique challenges for the civil justice system.

This RAND Institute for Civil Justice (ICJ) study is intended to provide objective data and analysis to stakeholders and policymakers so that they can address the key policy questions: How well is the current process working? Can it be improved?

Research Objectives

A clear understanding of the dimensions of asbestos litigation is essential to the design of an effective policy response to the litigation. What do past patterns of asbestos exposure tell us about the number of future claims that can be anticipated? How has the litigation evolved over time? How many claims are being filed? By whom? Against whom? For what injuries? How much are claimants recovering? How many defendants have been charged with responsibility, and what industries do they represent? How many bankruptcies have been attributed to asbestos litigation, and what are the overall economic effects of the litigation? More generally, what does the future hold? This study set out to answer those questions to the extent possible given the limitations in the data available.

Scope of This Study

As the questions posed in the previous section suggest, this study focuses on how the litigation system is performing in resolving asbestos claims. Within the available time and given the available resources, we could not examine the circumstances of those who were injured by asbestos exposure, nor could we investigate what companies that have been defendants in the litigation did or did not do to protect the health and safety of workers. Tens of millions of Americans were exposed to asbestos in the workplace over the past several decades. Of those, more than 700,000 have brought claims, and just as many, and possibly even more, claimants may come forward with claims in the future. We focus on what happened to those who claimed injury and what happened to the defendants in those cases.

Research Approach

The critical challenge to conducting research on asbestos litigation is that so little data are publicly available. There is no national registry of asbestos claimants. Some claims are not filed formally in court as lawsuits. Federal courts report the number of asbestos lawsuits filed, but in recent years most lawsuits have been filed in state courts, which do not routinely identify and report annual asbestos lawsuit filings.

The typical asbestos claimant brings a claim against many defendants. In recent years, defendants have typically named several dozen defendants, and each of those defendants generally settles claims separately and keeps its own records. Any one defendant knows about the claims against it and its settlements, but it usually does not know how much other defendants are paying on a claim. Claimants may receive money from settlements over a long period of time. They may settle with some defendants today and other defendants next year and still others later on down the line.

Further, because there are so many conflicting interests, and because so much money is involved, even the limited data possessed by those involved in the litigation are viewed as highly sensitive and confidential. So, answers to simple questions such as how many claims are there? and what does the litigation cost? are not readily available.

We approached this problem in a number of ways. First, we drew on data and knowledge gained in previous RAND Corporation research on asbestos and other mass toxic tort litigation (Kakalik et al., 1983; Kakalik et al., 1984; Hensler et al., 1985; Peterson and Selvin, 1991; Hensler, 1992; Hensler and Peterson, 1993; Hensler, 1995; Hensler et al., 2000). We drew on the knowledge we acquired in these studies to establish historical and interpretative contexts for new information.

Second, we collected publicly available data from a variety of sources, ranging from asbestos litigation reporters to corporations' Securities and Exchange Commission (SEC) filings. Where we found inconsistencies, we either note them or did not make use of the data. When corporations attribute their filing for bankruptcy to asbestos litigation, they often report the number of asbestos claims filed against them in their bankruptcy petitions. We obtained these data as well. Asbestos bankruptcy trusts (entities that are formed to pay asbestos claims after Chapter 11 reorganization) typically report the number of claims filed against them to the court that has jurisdiction over the bankruptcy. All of these records are public, although they are not always easy to locate.

Third, we obtained both public and confidential analyses from many of the financial analysts and insurance analysts who have conducted their own studies of asbestos litigation. If they used proprietary data in their studies, we asked the analysts to review their analytic methods with us. Most of the analysts we interviewed were willing to discuss their approach with us and show us how they arrived at their results, even if they could not share their data with us. We relied on only those studies that we determined were sound.

Fourth, we obtained confidential data from many participants in the litigation. In each instance, we specified the data we sought and conducted sufficient investigation (for example, comparing information from multiple sources) to assure ourselves that the data provided to us were reliable. We used only data that we confirmed with other data or with other participants in the litigation. In the first phase of the research, we obtained data, on a confidential basis, on each of the claims brought against almost 200 defendants and trusts through 2000. We then updated that dataset with data on claims brought against some of the major defendants and trusts in 2001 and 2002. Because time and resource constraints limited the second round of data collection, we did not attempt to update every data series we collected in the initial effort.

We obtained data on claimants from a number of defendants and insurers. Many defendants that have been prominent in the litigation have received claims from tens of thousands, and in some cases hundreds of thousands, of people. Because, as mentioned earlier, asbestos claimants typically file claims against multiple defendants, many of the claimants on the list for one defendant also appeared on the lists for other defendants. This overlap frequently allowed us to compare the information we obtained for a claimant from one defendant with the information we obtained for that claimant from other defendants to determine the reliability of the data. For our analysis, we included only those data that proved to be reliable in the sense that the data from different defendants agreed.

Some claimants filed two or more claims at different times and, occasionally, in different states. These claimants typically were those who brought a suit against some defendants at one time in one state and filed claims with one or more trusts at other times, possibly in another state. We counted each claimant only once—at the time and in the state in which that claimant first appeared in any of the data available to us. For example, the analysis of trends and patterns in filings by state reported in Chapter Three considers only the initial filing by any particular claimant and does not include any subsequent filings by that claimant. For this reason, the distributions of filings reported in that chapter undercount the total number of claims filed in any state in any time period, to the extent that the state saw filings against some defendants or trusts in that time period by persons who had filed asbestos claims against other defendants or trusts at an earlier date.

We also obtained aggregate annual data on indemnity payments and defense costs from a large number of defendants and insurers. Some defendants and insurers provided data going back to the early 1980s. Others were able to provide data only for the past few years. In all, the data include more than 60,000 defendant-year observations. Almost all the defendants for whom we have data had some insurance coverage, all of which had coverage limits. Because there is always the possibility that a defendant and insurer can dispute whether a coverage limit has been reached, both defendants and insurers have strong incentives to maintain accurate data on indemnity payments and loss adjustment costs. For that reason, we believe these data are accurate.

Finally, we conducted more than 60 interviews with key participants in the litigation, including plaintiff attorneys, corporate counsel, outside defense counsel, insurance company claims managers, investment analysts, and court-appointed "neutrals." All of these interviews lasted at least one hour, and some took considerably longer. In some instances, we conducted multiple interviews with a single source. The picture of the current state of asbestos litigation that emerged from these interviews was remarkably consistent. Where some interviewees had sharply different views of the litigation than others, they noted that themselves and discussed why their perceptions differed. All the interviews were conducted under the promise of confidentiality to encourage candor, and we explained the purposes of the study and our general approach to all the interviewees.

Differences Between This Report and an Earlier Interim Report on Asbestos Litigation

This monograph extends the work presented in an earlier RAND documented briefing on asbestos litigation (*Asbestos Litigation Costs and Compensation: An Interim Report*, DB-397-ICJ, 2002) in a number of ways. This report includes

- an expanded review of the epidemiological literature on asbestos-related injuries and a review of the most widely accepted projections of the number of mesothelioma cases that would occur between 1985 and 2009 (see Chapter Two)
- an updated discussion of the evolution of asbestos litigation, including more information on deferred and expedited dockets, consolidated trials and bankruptcy, and some additional details about trends in jury verdicts (see Chapter Three)
- updated estimates of the total number of individuals who had filed asbestos personal injury claims through 2002 and the total number of defendants named on those claims, and new analyses of the distribution of asbestos defendants across industries (see Chapter Four)
- more details about how we carried out the analysis, much of which is provided in the appendices to this report
- updated estimates of the total amount of money spent on asbestos personal injury claims through 2002, how much of that money was consumed by transaction costs, and how much ended up in claimants' pockets (see Chapter Five)

- updated estimates of the number of bankruptcies that have been attributed to asbestos litigation (see Chapter Six)
- discussion of asbestos litigation reform proposals (see Chapter Seven).

The revisions to the estimates published in the interim report are based on several considerations. Some estimates have changed because the analysis was incomplete when the interim report came out. For example, that report estimated that 6,000 defendants had been named in the litigation; this report updates that number to 8,400. The increase does not mean we that we estimated that 2,400 new defendants have been named on asbestos claims since the publication of the interim report. Rather, when we wrote the interim report, we had not completed the task of checking all the lists of defendants we had received from various sources for duplicates and subsidiaries. We estimated that the lists provided to us included well in excess of 6,000 defendants and, so, reported that estimate in the interim report. We have since completed checking those lists and estimate that 8,400 entities have been named as asbestos defendants.

Other estimates changed because we updated them. The interim report, for example, gave estimates of the numbers of claimants and total dollars spent on asbestos litigation through the year 2000. This report updates those estimates through 2002. Similarly, the interim report estimated the number of asbestos-related bankruptcies through spring 2002; we now provide an estimate of the number of asbestos-related bankruptcies through summer 2004. We also updated our discussion of the evolution of the litigation to include significant new developments.

It is important to note, however, that not all our data have been updated to 2002. Many of the estimates in this report still reflect data collected through 2000. We did not have the resources necessary to collect new data and revise the analysis in every case.

Terminology

We use a number of terms in this report that call for clarification at the outset.

Defendants

Several leading asbestos defendants filed for bankruptcy and subsequently emerged reorganized. The reorganizations included the formation of a trust funded by the defendant and its insurers. The trust is the only recourse for asbestos claimants, who are barred by injunction from pursing the reorganized company.[1] Rather than repeat the

---

[1] 68 B.R. at 624. The bar is known as a "channeling injunction" and has since been codified in the U.S. Bankruptcy Code at 11 U.S.C. §524(g).

phrase "defendants and trusts" in references to the entities against whom claims are brought or to the entities paying claims, we generally use the word *defendants* with the understanding that that word refers to both defendants and trusts.

Defense Costs

At various points in this report we refer to the *defense costs* (or *expenses* or *spending*) of defendants and insurers. These terms always refer to the amounts defendants spent on asbestos litigation, net of any reimbursement by insurers and the amounts insurers spent including both their own expenses and amounts they reimbursed defendants under various policies and excluding any contribution by other insurers under a reinsurance policy.

Claim

The typical asbestos lawsuit includes a number of claimants and names several dozen defendants. Commentaries on asbestos litigation sometimes use the word *claim* to refer to a lawsuit, regardless of the numbers of claimants and defendants included in the lawsuit. The word claim also is sometimes used to refer to a claimant regardless of whether that claimant's lawsuit also includes other claimants. Finally, the word claim is sometimes used to refer to an assertion by an individual claimant against an individual defendant. Most of our analyses focus on individual claimants, whether or not their claim was included in a lawsuit with other claims and independent of the number of defendants named by the claimant. Accordingly, in the subsequent discussion, we generally use the word "claim" to refer to an individual claimant. Thus, when we say a large fraction of the claims was filed by a small number of plaintiff law firms, we mean that a small number of plaintiff law firms filed claims on behalf of a large fraction of the individuals who brought claims against one or more defendants. Similarly, when we say defendants have spent X thousand dollars resolving claims for mesothelioma, we mean that the amounts of money paid to claimants who brought claims for mesothelioma and the legal fees and expenses incurred in the course of paying those claims added up to X thousand dollars.

Unimpaired

One of the most hotly debated issues in asbestos litigation concerns whether unimpaired asbestos claimants ought to be compensated. The term itself often introduces confusion because impairment can be taken to mean either an injury or a decrease in the ability to function in everyday activities. The American Medical Association's (AMA's) definition of impairment is synonymous with injury: *Impairment* is defined as "a loss, loss of use, or derangement of any body part, organ system, or organ function" (American Medical Association, 2001, p. 2). A scar on the lungs, in this sense, is impairment. *Impairment ratings,* however, as defined by the AMA, measure the functional limitations caused by an injury: Impairment ratings reflect "an individual's ability to perform common activities of daily living, excluding work" (American Medical Association, 2001, p. 4). "For example, an anatomic change such as a circumscribed pleural plaque would be an impairment based on an abnormality in anatomic structure. However, if there were no abnormality in lung function and no decrease in the ability to perform activities of daily living, the individual would be assigned a 0% impairment rating" (American Medical Association, 2001, p. 88). Under the AMA guidelines,

- a person may be injured, but not functionally impaired, and
- a person may be functionally impaired, while still being able to hold down a job.

In this report, we use the term *unimpaired* to refer to someone who experiences no decrease in the ability to perform the activities of daily life, even if he or she has evidence of an injury. In other words, the individual would be assigned a 0% impairment rating according to the AMA definition. It is important to note that claimants who are unimpaired in this sense when they file a claim may manifest more critical symptoms after an extended latency period. In most jurisdictions, those who are injured but not (yet) impaired by their exposure to asbestos have legally cognizable claims.

Injury/Disease

The term used to refer to a claimant's asserted condition is also a source of controversy. The word *disease,* as defined in Webster's *Collegiate Dictionary,* is "a condition of the living animal or plant body or of one of its parts that impairs normal functioning." Accordingly, some commentators object to the use of the word "disease" in referring to the entire population of asbestos claimants because it implies, in their view, a judgment that all claimants are impaired. In this report, when discussing all claimants taken together, we usually use the more neutral term: *injury.* Thus, when we say, the next chapter reviews the kinds of injuries associated with asbestos, we do not imply any judgment as to the severity of the various types of injuries and diseases asserted by claimants.

Organization of This Report

Chapter Two describes the kinds of injuries associated with exposure to asbestos and reviews the epidemiological studies that have estimated how many people are likely to eventually incur asbestos-related injuries. Chapter Three examines important aspects of the evolution of the litigation over the past two decades, including trends in jury verdicts. Chapter Four describes the numbers and types of claimants and defendants and shows how they have changed over time. Chapter Five describes costs of the litigation and compensation to plaintiffs, including distribution of total compensation amounts by type of injury. Chapter Six examines the economic effects of the litigation, focusing on the numbers of bankruptcies, characteristics of bankrupt defendants, and performance of personal injury bankruptcy trusts. Finally, Chapter Seven considers how well the tort system has performed and discusses recent efforts to devise alternatives to the current system for resolving asbestos injury claims.

CHAPTER TWO

Injuries from Asbestos Exposure

Asbestos litigation stems from widespread use of and exposure to asbestos, which is known to cause a variety of injuries. This chapter describes the nature of asbestos-related injuries and discusses why it has been difficult to estimate their occurrence. It concludes by summarizing the results of epidemiological studies that have estimated numbers of asbestos-related injuries through 2029.

Asbestos Use in the Workplace

Asbestos is abundant and inexpensive to mine and process. Because asbestos is strong, durable, and has excellent fire-retardant capability, it was widely used in industrial and other work and residential settings through the early 1970s. Asbestos consumption in the United States peaked in 1973 and then dropped dramatically over the next three decades (Alleman and Mossman, 1997).

Millions of American workers have been exposed to asbestos, some for long periods of time and/or at high levels. When the Occupational Safety and Health Act (OSHA) went into effect in 1970, industries imposed increasingly strict safety regulations governing workplace exposure to asbestos. In 1989, nearly 20 years later, the Environmental Protection Agency (EPA) proposed banning all products containing asbestos. That ban, however, was set aside in 1991 with a decision by the Fifth Circuit Court of Appeals (*Corrosion Proof Fittings v. E.P.A*).[1] Although the ban still applied to certain asbestos products and prohibited the use of asbestos in products that had not previously contained it, some uses of asbestos were permitted and remain legal to this day in the United States. The EPA notice on material containing asbestos notes the following: "EPA does NOT track the manufacture, processing, or distribution in commerce of asbestos-containing products" (EPA, 2003). Exposure to naturally occurring asbestos, which may also cause disease, is generally not regulated (Renner, 2000).

---

[1] 947 F.2d 1201 ([5th Cir. Oct. 18, 1991] [No. 89–4596]), *opinion clarified* (Nov. 15, 1991), *rehearing denied* (Nov. 27, 1991).

It is well documented that the dangers of asbestos were known before World War II (Brodeur, 1985; Tweedale, 2000). The managers of some asbestos manufacturing companies did not warn their employees of the risks of asbestos exposure or provide adequate protection for them, even though they were aware of those risks to the health of their workers (Brodeur, 1985; Castleman, 1996). In the 1950s, some manufacturers lobbied against stricter regulation of asbestos exposure in the workplace (Brodeur, 1985). It was these failures of public and private decisionmakers decades ago that precipitated what has been termed "the worst occupational health disaster in U.S. history" (Cauchon, 1999, p. 4) and set the stage for the current litigation.

Injuries Resulting from Asbestos Exposure

The groundbreaking work on injuries caused by asbestos exposure among U.S. workers was conducted by Dr. Irving Selikoff at the Mount Sinai School of Medicine in New York in the 1960s and 1970s (Selikoff, Churg, and Hammond, 1964 and 1965; Selikoff and Lee, 1978). We draw on that work in the following descriptions of the injuries caused by asbestos exposure, including mesothelioma, other cancers, asbestosis, and pleural thickening or plaques.

Mesothelioma

Mesothelioma is a cancer of the lining of the chest or abdomen. Asbestos is the only demonstrated cause of mesothelioma, although some mesothelioma cases have not been traceable to an asbestos exposure. Possible causes of mesothelioma other than asbestos have been suggested but have not been established based on epidemiologic evidence (Peterson et al., 1984; Strickler et al., 2003; Price and Ware, 2004). The incidence of mesothelioma among males has increased dramatically over the past several decades and is attributed to the use and production of asbestos in the preceding decades. Mesothelioma rates are much lower among females and have been stable over this period (Price and Ware, 2004). The disease is regarded as inevitably fatal, usually within a year or two of diagnosis. Mesothelioma can occur even with a relatively low level of exposure to certain types of asbestos fibers (EPA, 2003). Prior to 1999, the number of mesothelioma deaths in the United States could not be counted directly from public health reporting systems because mesothelioma was not recorded as a separate cause-of-death category on death certificates (Environmental Working Group, 2004). In the United States, the National Cancer Institute's Surveillance, Epidemiology, and End Results (SEER) Program, as part of the Centers for Disease Control and Prevention, now collects data on mesothelioma cases in certain areas. Mesothelioma is identified as a separate category in the SEER cancer registry data. The SEER data, however, cover only nine reporting areas (either states or metropolitan areas) that may not be representative of the rest of the United States.

Other Cancers

Other cancers have also been linked to asbestos, although they all have other causes besides asbestos exposure. Aside from mesothelioma, lung cancer is the most frequently claimed malignant disease. There is general agreement that asbestos exposure can cause lung cancer. The risk of lung cancer can be exacerbated by other factors as well, most notably smoking. Between 1940 and 1979, there were high rates of smoking among workers in the blue-collar industries where asbestos exposure was particularly high. In lung cancer cases, defendants often dispute plaintiffs' allegations that their cancer is attributable to asbestos exposure rather than to smoking.

Although an accurate count of lung cancer deaths is available from the Vital Statistics registration system in the United States, estimating the number of *asbestos-related* lung cancer deaths would be difficult. Lung cancer is coded as a separate cause of death on death certificates, but only a small proportion of all lung cancer deaths can be attributed to occupational asbestos exposure. Most lung cancer cases are caused by other factors, including cigarette smoking. Even if detailed smoking histories of lung cancer cases in the original asbestos worker cohorts were available, which they are not, it would be difficult to determine the appropriate proportion of lung cancer to attribute to occupational asbestos exposure. The same is true for lung cancer cases today.

Other cancers asserted by asbestos claimants include leukemia, and cancers of the bladder, breast, colon, esophagus, kidney, larynx, lip, liver, lymphoid, mouth, pancreas, prostate, rectum, stomach, throat, thyroid, and tongue. The relationship of these other cancers to asbestos is a subject of contention; defendants frequently dispute the causality of these cancer claims. No U.S. government agency monitors the incidence of asbestos-related cancers other than mesothelioma.

Asbestosis

Asbestosis is a chronic lung disease resulting from inhalation of asbestos fibers that can be debilitating and even fatal. However, a person diagnosed with asbestosis might be asymptomatic or only mildly impaired. Although decreased lung volume is a characteristic clinical feature of pulmonary asbestosis, it is not required for a diagnosis to be made (American Thoracic Society, 1996). Severe cases are usually the result of long-term, high-level exposure to asbestos, but "[e]vidence of asbestosis has been found many years after relatively brief but extremely heavy exposure" (American Thoracic Society, 1996).

The National Institute for Occupational Safety and Health (NIOSH) publishes limited data on U.S. deaths due to asbestosis, but no U.S. government agency monitors the prevalence of the disease. The NIOSH data indicate that deaths due to asbestosis have increased substantially over the past three decades, from 77 in 1968 to 1,265 in 1999 (NIOSH, 2004). (See Table A.2 in Appendix A for more details.) Because asbestosis is not always fatal, however, death certificates are not a good measure of the incidence of asbestosis, and the number of cases probably far exceeds the number of deaths. The only way to measure the number of asbestosis cases accurately would be to conduct a survey of workers exposed to asbestos that included a complete evaluation, documented occupational exposure, and provided X-ray, clinical, and physiologic evidence indicating the presence of physical changes associated with asbestosis.

Pleural Plaques, Pleural Thickening, and Pleural Effusion

Asbestos can cause other nonmalignant abnormalities of the pleura: pleural plaques and thickening, and pleural effusion (American Thoracic Society, 1996). Pleural plaques and thickening are scarring of the pleura, the membrane that lines the inside of the chest wall and covers the outside of the lungs. Pleural effusion is the presence of liquid in the pleural space. Pleural plaques and thickening can be diagnosed by a chest X-ray and can be accompanied by symptoms and diminished pulmonary function (Kilburn and Warshaw, 1990).

Controversy over the Unimpaired

One of the most hotly contested issues in asbestos litigation is the extent to which claimants are affected by their exposure: that is, how sick or "impaired" they are. Some commentators say that many claimants are "not sick" and, because the funds available to compensate asbestos claimants are limited, the funds should be allocated only to those who "are sick."

Others strongly disagree with this position, arguing that under the law of all 50 states individuals are entitled to compensation if they have suffered a tortious injury or disease. Under most state laws, workers who can show evidence of asbestos disease as defined above are eligible to claim compensation for injury.

In the United States today, there is no comprehensive database into which claimants' medical data have been consistently and reliably entered over time. The only direct information on the nature and severity of injuries claimed by asbestos plaintiffs, including the existence of impairment, comes from limited studies in which an analyst draws a sample of individual claims from defendants' files and reviews the medical information provided by the claimants to determine whether the information in the files offers evidence that a claimant was impaired. We discuss this evidence in Chapter Four.

Predicting Asbestos-Related Cancers

Estimating the numbers of asbestos-related deaths and diseases is complicated by the long latency periods associated with asbestos injuries. Typically, 20 to 40 years elapse between the first exposure to asbestos and disease manifestation. The Manville Trust found, for example, that the average year of first exposure to asbestos by claimants who filed a claim with the Trust during the 1980s and 1990s was generally about 40 years earlier (Claims Resolution Management Corporation, 2001, p. 20). Some people who are first diagnosed with a nondisabling condition may develop more serious diseases in the future, but others will not.

Several epidemiological studies aimed at projecting total asbestos-related disease in the United States were conducted in the late 1970s and 1980s (Higginson, 1980; Enterline, 1981; McDonald and McDonald, 1981; Peto et al., 1981; Nicholson et al., 1982; Walker et al., 1983; Lilienfeld et al., 1988). Each of these studies predicted the number of asbestos-related cases or deaths expected to occur in the future among persons occupationally exposed to asbestos over the previous several decades. Litigators still use the study by Nicholson et al. (1982) as the standard reference on occupational exposure to asbestos.

Because the study by Nicholson et al. (1982) is often cited in discussions of past and future asbestos litigation, we present a more detailed summary of their projections of asbestos-related cancer deaths (see Table 2.1). These projections estimated the number of "excess" (i.e., premature) asbestos-related deaths due to three types of cancer (mesothelioma, lung cancer, and gastrointestinal and other cancers), and the sum of these categories of cancer deaths for the years 1965 through 2029. Based on this study, 312,380 asbestos-related excess cancer deaths were projected to occur from 1965 through 2004, of which one-quarter are from mesothelioma (see Table 2.1). Nicholson et al. projected that excess deaths from asbestos-related cancers would peak during the 1990s, and then gradually decline. According to their projections, 120,085 asbestos-related cancer deaths will occur over the next 25 years (2005–2029). Of these future cases, four of five were predicted to occur in the next 15 years (2005–2019). The projections by Nicholson et al. (1982) end in the year 2029, although the number of asbestos-related cancer deaths in the last projection period (2025–2029) is still substantial at 8,695.

Because each of the early projection studies employed different methods, they generated vastly different estimates. Nicholson et al. (1982) examined asbestos-related diseases in industries and occupations judged to be "high-risk": that is, in industries and occupations in which workers incurred extensive exposure to asbestos. They estimated that 228,795 excess deaths due to asbestos-related cancers would occur from 1985 through 2009 as a result of exposure of workers to asbestos from 1940 through 1979 (see Table 2.2). Importantly, this number does not include deaths

Table 2.1
Projected Excess Deaths from All Asbestos-Related Cancers in Selected Occupations and Industries, United States, 1965–2029, Based on Study by Nicholson et al. (1982)

Years	Mesothelioma	Lung Cancer	Gastrointestinal and Other Cancers	All Cancers
1965–1969	4,505	11,720	4,280	20,505
1970–1974	5,410	16,430	5,170	27,010
1975–1979	7,125	21,840	5,950	34,915
1980–1984	8,875	25,275	6,880	41,030
1985–1989	11,990	27,360	7,475	46,825
1990–1994	13,740	27,485	7,470	48,695
1995–1999	14,845	26,295	7,125	48,265
2000–2004	15,300	23,465	6,370	45,135
2005–2009	14,995	19,605	5,275	39,875
2010–2014	13,305	14,935	4,060	32,300
2015–2019	10,410	10,540	2,820	23,770
2020–2024	7,475	6,270	1,700	15,445
2025–2029	4,585	3,230	880	8,695
1965–2004	81,790	179,870	50,720	312,380
2005–2029	50,770	54,580	14,735	120,085
1965–2029	132,560	234,450	65,455	432,465

NOTE: Estimates are based on annual projections in Table XXII (lung cancer), Table XXIII (mesothelioma), Table XXIV (gastrointestinal and other cancers), and Table XXV (all cancers) of Nicholson et al. (1982).

resulting from severe asbestosis, or from exposure to asbestos in other occupations and industries, or from post-1979 exposure to asbestos. Although estimates by Nicholson et al. (1982) are widely cited, they were disputed by some epidemiologists at the time of their publication. The Nicholson et al. estimates were derived from a study conducted by Irving Selikoff at the Mount Sinai School of Medicine under a contract with the United States Department of Labor.

Other studies conducted around the same time predicted far fewer excess cancer cases for 1985–2009 due to asbestos exposure. The lowest of these estimates, from a study by Walker et al. (1983), was 39,385 cases of mesothelioma and lung cancer among asbestos workers. The Walker study was conducted at the Harvard School of Public Health and the Epidemiology Resources Institute in Brookline, Massachusetts, under contract with the Johns-Manville Corporation and was itself subject to criticism. The Nicholson and Walker studies provide upper and lower bounds, respectively, for the credible projections of disease attributable to occupational asbestos exposure published during this time period (see Table 2.2).[2]

---

[2] An unpublished study by Bridbord et al. that was cited by Manton (1983) and by Lilienfeld et al. (1988) generated much higher estimates of cancer deaths from occupational exposure to asbestos. According to Manton, Bridbord et al. estimated that between 13 and 18 percent of all cancer mortality in the United States might be caused by occupational exposure to asbestos. Lilienfeld et al. reported that the Bridbord et al. study estimated that

Table 2.2
Projections of Asbestos-Related Cancers Among Asbestos Workers, 1985–2009

Study	Mesothelioma	Lung Cancer	Gastrointestinal and Other Cancers	Total[a]
Higginson (1980)	25,000	37,500	—	62,500
Enterline (1981)	16,650	63,525	—	80,175
Peto et al. (1981)	20,925	79,515	—	100,440
McDonald and McDonald (1981)	22,870	123,750	—	146,620
Nicholson et al. (1982)	70,870	124,210	33,715	228,795
Walker et al. (1983)	15,500–18,100	23,885[b]	—	39,385–41,985
Lilienfeld et al. (1988)	21,500	76,700	33,000	131,200

SOURCE: Lilienfeld et al. (1988), Table 2 (with minor corrections).
NOTE: — = Not reported.
[a] "Total" includes only the types of cancer reported in the projections.
[b] From Table 8 in Manton (1983).

Several other studies of trends in asbestos-related injuries have been conducted since these early studies, but most of those other studies focused on asbestos-related injuries outside the United States (e.g., Banaei et al. [2000] in France; Kjaergaard and Andersson [2000] in Denmark; Magnani et al. [2000] in Italy, Spain, and Switzerland; and Peto et al. [1999] in Western Europe). Litigation experts have also used the Nicholson et al. (1982) estimates, more recent studies, and other data to project the number of future asbestos claims (Manville Personal Injury Settlement Trust, 2001; Stallard, 2001).

Another recent study (Price and Ware, 2004) has updated predictions of mesothelioma for the coming decades in the United States. In Table 2.3, we present these projections of mesothelioma cases from 1990 through 2049 in the United States, including males and females. The basis for these predictions is the best available population-based rates from the SEER Program. This study predicts 89,305 cases of mesothelioma will occur in the United States between 2005 and 2049, with more than half of the cases occurring in the next 20 years. The decreasing number of mesothelioma cases among males beginning in the year 2005 reflects the decreased production and use of asbestos in the United States since 1976.

1.6 million cancer deaths, including 1.44 million lung cancer deaths, would occur among asbestos workers between 1980 and 2010. Also according to Lilienfeld et al., the Bridbord study estimated that 10,000 mesothelioma deaths would occur each year as a result of occupational asbestos exposure.

Table 2.3
Projected Cases of Mesothelioma, United States, 1990–2049, Based on a Study by Price and Ware (2004)

Years	Males	Females	Total
1990–1994	8,874	2,310	11,184
1995–1999	9,640	2,385	12,025
2000–2004	10,040	2,460	12,500
2005–2009	9,960	2,535	12,495
2010–2014	9,472	2,610	12,082
2015–2019	9,018	2,685	11,703
2020–2024	8,274	2,760	11,034
2025–2029	7,242	2,835	10,077
2030–2034	6,212	2,910	9,122
2035–2039	5,286	2,985	8,271
2040–2044	4,508	3,060	7,568
2045–2049	3,818	3,135	6,953
1990–2004	28,554	7,155	35,709
2005–2049	63,790	25,515	89,305
1990–2049	92,344	32,670	125,014

NOTE: Numbers of mesothelioma were estimated from Figure 2 of Price and Ware (2004).

Evaluating the Predictions

Although 20 years of the projection period in the earlier studies have elapsed, the projections from these studies are still difficult to validate using actual data. No projection studies have been published that update the estimates of Nicholson et al. or Walker et al. with actual data substituted for the early time periods of their projections or that independently project the number of asbestos-related health outcomes. The Nicholson and Walker projection studies used complicated models and required detailed and voluminous input (e.g., labor data to estimate the number of asbestos workers). These factors would make replication of those studies both time-consuming and expensive.

We conducted a limited test of Nicholson's projections in the case of mesothelioma alone by applying actual incidence rates for 1977–1997 from the SEER Program to the population of the United States. Our comparison between the two sources is limited to the five years shown in Table 2.4 for which data from the Nicholson study and mesothelioma rates for the SEER areas are available. Based on the number of mesothelioma cases shown in Table 2.4, we conclude that Nicholson's projections are similar to those based on actual SEER incidence rates, with the Nicholson estimates ranging from 20 percent higher to 10 percent lower than those based on the SEER rates. In these calculations, we assumed that Nicholson's estimates of the total number of workers exposed to asbestos (27.5 million) accurately represent all people exposed to asbestos, and that all cases of mesothelioma in the United States would occur within that group.

A more detailed discussion of the comparison of early projections of asbestos-related diseases is provided in Appendix A, and an explanation of the estimating procedures we used to test Nicholson et al.'s mesothelioma projections is provided in Appendix B.

Table 2.4
Estimated Cases of Mesothelioma in the United States, 1977–1997, Based on the Nicholson et al. (1982) Study and SEER Incidence Rates

Year	Number of Asbestos-Related Mesothelioma Deaths from Nicholson et al.	Number of Cases of Mesothelioma Estimated from SEER Incidence Rates
1977	1,425	1,200
1982	1,775	1,764
1987	2,398	2,157
1992	2,748	2,991
1997	2,969	2,604

CHAPTER THREE

Asbestos Litigation Dynamics

Background

Asbestos litigation is the longest-running mass tort litigation in the United States. It arose out of the exposure of millions of workers to a useful but injurious product and out of product manufacturers' failure to warn of the risks of exposure. Asbestos litigation over time has been shaped by changes in substantive and procedural law, the rise of a sophisticated and well-capitalized plaintiff bar, heightened media attention to litigation generally and toxic tort litigation in particular, and wider use of computer technology. In turn, asbestos litigation has made a significant contribution to the evolution of mass civil litigation, providing a model for some to emulate and others to avoid.

Most mass toxic tort litigation arises relatively soon after information related to litigation first appears, suggesting a link between product use or exposure and injury or disease. Within a few years, the litigation is either extinguished—as a result of new information disputing earlier claims of injury causation or court rulings in favor of defendants—or resolved in one or a few large-scale settlements. Because the history of these cases is relatively short, the substantive and procedural law and social and technological practices that prevail at the beginning of the litigation are likely to determine the litigation's progress and ultimate outcomes.

The long latency period of asbestos-related diseases, along with widespread exposure to asbestos over many decades, has created a dramatically different profile for asbestos litigation, which has been ongoing for more than three decades and is expected to continue long into the future. The distinguishing feature of asbestos litigation has been its tendency to reshape itself over time. The focus of the litigation has shifted from federal to state courts, and now, increasingly, to bankruptcy courts. Trial judges who developed innovative procedures to manage large asbestos caseloads have moved on to the appellate bench or private practice, leaving different judges to rediscover those procedures or substitute different procedures of their own. Law firms that played leading roles in asbestos litigation in the 1980s have left the field and been replaced by new firms with new litigation strategies and business models. Corporations that were perceived to have little or no exposure to asbestos-related liability have found themselves at the center of the litigation. As in the case of generals whose strategies seem to be based on fighting the last war, those engaged in asbestos litigation often find themselves primed to deal with a litigation whose character has dramatically evolved since they last reviewed their strategic options. This chapter describes that evolution, highlighting the features of the litigation that public policymakers most need to understand when considering how to respond to calls for asbestos litigation reform.[1]

The Early Years

Although Irving Selikoff's landmark studies of asbestos disease among insulation workers were widely publicized in the 1960s, it was not until the 1970s that lawyers representing asbestos workers scored significant victories against asbestos manufacturers. In *Borel v. Fibreboard*,[2] the Fifth Circuit Court of Appeals upheld the application of strict liability to latent injury torts and found defendants jointly and severally liable for injury to an asbestos insulation worker. In the following years, plaintiff lawyers in several states successfully challenged the exclusivity of workers' compensation for asbestos manufacturers' employees, freeing these workers to seek damages in tort (Hensler et al., 1985).

In the first successful cases against asbestos manufacturers, plaintiff attorneys introduced evidence that several major manufacturers had known about the dangers of asbestos exposure as early as the 1930s but had concealed this information from their employees. When defendants challenged the relevance of this evidence to claims from workers installing asbestos insulation, plaintiff attorneys sought to uncover evidence that asbestos manufacturers were aware that asbestos exposure was causing disease among insulators as well as asbestos factory workers (Hensler et al., 1985).

With the application of substantive legal doctrines to latent injuries still uncertain, pursuing individual claims against asbestos manufacturers in those early years was risky for plaintiff law firms. Moreover, each claim required the presentation of scientific evidence on the causal link between asbestos exposure and disease, plus extensive factual investigation to demonstrate a causal link between the specific plaintiff's injury and the defendant's products, meaning that asbestos claims were far more expensive to prosecute than ordinary personal injury claims. The defendants were large corporations that could afford to invest in protracted litigation and to adopt aggressive litigation strategies in response to plaintiffs' suits. As a result, few plaintiff

---

[1] Previous studies have detailed the evolution of asbestos litigation over time—e.g., Brodeur (1985); Hensler et al., (1985); Castleman (1996); and Hensler (2002). Although we provide some historical context in this chapter, our purpose is to highlight features of the litigation that pose challenges for lawyers, judges, and policymakers.

[2] 493 F.2d 1076 (5th Cir. 1973).

lawyers were willing to take on asbestos workers' claims, and those that did faced significant challenges and sometimes assumed substantial personal financial risks. It was these lawyers who laid the groundwork for the plaintiff successes that followed (Brodeur, 1985).

Growth of Mass Litigation

Initially, asbestos manufacturers vigorously defended themselves against workers' claims, raising a host of issues, including the risks of exposure to asbestos, whether the plaintiffs had been exposed to the defendant's products, and whether the statutory period for filing had passed (Hensler et al., 1985). By the mid-1980s, however, plaintiff law firms in parts of the country where people were heavily exposed to asbestos, such as jurisdictions with shipyards or petrochemical facilities, had learned that they could succeed against asbestos defendants by filing large numbers of claims, grouping them together, and negotiating with defendants on behalf of the entire group. Often, defendants would agree to settle all of the claims that were so grouped, including weaker as well as stronger claims, to reduce their overall costs of litigation. By agreeing to pay weaker smaller-value claims in exchange for settling stronger and larger-value claims, defendants could also contain their financial risk. Some plaintiffs might receive lower values for claims that were settled as part of a group rather than litigated individually, but litigating claims en masse lowered the cost and risk per claim for plaintiff law firms (Hensler, 2002; McGovern, 2002). At the same time, some defendants reportedly agreed to pay a few hundred dollars per claim for virtually all claims filed against them, without much attention to the facts of individual claims, in order to avert litigation costs.

To identify more potential claimants, plaintiff law firms began to promote mass screenings of asbestos workers at or near their places of employment (Hensler et al., 1985). Plaintiff law firms would bring suit on behalf of all the workers who showed signs of exposure, sometimes filing hundreds of cases under a single docket number (Hensler et al., 1985). Given the profile of asbestos disease, these groups of claimants had injuries of varying severity, ranging from fatal mesothelioma and other malignant diseases to disabling asbestosis to milder asbestosis to pleural plaques and scarring not accompanied by functional impairment.

Concentration of Plaintiff Representation

As asbestos litigation geared up in the 1970s, the risks and expense of representing asbestos workers and the development of mass filing strategies for litigating against corporate defendants with substantial resources led to the development of a small but sophisticated plaintiffs' asbestos bar, which represented a large fraction of all asbestos claimants. By 1985, ten firms represented one-quarter of the annual filings against major defendants. By 1992—about 20 years after the landmark *Borel* decision—just ten firms represented half of the annual filings against major defendants. Three years later, ten firms (many, but not all, of the same firms that had been in the 1992 "top ten") represented three-quarters of the annual filings against asbestos defendants, even though the filings themselves had increased by a third. The concentration of claims in a small number of firms facilitated mass litigation strategies, which in turn facilitated control of the litigation by these firms. More recently, the degree of concentration of asbestos cases has diminished somewhat, as new law firms—some of them spin-offs of older well-established firms—have entered the asbestos litigation market (see Table 3.1). But asbestos litigation has remained highly concentrated, with ten firms representing nearly half of all filings in 2000.

Adapting Legal Doctrine to Long-Latency Torts

Legal doctrines that determine whether and when injury victims can sue to obtain compensation were developed for victims of traumatic injury, not disease. The long latency period associated with asbestos disease posed challenges for the civil justice system to which courts in many jurisdictions were slow to respond.

Table 3.1
Data on Law Firms with Large Asbestos Caseloads

	Percentage of Cases Filed by Law Firms in Top 10 for Annual Asbestos Filings	Number of Law Firms with 100 or More New Filings	
		New Firms	Existing Firms
1985	24	0	102
1986	32	6	58
1987	40	14	61
1988	40	11	60
1989	38	15	67
1990	37	13	68
1991	35	12	64
1992	51	14	66
1993	51	11	64
1994	53	12	65
1995	76	7	63
1996	76	9	69
1997	59	12	77
1998	50	28	93
1999	51	17	82
2000	48	23	75

Statutes of Limitation and Definitions of Compensable Injury

Significant obstacles for asbestos plaintiffs during the early years of the litigation were statutes of limitation, which generally require injury victims to file legal claims within a year or two after injury. Initially, many state courts held that asbestos plaintiffs' injuries had occurred many years earlier when the workers were first exposed, and therefore the allowable time for filing claims had expired. Later, many legislatures adjusted their statutes of limitation so as to require that latent-injury victims file suit within one or two years of when they know or should have known that they were injured (Hensler et al., 1985), rather than within a few years of the time of first exposure, thereby significantly increasing the number of claimants who had been exposed to asbestos many years ago who were eligible to bring suit

The application of statutes of limitation to asbestos cases has important consequences for asbestos victims. If a worker learns that he or she has been exposed to asbestos, seeks a medical examination to determine whether there has been a serious health consequence (e.g., cancer), and discovers that he or she has pleural plaques or scarring but no other symptoms of injury or impairment, in most jurisdictions a legal claim must be filed within a short time in order to protect the worker's chance of seeking compensation, as these physiological changes have been held to trigger a cause of action. Under traditional tort doctrine, only a single claim can be filed for any tort, even if that tort causes multiple injuries to a person. Therefore, in jurisdictions that follow this traditional rule, a worker who files a claim for pleural plaques or nondisabling asbestosis cannot file another claim if he or she develops more serious disease, such as cancer, in the future. However, in some jurisdictions, the worker may be able to recover compensation for fear of developing a later disease or for medical monitoring of his or her health (Behrens, 2002).

Over time, many jurisdictions have adopted special doctrines and rules to adjust the application of these traditional tort doctrines to long-latency asbestos disease claims. Most jurisdictions now follow the rule that the statute of limitations begins to run when workers discover that they have been injured, rather than at the time of first exposure. In California, the statutory period for filing an asbestos claim does not begin until a plaintiff's ability to work at his or her ordinary occupation is impaired (CA Civ Proc §340.2). Some courts have held that asymptomatic pleural thickening is not a compensable injury; hence, the statute of limitations in asbestos cases does not begin to run when a worker discovers such thickening.[3] Many states have adopted a "two-disease" rule that allows asbestos plaintiffs who have filed claims for

---

[3] See, e.g., *In re Hawaii Fed. Asbestos Cases*, 734 F. Supp. 1563 (1990); *Owens-Illinois v. Armstrong*, 87 Md. App. 699 (1991); and *Simmons v. Pacor, Inc.*, 543 Pa. 664 (1996).

nonmalignant diseases to bring a second lawsuit if and when a malignancy is diagnosed.[4]

Inactive and Expedited Dockets

Some jurisdictions have established inactive dockets (sometimes called "pleural registries") that enable asbestos plaintiffs who show signs of exposure but are not functionally impaired to satisfy statutes of limitation by filing their lawsuits but delay processing and resolving those lawsuits until the plaintiffs' injuries have progressed further (Schuck, 1992; Rothstein, 2001; Behrens, 2002). Nonmalignant claims are removable from the inactive docket only if they meet prespecified clinical criteria (e.g., diagnosis of malignancy, certain radiological exam results, and pulmonary function test ratings) or if a claimant's lawyer is otherwise able to persuade the court that a claim should be activated. State courts in Massachusetts (Commonwealth of Massachusetts, 1986), Cook County, Illinois,[5] and Baltimore, Maryland,[6] established inactive dockets in the late 1980s and early 1990s. In a variation on this policy, some courts have established "expedited dockets" that give priority to cancer claims, placing the claims of those without functional impairment at the back of the queue.[7]

Although registries preserve plaintiffs' rights to pursue compensation in the future, they do not provide compensation for whatever losses a plaintiff might already have suffered or for monitoring his or her health going forward. In courts such as Cook County, where discovery does not begin until a case is transferred from the inactive to the regular (active) docket, attorneys who have agreed to represent plaintiffs who are not currently functionally impaired do not have to invest time and money to investigate the case ("Inactive Asbestos Dockets . . . ," 2002). But the plaintiff lawyers who represent non-impaired plaintiffs also cannot secure fees immediately, making it harder for them to spread the risks of litigating more serious cases and perhaps making it less financially attractive for them to represent asbestos plaintiffs generally. Not surprisingly, some plaintiff attorneys have been unenthusiastic about pleural registries, and in some jurisdictions (e.g., Baltimore), plaintiff attorneys have vigorously contested their establishment or requirements.

---

[4] See, e.g., *Eagle-Picher Industries, Inc. v. Cox,* 481 So. 2d 517 (1985); *Devlin v. Johns-Manville Corp.,* 202 N.J. Super. 556 (1985); *Marinari v. Asbestos Corp.,* 417 Pa. Super. 440 (1992); and *Sopha v. Owens-Corning Fiberglas Corp.,* 230 Wis. 2d 212 (1999).

[5] *In re Asbestos Cases,* Order to Establish Registry for Certain Asbestos Matters (Cir. Ct. Cook Cty., Ill., May 26, 1991).

[6] *In re Asbestos Pers. Injury and Wrongful Death Asbestos Cases,* Order Establishing an Inactive Docket for Asbestos Pers. Injury Cases, No. 92344501 (Cir. Ct. Baltimore City, Md., Dec. 9, 1992).

[7] See, e.g., *In re Cuyahoga Cty. Asbestos Cases,* Gen. Pers. Injury Asbestos Case Mgmt. Order No. 1 (as amended Jan. 4, 2002) (Cleveland, Ohio); and *In re New York City Asbestos Litig.,* Order Amending Prior Case Mgmt. Order (S. Ct. N.Y. City, N.Y., Dec. 19, 2002).

From the perspective of defendants, pleural registries are attractive because they reduce the number of claims paid out annually by eliminating payments for those who are not functionally impaired, who in recent years have constituted the majority of all claimants (see Chapter Four). And, in jurisdictions where placement on pleural registries is mandated, if nondisabled plaintiffs never develop injuries that meet the criteria necessary to be removed from the registry, defendants will pay fewer claims in total over time and likely less in total compensation to all those who have been exposed to asbestos.

Although only a small number of jurisdictions had established inactive dockets up until 2000, inactive dockets have attracted renewed attention over the past few years. Courts that have established inactive dockets in recent years include New York City,[8] Seattle, Washington,[9] and Madison County, Illinois,[10] all of which now have substantial numbers of asbestos cases on their inactive dockets. Some judges have issued case management orders dismissing claims filed by certain law firms on behalf of nonfunctionally impaired plaintiffs with nonmalignant claims, while also tolling the statute of limitations for these claims.[11] On several occasions, federal judge Charles Weiner, to whom all asbestos lawsuits filed in federal courts have been transferred for pretrial management since 1991, has ordered the administrative dismissal of claims of plaintiffs without malignancies or current functional impairments.[12] Orders issued by state court trial judges usually apply to their courts only, but in states in which all asbestos cases are transferred to a single court for coordination the scope of a case management order may be effectively statewide. In January 2004, the Michigan State Supreme Court heard arguments on a petition filed by 60 corporate defendants asking the court to establish a statewide inactive docket for asbestos plaintiffs without malignancies or current functional impairments ("Michigan High Court Hears Docket Arguments," 2004). In June 2004, Ohio enacted legislation requiring that all

---

[8] *In re Asbestos Litigation,* Order Amending Prior Case Management Orders (S. Ct. N.Y. City, N.Y., Dec. 19, 2002).

[9] Letter from Judge Sharon Armstrong, King County, Washington, to Counsel of Record, December 3, 2002.

[10] *In re All Asbestos Litigation Filed in Madison County,* Order Establishing Asbestos Deferred Registry (Cir. Ct. Madison County, Ill., Jan. 23, 2004).

[11] See, e.g., *In re Wallace & Graham Asbestos-Related Cases,* Case Management Order (Greeneville County, S.C., 2002; *In re All Asbestos Cases,* Order Establishing an Inactive Docket for Cases Filed by the Law Offices of Peter T. Nicholl Involving Asbestos-Related Claims, No. CL99-399 (Portsmouth City Circuit Court, 2004).

[12] *In re Asbestos Prod. Liab. Litig. (No. VI),* MDL 875, Civil Action No. 2 (Maritime Actions), Order at 9, 13, 15 (E.D. Pa. May 1, 1996); *In re Asbestos Prod. Liab. Litig. (No. VI),* MDL 875, Order (E.D. Pa. Oct. 16, 1997); and *In re Asbestos Prod. Liab. Litig. (No. VI),* MDL 875, Admin. Order No. 8 (E.D. Pa. Jan. 14, 2002). The statute of limitations is tolled and plaintiffs may re-file when they can show "manifest injury" due to asbestos exposure.

asbestos plaintiffs meet specified injury criteria; in the absence of malignancy, the law requires proof of functional impairment.[13]

Judicial Case Management

As asbestos cases flooded courts in areas of the country where there had been heavy exposure to asbestos, federal and state courts struggled to manage asbestos caseloads more efficiently in order to reduce private and public transaction costs (Hensler et al., 1985; Hensler, 1995; McGovern, 1986, 1989a, 1997; Peterson and Selvin, 1991; and Willging, 1985). The initiatives taken in the 1980s by innovative judges to improve efficiency were widely admired and imitated by fellow judges as the litigation progressed (McGovern, 1995).

A key feature of judicial management in asbestos litigation—and now, in mass torts generally—is the aggregation of cases for pretrial processing. Judges issue case management orders that apply to all asbestos cases filed in their courts, not just the single case that might be before them at a particular time. Often, judges will schedule hundreds or more cases filed by a single law firm for pretrial settlement discussion, hoping that having the entire set of cases before them for evaluation will facilitate settlement negotiations between plaintiff and defense counsel. Sometimes the cases will be grouped by plaintiffs' place of employment, but in other instances they may include claims from diverse sites and occupations. Typically, these large groups of cases include claims of varying injury severity.

Aggregation Across Jurisdictions

In 1991, by order of the Judicial Panel on Multidistrict Litigation (JPMDL), under authority granted by 28 U.S.C. §1407, all asbestos cases filed in the federal courts were transferred to Judge Charles Weiner of the Eastern District of Pennsylvania for pretrial management.[14] Under the statute, when Judge Weiner deems the cases ready for trial, he is required to remand them to the jurisdictions in which they were originally filed.[15] By September 2004, 100,412 asbestos suits had been transferred to Judge Weiner. (In addition, 7,468 cases have been filed in the Eastern District of Pennsylvania and assigned to Judge Weiner.) Of these, 74,152 have been dismissed and 366 have been remanded to their filing district for trial ("Statistical Analysis of Multidistrict Litigation," 2004). Most of these cases were closed administratively without liability being decided or compensation being paid.

---

[13] OH LEGIS 88 (2004), 2004 Ohio Laws File 88 (Am. Sub. H.B. 292). The Ohio statute also sets other conditions for filing asbestos lawsuits.

[14] *In re Asbestos Prods. Liab. Litig. (No. VI),* 771 F.Supp. 415 (J.P.M.L. 1991).

[15] *Lexecon v. Milberg, Weiss, Bershad, Hines & Lerach,* 523 U.S. 26 (1998).

In some states, courts have adopted rules that call for transferring all asbestos cases filed in courts within the state to a single court (Hensler et al., 1985; McGovern, 1986). These rules frequently provide for trial as well as case management in the transferee court. In 1991, cases filed in four West Virginia counties were consolidated for trial in Monongalia County ("Cases in Four West Virginia Counties Consolidated," 1991).[16] In 1999, West Virginia promulgated TCR 26.01, which provides for transfer of mass tort cases filed in any county in the state to a single judge for case management and trial.[17]

Aggregation may also be accomplished by certification of a class under F.R.C.P. 23 or its state law counterparts. Class actions may include claims filed in many different state and federal courts (as well as claims that have not yet been filed in court). However, the requirements for class certification are more precise and arguably more difficult to satisfy than the requirements for consolidation, and class actions have been few—albeit significant—in shaping asbestos litigation.

In Mississippi, until September 2004, plaintiffs from outside the state who wished to join litigation in Mississippi could do so under the provisions of a unique mass joinder rule (M.R.C.P. 20) that required only that a single plaintiff meet state venue requirements.[18] The rule drafters' comments to Mississippi's joinder rule indicated that their intention was to allow "virtually unlimited joinder at the pleading stage" and give the judge wide latitude to "shape the trial to the necessities of the particular case."[19] However, the Mississippi State Supreme Court recently handed down an opinion restricting the application of joinder under Rule 20.[20] Prior to 2003, under the Mississippi rule, thousands of plaintiffs—including many from outside the state—filed asbestos claims in Mississippi courts.

---

[16] When the consolidation order was announced, plaintiff attorneys said they did not know how many cases it covered. See *State of West Virginia Ex Rel. Mobil Corp. v. Gaughan,* Judge, Supreme Court of Appeals of West Virginia, April 2002, No. 30314.

[17] On the adoption of TCR 26.01, see *State ex rel. Mobil Corp. v. Gaughan,* 211 W. Va. 106 (2002). The West Virginia Supreme Court has held that case law setting requirements for Rule 42(a) trial consolidations (discussed in the next section) does not apply to cases consolidated under TCR 26.01 (*State ex rel. Mobil Corp.,* 2002). Other states also have rules for transferring similar cases to a single jurisdiction. See, e.g., Maryland Rule 2-327(d); New Jersey Rule 4.38-1(b); and Kansas State Acts 60-242.

[18] Mississippi Code, Section 11-11-3. The amended statute requires each plaintiff to meet venue requirements. It applies only to cases filed after September 2004. Mississippi law does not provide for class actions.

[19] Challenges to joinder are reviewed under an abuse of discretion standard. *Illinois Central Railroad v. Travis,* 808 So. 2d 928 (Miss. 2002); *Am. Bankers Ins. Co. of Florida v. Alexander,* 825 So. 2d 8 (Miss. 2002).

[20] *Janssen Pharmaceutica, Inc. v. Armond,* 866 So. 2d 1092 (Miss. 2004) (rejecting joinder of 56 plaintiffs alleging injury from the prescription drug Propulsid). The court noted that although the rule drafters asserted that the "general philosophy" behind Rule 20 was to permit "virtually unlimited joinder," the comments to Rule 20 also state that "joinder of parties . . . is not unlimited" and set two conditions for joinder. *Janssen Pharmaceutica* (2004) at 1097.

Consolidation

Within jurisdictions, rather than simply relying on scheduling orders to aggregate cases for settlement discussions, some judges have formally consolidated cases for pretrial, and sometimes for trial as well. Consolidation within a single court jurisdiction is provided for by Rule 42(a) of the Federal Rules of Civil Procedure. Many states have adopted Rule 42(a) in its entirety, although a handful of states have not. Under Rule 42(a), trial judges have broad discretion to consolidate cases that share common legal or factual issues,[21] but they are required to balance the potential savings of time and cost resulting from consolidation against the possibility of prejudice against the parties.[22] A judge may consolidate cases completely or for limited proceedings without the consent of the parties. For example, in 1983, Judge Tom Lambros consolidated all asbestos cases then pending in his court for case management and settlement.[23]

In the early 1980s, a few judges experimented with consolidating cases for *trial*, hoping to minimize duplicative testimony on crosscutting issues such as disease causation. Ordinarily, in a unitary consolidated trial, the jury hears crosscutting evidence once, and then hears evidence specific to each of the cases; after deliberating, the jury issues verdicts in each of the cases, based on all the evidence it has heard. Sometimes, consolidated trials are bifurcated: The jury hears liability and other cross-cutting evidence (e.g., causation, punitive damages) first and decides those issues, and then, if the jury decides against the defendant(s), the jury hears and decides the individual issues in each case, which it may also hear and decide in a single sitting.[24] Occasionally, cases may be "reverse bifurcated" meaning that the jury first hears damages evidence and issues a compensatory award and then hears liability evidence. (The supposition is that knowing the value a jury places on damages may facilitate settlement, thus obviating the need for a potentially complex trial of liability evidence.)

Unitary consolidated trials are most practical when the number of cases consolidated is relatively small. If a large number of cases is consolidated for trial, unitary trials become unwieldy. Some judges address this problem by consolidating large numbers of cases for trial, and then dividing the consolidated cases into smaller groups (called "panels" or "flights") and trying the grouped claims together. Often,

---

[21] *Malcolm v. National Gypsum Co.*, 995 F.2d 346 (2d Cir. 1993); *Saudi Basic Industries Corp. v. Exxon Mobil Corp.*, 194 F. Supp. 2d. 378 (D.N.J. 2002).

[22] *Arnold v. Eastern Airlines, Inc.*, 681 F.2d 186, 193 (4th Cir. 1982), *cert. denied*, 460 U.S. 1102; *Daniels v. Loizzo*, 178 F.R.D. 46 (S.D.N.Y. 1998).

[23] *In re Ohio Asbestos Litig.*, N. 83-OAL (N.D. Ohio, June 1, 1983) (General Order No. 67, OAL Order No. 1). Judge Lambros informally coordinated his docket for case management purposes with the state court in Cuyahoga County.

[24] Authority to bifurcate cases is provided by F.R.C.P. 42(b). Individual trials may also be bifurcated. Experimental research suggests that bifurcating issues for trial may change outcomes, in comparison with trying all issues at once in a unitary trial (Horowitz and Bordens, 1990).

the judges hope that the verdicts in the first few trials will lead parties to settle the remainder of the consolidated cases, as (under the doctrine of *collateral offensive estoppel*)[25] liability verdicts against the defendants might preclude these same defendants from contesting liability in future trials.

To increase trial efficiency (and parties' motivation to settle) in large-scale consolidations, some judges select a few representative cases for trial of liability and other crosscutting issues. The jury decides those issues and then decides damages (if necessary) in the representative cases. The jury's decisions on the crosscutting issues are applied to *all* cases in the consolidation, and other juries then hear damages issues in the other cases that are part of the consolidation. In practice, these large-scale consolidations resemble trials of class actions, in which class-wide issues are usually tried to a single jury and followed, if necessary, by trials of individual class members' claims. But whereas a jury's decision on group-wide issues in a consolidated trial binds only the named parties that are before the court, in a Rule 23 class action the jury's decision on class-wide issues binds all members of the class, including absent parties.[26] While there is case law regarding the selection of representative parties in class actions, there is little or no case law regarding the selection of representative parties for non–class action consolidated trials, and judges appear to make the selection—often with the advice of the attorneys—on an ad hoc basis.[27]

The organization of trials in Rule 42(a) and other consolidations and Rule 23 class actions is specified by judicial case management orders, which, in asbestos litigation, have produced considerable variation on the trial models described in this section. In the early 1980s, in the Philadelphia Court of Common Pleas and the federal court in East Texas, several juries were seated to hear testimony common to several cases at the same time and then separated to hear testimony specific to each case and to decide those cases' outcomes. When, after hearing the same evidence, the different juries returned conflicting verdicts on the common questions, this experiment was abandoned (Hensler et al., 1985). Thereafter, when judges consolidated cases for trial, they generally put together a few cases, and tried those cases together to a single jury, which delivered individual verdicts for each case. In 1984, federal judge Robert Parker consolidated 30 cases for trial in East Texas and selected four cases from the larger consolidated group for trial to a single jury. As the judge anticipated, the verdicts in the tried cases provided benchmarks for settling all of the remaining cases; however, had settlement not ensued, each of the cases that had been aggregated

---

[25] *Parklane Hosiery Co. v. Shore*, 439 U.S. 322 (1979).

[26] When a class is certified under F.R.C.P. 23(b) (3), class members who do not wish to be bound by the case's outcome may opt out of the class litigation.

[27] But, see *In re Ethyl Corp.*, 975 S.W.2d 606, 620 (Tex. 1998) (reviewing case law on the criteria for consolidation and discussing in passing the selection of representative cases).

would have been tried (several at a time) to a jury (Selvin and Picus, 1987). At the time, it was the largest nonclass consolidation of asbestos cases for trial ever.[28]

Although most consolidated trials in the early years involved relatively small numbers of plaintiffs, a few judges in jurisdictions with large asbestos caseloads consolidated thousands of cases for trial. In 1985, Judge Parker certified the first class action of asbestos workers' injury claims in East Texas, and scheduled a trial of four class-wide questions, including punitive damages.[29] The class comprised about 800 asbestos claims then pending in federal court in Texas. Judge Parker's certification decision specified that if liability were found against the defendants, plaintiffs' damages claims would be decided in "mini-trials" of four to ten claims. The class action settled for $137 million five weeks into trial (McGovern, 1989). Judge Parker later certified another class action comprising some 3,000 claims, which were tried in 1990 in a novel format that applied the jury's liability verdict to the entire class and extrapolated the damages verdicts in sample cases to similar class members (Saks and Blanck, 1992; Bordens and Horowitz, 1998).[30] In 1989, the state court in Kanawha County, West Virginia, tried several hundred cases together, ordering a single jury to decide six common issues, including the award of punitive damages.[31] Three years later, asbestos cases filed in four West Virginia counties were consolidated for trial in the Monongalia County, West Virginia, state court ("Cases in Four West Virginia Counties Consolidated," 1991).[32] In 1991, New York State Court judge Helen Freedman consolidated 850 cases arising out of asbestos exposure to powerhouse workers.[33] About the same time, Judge Freedman and federal judge Jack Weinstein (sitting in the Eastern and Southern Districts of New York) consolidated for trial approximately 600 cases arising out of asbestos exposure to workers in the Brooklyn

---

[28] *Newman v. Johns-Manville*, Civil No. M-79-124-CA (E.D. Tex.). *Newman* was filed against multiple defendants, including Johns-Manville. The litigation against Manville was stayed after its 1982 filing for Chapter 11 reorganization, but the case moved forward against the other defendants. At the time of the trial, ten defendants remained.

[29] *Jenkins v. Raymark Industries, Inc.*, 109 F.R.D. 269 (E.D. Tex. 1985), *aff'd*, 782 F.2d 468 (5th Cir. 1986).

[30] *Cimino v. Raymark Indus.*, 751 F. Supp. 649 (D. Tex. 1990). Subsequently, the 5th Circuit held that the trial consolidation violated defendants' due process rights, and the verdicts were vacated. *Cimino v. Raymark Indus.*, 151 F.3d 297 (5th Cir. 1998).

[31] *Turley v. Owens-Corning Fiberglass In re Asbestos Case*, Nos. 84-C-3321 (Cir. Ct., Kanawha Co., W. Va., Feb. 15, 1989). The order consolidated all cases on which the firm of Ness, Motley, Loadholt, Richardson & Poole, a leading South Carolina asbestos law firm, was associated. The cases were consolidated under Rule 42 of the West Virginia Rules of Civil Procedure. See *State of West Virginia Ex. Rel. Mobil Corporation v. Gaughan*, West Virginia Supreme Court of Appeals, slip op. No. 30314 (April 2002). It is unclear how many cases initially were covered by the trial consolidation order, but 315 cases were actually tried in the first phase. See "Trials: Damages Awarded in West Virginia Second Phase," 1990.

[32] When the consolidation order was announced, plaintiff attorneys said they did not know how many cases it covered ("Cases in Four West Virginia Counties Consolidated," 1991).

[33] *In re New York City Asbestos Litigation*, Re: All Powerhouse Cases, N.Y. Sup. Ct., N.Y. Co. (1991).

Navy Yard. Most of the Navy Yard cases settled before trial,[34] but 79 cases were tried in a multiphase trial before a single jury.[35]

By the beginning of the 1990s, both the frequency and scale of consolidation seemed to be increasing. In 1990, 8,555 claims against more than 100 defendants were consolidated for trial in state court in Baltimore, Maryland. The judge's order called for two trials of different groups of defendants. Under the trial plan, if the jury found liability for any of the defendants, damages trials (with different juries) would be held subsequently for small groups of plaintiffs, until all plaintiffs' cases had been either tried or settled. The first jury to hear cases would also be asked to set a punitive damage multiplier for all defendants against whom it decided punitive damages were merited. By the time of the first trial, in 1992, claims against all but 15 of the defendants had been dismissed or settled, and during the trial nine of these defendants settled. The jury found some but not all of the remaining defendants liable and set a punitive damage multiplier for some of the latter defendants; it awarded compensatory damages to some but not all of the representative plaintiffs.[36] In 1993, the largest consolidated trial to date was heard in a Jackson County, Mississippi, state court. The trial was held in a courtroom at the county fairgrounds constructed just for this trial and lasted four and a half months (Abbott and Mallette, 1994). Six of nine sample plaintiffs were awarded $9.26 million in compensatory damages, while defense verdicts were delivered in the remaining three cases. A punitive damages multiplier was set at ten cents for every dollar of compensatory damages, which was applicable for the remaining plaintiffs in the 9,600-plaintiff trial.[37]

Trying thousands of cases together raises due process questions for plaintiffs and defendants alike (Trangsrud, 1989). If, as is common, the liability phase is tried first with representative plaintiffs, and the jury decides in favor of the defendant, all of the plaintiffs, not just those whose cases were presented to the jury, lose—as indeed happened in a trial of 800 cases alleging birth defects arising out of the use of Bendectin

---

[34] *In re New York City Asbestos Litigation*, 142 F.R.D. 60 (E.D.N.Y. & S.D.N.Y. 1992).

[35] *In re Eastern & Southern Dists. Asbestos Litig.*, 772 F. Supp. 1380 (E.D.N.Y. & S.D.N.Y. 1991), *aff'd in part, rev'd in part* 971 F.2d 831 (2nd Cir. 1992).

[36] See *ACandS, Inc. v. Godwin et al.*, 340 Md. 334 (1995). Two other defendants who had settled with the plaintiffs who brought suit against them elected to have their cross-claims heard in the common issues trial, so that the jury actually decided claims against eight defendants. The Maryland appellate court upheld the consolidation on appeal but reversed the jury's punitive damages awards, with the result that in the subsequent trials plaintiffs could obtain only compensatory damages. (See *ACandS, Inc.*, 1995). The mass consolidation followed a period in which the court had attempted to manage its asbestos cases by consolidating first six, and later ten, cases for trial (*ACandS, Inc.*, 1995). The first consolidation, known as Abate I, was followed by a second consolidated trial of other defendants and cross-claims, known as Abate II. See *ACandS, Inc. v. Abate*, 121 Md. App. 590 (1998).

[37] *In re Asbestos Personal Injury Cases, Abrams et al.*, (Jackson Co. Cir. Ct., 19th Jud. Dist. Miss. 1993). This was apparently the second phase of a multiphase trial in which the different phases involved different sets of defendants. When the case was first scheduled for a consolidated trial, it was estimated to comprise some 6,000 claims. (See "Judge Hopes to Resolve 6,000 Cases in Consolidated Trial," 1991).

(Green, 1996). In a class action trial, the risk is magnified, as the outcomes of a class-wide trial apply to all class members including absent unnamed parties. Moreover, experimental social-psychological research suggests that consolidating cases for trial may change jurors' assessments of liability and damages. Horowitz and Bordens (1988) found mock juries in simulated trials with representative plaintiffs were more likely to find the defendant liable when the juries were aware that a large number of plaintiffs were represented by the case in front of them.

Defendants believe that large-scale consolidation, especially when accompanied by the risk of huge punitive damage awards, tilts the playing field against them. As a result, when faced with a consolidated or class-wide trial of thousands of cases, they are very likely to settle. For example, just before the 1991 first phase of the large-scale consolidated trial in Jackson County, Mississippi, several defendants settled with 5,500 plaintiffs ("5,500 Mississippi Plaintiffs Settle . . . ," 1991). In recent years, defendants have challenged large-scale consolidations on due process grounds. In 1998, the Fifth Circuit Court of Appeals vacated the results of the East Texas class action trial in which verdicts for 160 plaintiffs were extrapolated to a class of more than 3,000 plaintiffs.[38] The court held that the trial plan violated the Seventh Amendment right to trial. However, the West Virginia Supreme Court has supported mass consolidations in that state.[39] To date, the U.S. Supreme Court has not agreed to hear appeals of mass consolidations. Consolidated trials of small numbers of cases may also raise due process concerns for plaintiffs and defendants, as information about one plaintiff's injuries or damages may skew the awards for other plaintiffs upward or downward in a process known as "anchoring" (Sunstein et al., 1998). In experimental research using mock juries and simulated trials, Horowitz and Bordens (1988) found that in a group trial the presence of an "outlier" plaintiff with more-severe injuries led to higher awards for the other plaintiffs in the group. Trying small numbers of claims together does not seem to have engendered the same level of controversy as mass consolidations, but outcomes of consolidated trials are often appealed, in part, on the grounds that consolidation was inappropriate.[40]

To determine the proportion of asbestos claims tried singly and in groups in recent years, we searched *Mealey's Litigation Report: Asbestos* from January 1, 1993, to

---

[38] *Cimino v. Raymark Indus.*, 151 F.3d 297 (5th Cir. 1998).

[39] *State of West Virginia ex. rel. Mobil Corp. v. Gaughan*, West Virginia Supreme Court of Appeals, slip op. No. 30314 (April 2002).

[40] See, e.g., *Malcolm v. National Gypsum Co.*, 995 F.2d 346 (2d Cir. 1993) (holding judge erred in consolidating 48 New York State cases of powerhouse workers who were employed at different sites); *Cain v. Armstrong World Industries*, 785 F. Supp. 1448 (S.D. Ala., 1992) (holding trial court erred in consolidating 13 diverse actions, including personal injury and wrongful death actions); *In re Ethyl* 975 S.W.2d 606 (1998) (reviewing prior appellate opinions on trial consolidation and suggesting consolidating small numbers of claims may be acceptable, where large-scale consolidations would not).

2001.[41] We found 526 trials that reached verdicts on 1,570 plaintiffs' claims. About 60 percent of the trials involved a single claim; most of the remainder involved fewer than ten claims (see Figure 3.1). But the proportion of all *claims* that were tried individually was only about one-quarter; about half were tried in groups of six claims or more (see Figure 3.2).

The distribution of claims by number of claims tried together remained roughly the same over the time period, although a somewhat larger proportion of claims was tried individually in the last few years studied (see Figure 3.3).

Some claims are filed in groups (i.e., under a single docket number)[42] and then tried together as if they were a single case, without a case management order consolidating claims for trial. Most large-scale consolidations either are settled or are resolved by group-wide trials on liability issues (and sometimes punitive damages),

Figure 3.1
Distribution of Trials by Number of Claims Tried Together (Claims Tried to Verdict, 1993–2001)

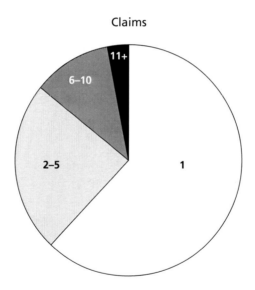

Claims

RAND *MG162-3.1*

---

[41] There is no national database of civil jury outcomes. *Mealey's* is a subscription service for litigators that is now available online (www.mealeysonline.com). *Mealey's* has been following asbestos litigation closely for many years and is often used as a reference for the field. For further details on our selection and processing of data from *Mealey's*, including data limitations, see Appendix C.

[42] For example, an Illinois decision references a complaint filed in Cook County in 1987 on behalf of 134 plaintiffs against 20 or more defendants. See *In re Asbestos Cases*, 224 Ill. App. 3d 292, 293 (Ill. App. Ct. 1991). But see *Abdullah v. Acands, Inc.*, 30 F.3d 264 (1st Cir. 1994) ("The Massachusetts Mass Joinder Cases") (upholding Massachusetts federal court's dismissal of a single complaint filed on behalf of 1,000 plaintiffs on grounds that the complaint did not meet joinder requirements).

Figure 3.2
Distribution of Claims by Number Tried Together (Claims Tried to Verdict, 1993–2001)

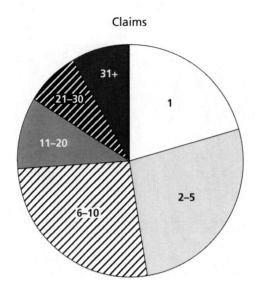

RAND *MG162-3.2*

NOTE: The 31+ category is accounted for entirely by a consolidated trial of 129 claims.

Figure 3.3
Percentage of Claims Tried Singly and in Groups over Time (Claims Tried to Verdict, 1993–2001)

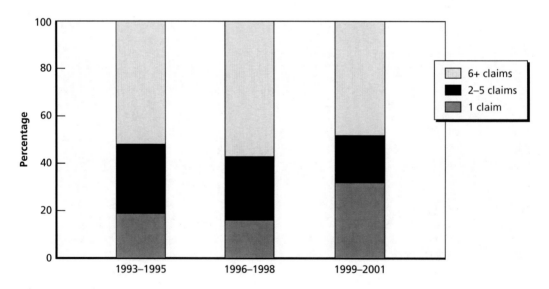

RAND *MG162-3.3*

followed by damages trials of small groups of claims. Jury verdict reporters do not always distinguish among these situations. Therefore, one cannot determine the frequency of trial consolidation or the magnitude of large-scale consolidations by simply counting the number of group trials or the number of claims tried together, as reported by *Mealey's* or other litigation subscription services. To further explore the frequency and magnitude of large-scale consolidations, we closely read descriptions of all cases identified as "consolidated" in *Mealey's Litigation Report: Asbestos* from 1993 to 2003, including cases in which few claims reached trial.

Excluding consolidations for pretrial purposes only—such as the consolidation of federal cases under 28 U.S.C. §1407 and a consolidation of cases in Kansas under a rule modeled after the federal multidistrict statute—we found 15 consolidations each of which comprised 100 claims or more, which proceeded in seven states (see Table 3.2). All but one of these large-scale consolidations resulted in trials, including trials of subgroups of cases as well as trials with representative plaintiffs. In some instances, a consolidation led to multiple trials of representative plaintiffs against different subgroups of defendants.

Table 3.2 includes only consolidations that were either tried or scheduled for trial but settled during the ten-year period (1993–2003) we studied. Some of the cases listed in Table 3.2 were first consolidated before 1993, and in one case, an initial trial phase took place before 1993, and then a second phase occurred during the period under study. As discussed previously, some large-scale trial consolidations, including trials of class actions and (in Mississippi) mass joinders, were completed before 1993 and therefore are not included in Table 3.2.[43] In the final phase of preparing this report, we identified an additional large-scale consolidation, comprising about 5,000 cases, which went to trial in 2004 and therefore is also not included in Table 3.2. On the other side of the ledger, some of the consolidations listed in Table 3.2 might not sustain appeal today: In 2004, the Mississippi Supreme Court articulated stricter requirements for Rule 20 joinders;[44] subsequently, the Mississippi state

---

[43] Many claims have been filed in Mississippi under its permissive joinder rule (Rule 20). Table 3.2 includes only mass joinder cases that were scheduled during the study period for a consolidated trial (typically under Rule 42). Mass joinders of 100 claims or more that we identified in our legal research, but for which we did not find reports of consolidated trials, include *Abercrombie v. Pittsburgh Corning Corp.* (214 plaintiffs); *Abner v. Westinghouse Elec. Corp.* (1,123 plaintiffs); *Barksdale v. Pittsburgh Corning Corp.* (130 plaintiffs); *Bell v. Combustion Engineering* (1,123 plaintiffs); *Hedrick v. Metropolitan Life Ins. Co.* (2,856) plaintiffs; *Noble v. E.H. O'Neill* (4,667 plaintiffs); and *Stephens v. Combustion Engineering* (2,500 plaintiffs). See *Prepared Statement of Steven Kazan, Hearing on Asbestos Litigation Before the Committee on the Judiciary, U.S. Senate*, September 25, 2002 (citing data reported in an amicus brief of the Mississippi Manufacturers Association in *American Bankers Ins. Co. of Fla v. Alexander*, filed July 14, 1999). On the number joined in *Stephens*, see Clark (2001, pp. 371–372). After filing the mass joinder, the plaintiff attorneys in Stephens amended the complaint to remove most of plaintiffs, leaving only some 300 (Clark, 2001, footnote 60).

[44] *Janssen Pharmaceutica, Inc. v. Armond*, 866 So. 2d 1092 (Miss. 2004).

Table 3.2
Large-Scale Trial Consolidations, 1993–2003

State	Case Title	Year[a]	Number of Claims	Was There a Trial? What Form?	Outcome(s) to Date
Illinois	*In re Asbestos*[b]	1996	220	No	Settled
Louisiana	*In re Asbestos Plaintiffs v. Bordelon*[c]	1994	2,995	Yes, some cases tried in groups of ten or fewer claims.	Mix of plaintiff and defense verdicts, dismissals and settlements.
Louisiana	*Abadie v. Metropolitan Life*[d]	1995	1,000+	Yes, some cases tried in small and large groups.	Mix of plaintiff and defense verdicts, judgments notwithstanding the verdict (JNOVs) and settlements.
Louisiana	*Bickham v. Metropolitan Life*[e]	1999	1,400	Yes, some cases tried in small groups.	Defense verdicts; outcomes of other consolidated claims unknown.
Maryland	*Abate v. AC&S* ("Abate II")[f]	1994	1,300	Yes, single multiphase trial with five representative plaintiffs, followed by mini-trials of damage claims. Trial also resolved some claims pertaining to 8,555 plaintiffs whose claims were tried in prior consolidated trial ("Abate I").	Liability found and compensatory and punitive damages awarded; JNOV granted to some defendants re punitive damages; liability of some defendants reversed by appellate court; liability of other defendants vacated and remanded for retrial; 6,800 claims ultimately resolved by settlement prior to mini-trials.
Mississippi	*In re Asbestos Personal Injury Cases* (Abrams)[g]	1993	9,600	Yes, multiphase trial with nine representative plaintiffs. Claims against different defendants were tried in separate phases.	Mix of plaintiff and defense verdicts; punitive damage multiplier specified for all plaintiff verdicts.

Table 3.2—Continued

State	Case Title	Year[a]	Number of Claims	Was There a Trial? What Form?	Outcome(s) to Date
Mississippi	*Cosey v. Bullard*[h]	1998	3,464	Yes, 12 plaintiff cases tried together; judge reportedly planned to try additional cases to same jury.	Plaintiff verdicts in all cases against some or all defendants. All defendants found liable for punitive damages. All cases settled before amount of punitive damages was decided. Remaining cases in mass joinder settled with most defendants, along with another mass joinder case, *Rankin v. A-Bex Corp.*
Mississippi	*Curry v. ACandS*[i]	2001	154	Yes, ten cases set for trial; two were dismissed and two settled before trial. Additional trials planned for groups of ten cases.	Plaintiff verdicts against all non-settling defendants. No punitive damages awarded.[j]
Texas	*In re Ethyl Corp.*[k]	1998	459	348 settled. Of the remaining 111, 25 were selected for trial (later reduced to 22).	Consolidation of 25 claims appealed but upheld. Final outcomes unknown.
Virginia	*In re Asbestos Cases*[l]	2002	1,296	Yes, bifurcated trial against eight defendants. One defendant dismissed, four settled.	One of three remaining defendants found liable; no punitive damages. Case may have settled; damages phase not reported.

Table 3.2—Continued

State	Case Title	Year[a]	Number of Claims	Was There a Trial? What Form?	Outcome(s) to Date
West Virginia	*Mobil Corp. v. Gaughan*[m]	2002	7,715[n]	Multiple trial plans proposed by judge. At one time, five trial phases, each of one or more groups of 25 claims, except for one group of 20 cancer claims. All trials in unitary format, to resolve only the claims before the jury.[o] Plaintiffs to decide trial groupings.[p] At another time, three judges and juries to hear and to decide common issues, followed by mini-trials on causation and damages with other juries, apparently of groups of claims.[q] As held, Phase I group-wide trial on liability, with Phase II mini-trials on damages, including punitive damages, to follow.	Trial began against "a few defendants"; case was dismissed against one, others settled, leaving one defendant to proceed, which the jury found liable.[r]
West Virginia	*Mon-Mass Ii*[s]	1998	7,000	At time of consolidation, more than 140 defendants; reduced to 80 defendants as trial approached; only three remaining by verdict. Phase I trial of liability and punitive damages. Mini-trials on damages to follow.	Liability found against three defendants and punitive multiplier specified.
West Virginia	*In re Asbestos Cases* (Kanawha III)[t]	1994	9,000–10,000	Reported to be tried to two juries and two judges, "perhaps coming together," with one trial with sample plaintiffs but the other not.	Mix of defense and plaintiff verdicts; punitive damages assessed against one defendant; most defendants settled before verdict.[u]
West Virginia	*In re Asbestos Cases* (IV)[v]	1995	"Up to" 1,000	Phase I trial on product defect against six manufacturers of welding rods, wires, and cables; no punitive damages claims.	Mix of liability ("defective") and no-liability; outcomes of damages claims not reported.

Table 3.2—Continued

State	Case Title	Year[a]	Number of Claims	Was There a Trial? What Form?	Outcome(s) to Date
West Virginia	*In re Asbestos Cases* (Kanawha IV)[w]	1996	1,000+	Multiphase trial plan, Phase I on liability, organized by 33 premises and 17 owners. Phase II individual claims against defendants held liable in first phase.[x]	Liability found against defendants. Verdict said to apply to "all current and future plaintiffs" claiming exposure to products manufactured by these defendants. Outcomes of damages claims not reported.

[a] Generally, this is the year of trial. In some instances, cases were ordered to be consolidated some years earlier. In some instances of multi-phase trials, earlier trial phases occurred before the period under study.

[b] *In re Asbestos Litigation*, Master File Asbestos Litigation No. 95 L 00000 (Ill. Cir., Cook Co.).

[c] *Asbestos v. Bordelon, Inc.*, 726 So. 2d 926, 978 (La. Ct. App. 1998).

[d] *Abadie v. Metro. Life Ins. Co.*, 784 So. 2d 46 (La. Ct. App. 2001).

[e] *Bickham v. Metropolitan Life Ins. Co.*, 764 So. 2d 345 (La. Ct. App. 2000).

[f] Details of the trial plan in Abate II are reported at *ACandS, Inc. v. Abate*, 121 Md. App. 590 (1998). This second consolidated trial in the long-running Baltimore City asbestos litigation included both third-party and cross-claims pertaining to the original 8,555 plaintiffs whose cases were tried in 1992 and the liability and compensation claims of an additional 1,300 plaintiffs whose claims were filed after the claims of the 8,555 whose cases were tried in Abate I. The 1998 appellate court opinion notes that there is uncertainty about how many plaintiffs' and defendants' cases were decided in the 1994 trial.

[g] *In re Asbestos Personal Injury Cases: Abrams et al.*, Jackson Co. Cir. Ct. Miss. About 5,500 plaintiffs settled with some defendants prior to trial. See "5500 Mississippi Plaintiffs Settle . . . " (1991).

[h] *Cosey v. Bullard Co. et al.* (No. 95-0069, Miss. Cir. Jefferson Co.). On the number of cases joined in *Cosey,* see "Trade Association Asks Mississippi High Court . . ." (1999). On the trial outcomes, see "Mississippi Jury Awards $48.5 Million . . ." (1998). On the settlement of *Cosey* and *Rankin,* said to include "nearly 4,000 plaintiffs," see "Plaintiffs Question Allocation . . ." (2000). Later reports describe the post-*Cosey* settlement as covering more than 6,100 plaintiffs. See "Tobacco Lawyers Want New Asbestos Trial Site" (2001, p. 10A). We also found references to other mass joinder cases in Mississippi: *Noble v. O'Neil* (4,667 plaintiffs); *Bell v. Combustion Engineering* (987 plaintiffs); and *Stephens v. Combustion Engineering* (2,500 plaintiffs). None of these appears to have reached trial in consolidated form. On the number of cases joined in *Noble* and *Bell,* see "Trade Association Asks Mississippi High Court . . ." (1999). On the number joined in *Stephens,* see Clark (2001, pp. 371–372). After filing the mass joinder, the plaintiff attorneys in *Stephens* amended the complaint to remove most of the plaintiffs, leaving only some 300 (Clark, 2001, footnote 60).

[i] *James Curry et al. v. ACandS Inc. et al.* (No. CV 00-181, Miss. Cir. Holmes Co.). For a description of trial and outcomes, see "Miss. Jury Returns $150 Verdict . . ." (2001). In some reports, this case is cited as *Johnson v. ACandS.*

[j] 3M has appealed the verdicts against it. *3M Co. v. Johnson*, 2004 Miss. LEXIS 1102 (Miss. 2004).

[k] *In re Ethyl Corp.*, 975 S.W.2d 606, 620 (Tex. 1998) (upholding consolidation).

[l] *In re Asbestos Cases*, No. CL-99-20000-00, Va. Cir. Newport News (petition for writ of mandamus against judge ordering consolidation denied). *In re Hopeman Bros., Inc.* 569 S.E.2d 409 (Va. 2002). Cert. denied. *Hopeman Brothers Inc. v. Clarence L. Acker et al.*, No. 02-520, U.S. Sup. For a description of the trial, see "Jury Returns Mixed Verdict . . ." (2003).

[m] *Adkins v. Mobil Oil Corp.*, No. 01-50987, Kanawha Co. Cir. Ct., W. Va. This was the first case consolidated under West Virginia TCR 26.01.

[n] Originally reported to include more than 8,000 plaintiffs and more than 250 defendants; by the time of trial, about 5,000 plaintiffs and "a few" defendants remained.

[o] *State ex rel. Allman v. MacQueen*, 209 W. Va. 726, 729 (2001).

[p] *State ex rel. Allman* (2001, at 732).

q *State ex rel. Mobil Corp. v. Gaughan*, 211 W. Va. 106, at 109 (2002). The trial judge noted that he was also considering applying a "damage matrix" to assess damages for the individual claims (*State ex rel. Mobil*, 2002, at 110).

r "Union Carbide Liable . . ." (2002).

s *In Re: Mon-Mass II*, C.A. No. 93-C-362, et al. W. Va. Cir., Monongalia Co.

t No. 92-C-8888, Kanawha Co. Ct., W. Va.

u See "OCF Admits to Liability . . ." (1994); "MetLife Settles 35,000 Cases . . ." (1994); "Rapid American Hit with . . ." (1994).

v No. 92-C-8888, Kanawha Co. Ct. W. Va. For a description of the trial and outcomes, see "Welding Rod, Wire, and Cable Defendants . . ." (1995).

w No. 92-C-8888, Kanawha Co. Ct., W. Va. In all, there were six consolidated trials in Monongalia and Kanawha counties prior to the adoption of TCR 26.01, which were said to have resolved more than 20,000 cases. See *State ex rel. Allman v. MacQueen*, 209 W. Va. 726 (2001), Note 6. The first consolidated case in Kanawha County was tried in 1990 ("Damages Awarded in West Virginia Second Phase," 1990).

x *State ex rel. Appalachian Power Co. v. MacQueen*, 198 W. Va. 1 (1996). At the time of the Supreme Court's ruling upholding the trial consolidation, the plans for Phase II had not yet been announced (*State ex rel. Appalachian Power Co.*, 1996, at 6).

legislature amended state venue rules to limit joinders to plaintiffs who would satisfy state venue requirements,[45] effectively eliminating mass joinders of out-of-state plaintiffs. The Texas Supreme Court, while upholding consolidation in *In re Ethyl*, articulated consolidation guidelines that arguably restrict future mass consolidations in that state.[46]

Although we supplemented our reading of litigation reporters with traditional legal research, determining whether trials took place and what form they took proved to be extraordinarily difficult.[47] As a result, we regard the information shown in Table 3.2 as being suggestive of the frequency and scale of large-scale consolidations during the period studied; some large-scale consolidations may not be included, and the numbers of claims reported may be approximate.

All of the consolidated trials listed in Table 3.2 were complex. Of the 14 large-scale consolidations we identified where some trials took place, eight used representa-

[45] Mississippi Code, Section 11-11-3.

[46] *In re Ethyl Corp.*, 975 S.W. 2d 606 (1998) (setting requirements for consolidation under Tex. R. Civ. P. (a) but denying mandamus on grounds that the trial court record was silent regarding relevant factors and trial court order is reviewed for abuse of discretion).

[47] The numbers of cases consolidated change as the litigation progresses, and some cases settle with some or all defendants while others are apparently added to the original consolidation order. Decisions sometimes refer to general titles for the consolidated litigation ("In re asbestos"), sometimes refer to lead plaintiffs, and sometimes rely on colloquial descriptions ("the mass consolidations in Monongalia county"), making it easy to undercount or over-count cases. Court decisions often are either silent or vague about the number of cases affected by the decisions; indeed, sometimes courts comment that they are unsure about the number themselves. See, e.g., *ACandS, Inc. v. Abate*, 121 Md. App. 590 (1998); *State ex rel. Mobil Corp. v. Gaughan*, 211 W. Va. 106 (2002), note 3; and *State ex rel. Allman v. MacQueen*, 209 W. Va. 726 (2001), note 1. We even found one instance in which the parties themselves argued about how many cases had been decided by a consolidated trial. Although we tried to identify cases that were consolidated for trial but settled entirely before a trial took place, it seems likely that litigation reporters would be more prone to miss such cases than to miss cases in which trial commenced. We believe Table 3.2 presents the most accurate count of large-scale consolidations possible without extensive interview-based research with attorneys involved in these consolidations, which was beyond the scope of this study.

tive plaintiffs to try liability (and sometimes punitive damages) against defendants. In the remaining six trials, plaintiffs were grouped for unitary ("all issues") trials, including one trial in which a single jury heard all 129 claims in full and was instructed to fill out a special verdict form for each.[48] Although only half of the consolidated trials were structured so that the jury's verdict in the liability phase would bind all of the consolidated claims, descriptions of the unitary trials of small groups of claims suggest that judges anticipated that the initial trials would lead to settlement of all the remaining consolidated claims.

Some of the trials listed in Table 3.2 were extraordinarily complex. For example, the 1994 Baltimore City trial known as "Abate II" (which was the second stage of the 1992 trial, "Abate I," described above), the jury was asked to decide liability and punitive damages against defendants sued by some 1,300 plaintiffs whose cases were filed after 1992, and *also* some claims against these defendants brought by the original set of 8,555 plaintiffs whose claims were tried in 1992 to a different jury. In its decision on the trial appeal brought by some defendants, the appellate court noted that it was uncertain how many plaintiffs' and defendants' cases were decided in the 1994 trial.[49]

The challenge of trying thousands of sometimes quite disparate claims against scores of defendants is illustrated by the succession of different trial plans that were announced in some cases. For example, in *Adkins v. Mobil Oil Corp.*,[50] a 2002 consolidation of 7,715 claims in West Virginia, the judge at one time indicated that there would be five trial phases, each involving one or more groups of 25 claims each, except for one group of 20 cancer claims, with the plaintiff attorneys to decide on how cases would be grouped. All claims would be tried in unitary format, meaning the outcomes would apply only to this specific group of claims.[51] Later, it was reported that three judges and juries would be assigned to hear and decide common issues among the consolidated claims, perhaps with mini-trials of damage claims to follow, but perhaps with some procedure aimed at applying a "damage matrix."[52] Ultimately, there was a single bifurcated trial, with phase I deciding group-wide liability issues. The judge intended that phase to be followed by mini-trials to decide com-

---

[48] *Abadie v. Metro. Life Ins. Co.*, 784 So. 2d 46 (La. Ct. App., 2001).

[49] *ACand S, Inc. v. Abate,* 121 Md. App. 590 (1998). The Maryland court was not the only court to express uncertainty about how many cases were involved in consolidations. See, e.g., *State ex rel. Mobil Corp. v. Gaughan,* 211 W. Va. 106 (2002), note 3, and *State ex rel. Allman v. MacQueen,* 209 W. Va. 726 (2001), note 1.

[50] No. 01-50987, Kanawha Co. Cir. Ct., W. Va.

[51] *State ex rel. Allman v. MacQueen,* 209 W. Va. 726, 729, 732 (2001).

[52] *State ex rel. Mobil Corp. v. Gaughan,* 211 W. Va. 106, 109–110 (2002).

pensatory and punitive damages, but the one defendant who remained at the time of the liability verdict apparently settled thereafter.[53]

In some instances, how the consolidated litigation would be organized for trial was still unclear at the time that the trial began. For example, at the time that some defendants appealed a trial consolidation plan for some 1,000 premises liability claims brought in Kanawha County, West Virginia, the West Virginia Supreme Court—upholding the plan—noted that while the judge had organized the liability phase of the trial, "the precise formula for the presentation of phase two of the trial has not been announced."[54] We could find no record of the judge's plan for trying successive waves of cases in the large-scale consolidation of *Cosey v. Bullard*,[55] a Mississippi mass joinder of 3,464 claims. In answer to our inquiry, one of the lawyers who tried the case told us that when the case settled—after the first 12 plaintiffs' claims reached verdicts and all defendants were found liable for punitive damages—the lawyers were still not certain how the trial would proceed.

Both defendants and plaintiffs sometimes appealed these trial consolidation plans (although defense appeals were more common). For example, when the West Virginia trial judge presiding over *Adkins* announced his plan for consolidating groups of claims and holding "all issues" unitary trials, defendants argued against any consolidated trial, and one group of plaintiffs argued against unitary trials, asking instead that the trial begin with a single liability phase that would apply to all of the consolidated claims.[56] More frequent than appeals, however, were the large-scale settlements that many defendants agreed to before trials commenced or before the juries reached verdicts.

The parties were not the only ones who opposed massive consolidations; some judges expressed doubts as to the fairness of proposed consolidations, especially in light of the U.S. Supreme Court's decision in *Amchem Products v. Windsor*,[57] reversing that large-scale consolidation of the claims of future plaintiffs. "Frankly, this case leaves me with a profound disquiet," wrote one of the West Virginia Supreme Court justices who ruled on the *Adkins* consolidation plan. "Mobil argues very persuasively and convincingly that the defendants have been denied due process in our courts. . . . I am deeply concerned that Mobil is probably correct and some federal court will eventually tell us so." Justice Maynard nevertheless concurred with colleagues on the bench in rejecting Mobil's challenge as untimely, because the trial plan for *Adkins*

---

[53] See "Union Carbide Liable for Thousands of Asbestos Claims . . . " (2002); "Union Carbide Left as Remaining Defendant . . . " (2002).

[54] *State ex rel. Appalachian Power Co. v. MacQueen,* 198 W. Va. 1 (1996), note 9.

[55] No. 95-0069, Miss. Cir. Jefferson Co.

[56] *State ex rel. Allman v. MacQueen,* 209 W. Va. 726 (2001).

[57] 521 U.S. 591 (1997).

had not yet been completed. Moreover, Judge Maynard concluded, "Notwithstanding the foregoing, there is another side to this issue which is equally thorny and troubling. If this mass litigation is simply halted, clearly all the plaintiffs would be denied their due process rights and their day in court. There should be a simple answer that would guarantee everyone's due process rights, but I cannot conceive or fashion one."[58]

Notwithstanding defendants' fears that consolidated trials will inevitably result in plaintiff awards, the cases for which we were able to determine trial outcomes displayed a mix of outcomes. Of the 13 consolidations for which we were able to determine at least some trial outcomes, six resulted in a mix of plaintiff and defense verdicts, six resulted in plaintiff verdicts in all cases against some or all defendants, and one resulted in defense verdicts. Punitive damages were not always claimed and not always awarded against all defendants when claimed. In two instances, trial judges dismissed claims against one or more defendants, and in two instances they reversed one or more jury verdicts. In one instance, an appeals court vacated some decisions and remanded the case for retrial. Interpreting this mix of outcomes is complicated by the fact that only those who are most certain of the strength of their cases (correctly or incorrectly) generally proceed to trial.

Settlement

In asbestos litigation, as in all other civil litigation in the United States, most cases settle. Some settlements are the result of judicial case management practices, including large-scale consolidations such as those described above. However, over time, many defendants have chosen to adopt independent settlement programs, negotiating settlements of thousands of cases outside the courts.

The "Futures" Problem

When a single plaintiff settles a torts case, the plaintiff generally is reasonably certain of the extent of his or her injuries, and the defendant offers an amount intended to cover future medical costs and work losses associated with the injury, as well as the costs incurred to date. In many mass tort cases, however, the plaintiffs include some people with little or no current injury who claim that they have a higher risk of injury in the future, because they have used or have been exposed to a defendant's product. Whether and under what circumstances these plaintiffs should be able to

---

[58] *State ex rel. Mobil Corp. v. Gaughan*, 211 W. Va. 330, 331, 333 (2002) (J. Maynard, concurring). On October 7, 2002, the U.S. Supreme Court rejected the defendants' appeal. *Mobil Corp. v. Adkins,* 537 U.S. 944 (2002), *cert. den'd.* By October 18, all but one defendant had settled the claims against them ("Union Carbide Left as Remaining Defendant . . . ," 2002).

collect damages from defendants has been a source of sharp controversy, and state laws regarding future injuries vary. However, as a practical matter, in order to achieve a comprehensive settlement of all claims associated with alleged product defects, defendants often offer payments to plaintiffs who are mainly seeking protection against future injury-related losses.[59]

In asbestos litigation, the problem of future injury costs is compounded by the long latency period of asbestos-related disease. Defendants who have been the targets of large numbers of claims in the past anticipate that claims will be brought against them for many years to come. Likewise, plaintiff attorneys who specialize in representing asbestos plaintiffs anticipate that they will represent similar plaintiffs, as they become ill, far into the future. Uncertainty about the extent of previous asbestos exposure and changing claiming rates and patterns—reflecting in large part the litigation strategies we have discussed in this chapter—have made it extremely difficult to predict the number and cost of future asbestos claims. But the certainty that future claims will emerge has encouraged settlement agreements that incorporate future claimants. How to make certain that these agreements will, in fact, provide for all future claimants who come forward, so that all who are eligible for compensation are properly compensated and all who are required to pay compensation have taken into account this responsibility in their business planning, has come to be called "the futures problem."

Some corporations that face mass asbestos filings have entered into standing settlement agreements with leading plaintiff attorneys' firms.[60] These agreements typically call for settling hundreds or thousands of cases per year at amounts specified in administrative schedules. The amounts reflect differences in injury severity and other claim characteristics, including the plaintiff lawyer's trial skills and willingness to go to trial, that affect the trial value of cases. Defendants' decisions to pay the negotiated sums are based on cost-benefit calculations that include the value of avoiding the risk and costs of trial, including the untoward effects on stock prices of large jury awards, and also a desire to smooth cash-flow demands to settle cases (Hensler, 2002). Settlement amounts may be renegotiated over time to reflect perceived changes in the values of asbestos claims.

---

[59] For example, plaintiffs who feared rupture of defective implanted Shiley Heart Valves obtained a settlement that offered medical monitoring and payment to remove the valves if they ruptured in the future. *Bowling v. Pfizer, Inc.*, 143 F.R.D. 141 (S.D. Ohio 1992), *appeal dismissed*, 14 F.3d 600 (6th Cir. 1993). Many of these plaintiffs' claims would not have survived motions to dismiss because they arose in jurisdictions that did not recognize claims for emotional distress arising from fear of future injury *(Bowling, 1992)*. Plaintiffs who feared future heart-valve injury as a result of taking the diet pill popularly known as "fen-phen" were included in a class action settlement that offered, inter alia, medical monitoring. *Brown v. Am. Home Prods. Corp. (In re Diet Drugs Prods. Liab. Litig.)*, 2000 U.S. Dist. LEXIS 12275 (D. Pa. 2000).

[60] See, e.g., "4th Circuit Rules That Ohio Plaintiffs Are Necessary . . ." (1999) (reporting settlement agreements between Owens Illinois and three West Virginia attorneys).

For plaintiff law firms, standing agreements offer a means of reducing transaction costs of litigation and also regularizing their firms' revenue stream over time. The agreements also expand the number of claimants on whose behalf the firms are able to obtain compensation. By "packaging" plaintiff claims, the lawyers are able to obtain compensation for claimants with weak claims who would have difficulty collecting damages if they were to proceed individually.

Plaintiff law firms that enter into these agreements demand that each defendant with whom they negotiate an agreement pay a share of the estimated total value of the plaintiff's claim that, in the plaintiff lawyer's view, reflects the share of liability attributable to that defendant. For many years, under the terms of such agreements, lead defendants—mainly asbestos product manufacturers—have paid substantial amounts, while peripheral defendants, whose connection with asbestos products was attenuated, paid more modest amounts.

The Search for Global Settlement

When federal asbestos cases were transferred to Judge Charles Weiner by the Judicial Panel on Multidistrict Litigation in 1991, many asbestos lawyers anticipated that Judge Weiner would help parties negotiate a global settlement of all federal cases against all defendants that would in turn provide a model for resolving state cases (Hensler, 2002). However, fashioning such a broad settlement among a large number of defendants and plaintiff attorneys who had diverse and opposing interests proved enormously difficult. Moreover, if defendants were to achieve their goal of "global peace"—resolving all claims, present and future, at a known price—the parties needed to craft a mechanism for dealing with claimants who had not yet come forward.[61]

Ultimately, the search for a single overarching settlement failed. Instead, a consortium of about 20 major asbestos defendants negotiated two settlements with leading asbestos plaintiff attorneys under the aegis of the multidistrict litigation transferee court, one a "private" (not judicially supervised) settlement of all claims those attorneys then had pending against the defense consortium, and the second, a class action settlement of *all claims that might be brought in the future by any plaintiff (and plaintiff attorney)* against the consortium.[62] The class action settlement provoked sharp attack from lawyers who were not part of the negotiated agreements, from public interest attorneys, and from legal ethicists (Baron, 1993; Hensler, 2002; Symposium, 1995), and was appealed first to the Third Circuit[63] and then to the

---

[61] While challenging, this requirement was not unique to asbestos litigation. For example, at the time of the Agent Orange settlement (resolving claims of Vietnam veterans who alleged injury due to dioxin exposure), the total size of the class was unknown (Schuck, 1987).

[62] *Georgine v. Amchem Products, Inc.*, 157 F.R.D. 246 (E.D. Pa. 1994).

[63] *Georgine v. Amchem Prods.*, 83 F.3d 610 (3d Cir. 1996).

U.S. Supreme Court. When the settlement was rejected by the U.S. Supreme Court in *Amchem Products v. Windsor*,[64] and when the Court, in *Ortiz v. Fibreboard*,[65] subsequently rejected a similar class settlement of asbestos claims against another major defendant in 1999,[66] efforts to achieve a global resolution of asbestos litigation through class action litigation collapsed (Cabraser, 1998).

Asbestos Litigation After *Amchem* and *Ortiz*

After the failure of the *Amchem* and *Ortiz* class action settlements in 1997 and 1999, the landscape of asbestos litigation began to change. Filings surged, perhaps in part as a result of the publicity engendered by the class action notices required by *Amchem* and *Ortiz* and the ensuing controversy, which was widely reported in the legal media. From 1998 on, the number of law firms filing more than 100 cases annually increased dramatically, and the number of firms that were new to such large-scale filings also shot up (See Table 3.1).

In an effort to achieve a comprehensive settlement of all present and future claims against it, Owens-Corning Fiberglass, a leading asbestos manufacturer defendant, announced a national settlement program comprising standing settlement agreements with multiple plaintiff law firms. In short order, that settlement program collapsed under the weight of an unanticipated flood of claims, and the company petitioned for bankruptcy reorganization. The consortium of defendants that had hoped to contain their asbestos litigation exposure through the *Amchem* settlement suspended operations, and many of their members also filed for Chapter 11 reorganization (Hensler, 2002).

As filings surged, many of the asbestos product manufacturers that plaintiff attorneys had traditionally targeted as lead defendants filed for bankruptcy. Plaintiff attorneys sought out new defendants and pressed defendants whom they had heretofore treated as peripheral to the litigation for more money. With new firms engaged in litigating on the plaintiffs' behalf, and new corporations drawn into the litigation or assuming a more central role, the old settlement agreements began to unravel.

---

[64] 521 U.S. 591 (1997). The Supreme Court had granted certiorari on the question of whether it is permissible for judges to certify a settlement class action in circumstances where it would (arguably) be impermissible to certify a litigation class. The Court did not reject the legitimacy of settlement classes generally but vacated approval of the settlement before it on the grounds that the diverse interests of class members were not properly represented by class representatives and class counsel (Hensler, 2002).

[65] 527 U.S. 815 (1999).

[66] *Ortiz v. Fibreboard Corp.*, 527 U.S. 815 (1999).

Jury Verdicts

Predictions of jury trial outcomes shape settlements in ordinary and mass tort litigation. Parties estimate expected value from previous jury verdicts in similar cases (Mnookin and Kornhauser, 1979; Galanter, 1993). Because few cases go to trial, cases that reach verdict are not likely to be representative of the typical lawsuit. How attorneys adjust settlement values to reflect this selection bias is not well understood. But it is widely assumed that trends in settlement values of cases reflect trends in jury awards (perhaps with some lag).

There is no national databank or tracking system for jury verdicts, including asbestos cases. To investigate trends in asbestos jury verdicts, we searched *Mealey's Litigation Report: Asbestos* from January 1, 1993, to 2001. As we discussed previously, we found 526 trials that delivered verdicts on 1,570 plaintiffs' claims, which constitute the database for our jury verdict analysis.[67] Our analysis generally focused on verdicts on the 1,570 claims, whether tried singly or together.

Trends in Numbers and Types of Claims Tried to Verdict

The annual number of claims decided by a jury declined over the period studied, but, as Figure 3.4 shows, that decline occurred primarily between 1993 and 1994, when claims tried to verdict fell by more than 50 percent.[68] After that, juries decided between 50 and 250 claims per year.

The peak number of jury verdicts in 1996 was the result of the consolidated trial of the claims of 129 shipyard workers in Louisiana, which accounted for more than half of all jury verdicts in that year.[69] In 1999, the number of asbestos jury verdicts hit their lowest point since 1993 and then began to increase again. The increases from 1999 to 2001 may reflect the destabilization of the litigation that took place after the U.S. Supreme Court announced its decisions in *Amchem* and *Ortiz.*

Reflecting the composition of the population of asbestos claims generally, most claims that reached verdict in the period studied were for nonmalignant injuries.

---

[67] We excluded asbestos property damage cases from our analysis and cases in which asbestos exposure was tangential to the claim—for example, tobacco suits.

[68] There is no statistically significant time trend in the number of claims tried to jury verdict from 1994 to 2001 (coeff = −5.94, p = .518). Further investigation revealed that 1993 is not an aberration, but the last of a few years with high levels of claims presented to juries. A search of the *Mealey's Litigation Report: Asbestos* for 1992 revealed an even larger number of claims tried to verdict than for 1993. A reviewer of a preliminary draft of this report suggested that two factors may explain the sharp drop in the number of claims tried to verdict from 1993 to 1994: (1) a number of defendants known for "aggressive" litigation strategies, including Raymark, Celotex and Keene, filed for Chapter 11 reorganization, effectively ending their role in the litigation; and (2) the stay of litigation against the Center for Claims Resolution (representing some 20 defendants) that prevailed during the negotiations of the *Georgine* class action settlement and its aftermath.

[69] *Abadie v. Metro. Life Ins. Co.*, 784 So. 2d 46 (La. Ct. App. 2001).

Figure 3.4
Number of Claims Reaching a Jury Verdict

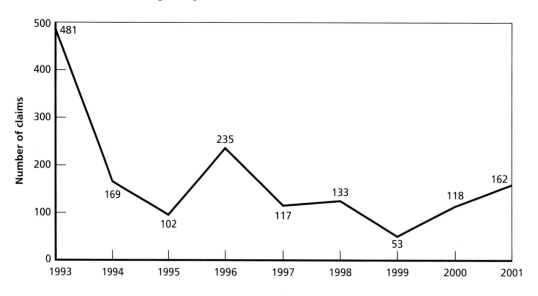

RAND *MG162-3.4*

Among the claims that reached verdict, asbestosis claims were the most numerous, followed by claims for other nonmalignant conditions, including pleural plaques (see Figure 3.5).

Figure 3.5
Distribution of Claims Tried to Verdict by Injury Type

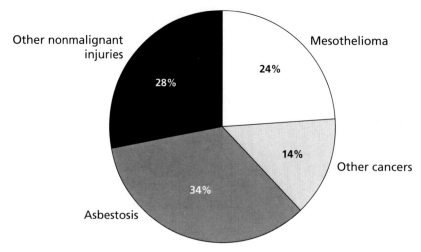

RAND *MG162-3.5*

The distribution of claims tried to verdict by injury type did not change much over the period studied (see Figure 3.6).[70] The large fraction of nonmalignant claims among the 1996 verdicts is attributable to the consolidated trial of 129 claims described above. (Two of the plaintiffs in that trial had mesothelioma, two had other cancers, and two had disabling asbestosis. The remainder claimed other nonmalignant injuries.)

Trends in Plaintiff Success and Award Sizes

During the period studied, plaintiffs with mesothelioma were most likely to win at trial, followed by plaintiffs with asbestosis. Plaintiffs with malignancies other than mesothelioma were least likely to win (see Figure 3.7).[71]

Figure 3.6
Distribution of Claims Tried to Verdict by Injury Type over Time

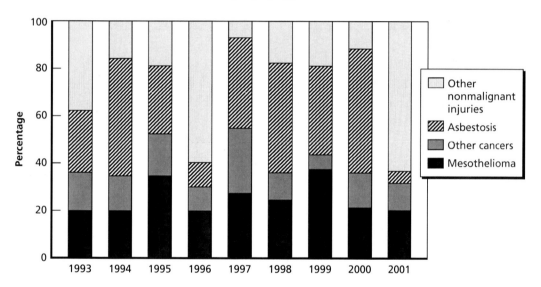

RAND *MG162-3.6*

---

[70] None of the changes observed is statistically significant. We rely on the litigation reporter's description of injury type in this analysis.

[71] All pairwise comparisons are statistically significant except for the comparison between other cancers and other nonmalignant injuries (coeff = .042, p = .312). (*Coeff* [coefficient] is a measure of the difference between the proportions, and *p* [probability] is the statistical significance of the difference.) The differences in the probability of a plaintiff award between cancer claims and nonmalignant injury claims are: coeff = .061, p =.017; the differences in the probability of a plaintiff award between mesothelioma claims and other cancer claims are: coeff = .225, p = .000; the differences in the probability of a plaintiff award between asbestosis claims and other nonmalignant injury claims are: coeff = .072, p =.028; and the differences in the probability of a plaintiff award between mesothelioma claims and asbestosis claims are: coeff = .112, p = .001.

Figure 3.7
Probability of Plaintiff Award by Injury Type

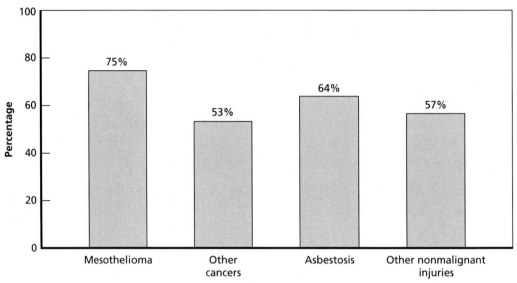

RAND *MG162-3.7*

During the period studied, there was considerable change in plaintiff success among all injury groups (see Figure 3.8). Over time, the probability of winning generally increased for asbestosis plaintiffs,[72] whereas the probability of winning declined somewhat for mesothelioma plaintiffs, only to rise again toward the end of the study period.[73]

On average, successful mesothelioma plaintiffs received the largest jury awards, and successful asbestosis plaintiffs the next-largest awards (see Figure 3.9).[74] During 1993–2003, the average mesothelioma award topped other award averages in all but one year (see Figure 3.10).[75] The relative size of average awards in other injury categories changed from year to year, often as the result of a few dramatically large jury verdicts in a specific injury category. For example, in 1998, a jury in Texas awarded $5.6 million to each of 18 asbestosis plaintiffs whose cases were tried together. Three years later, a jury in Mississippi awarded $25 million to each of six plaintiffs whose

---

[72] coeff = .033, p = .003.

[73] Net decrease over time, coeff = −.017, p = .059. Other observed changes are not statistically significant.

[74] All pairwise comparisons are statistically significant (p < .001).

[75] The observed changes over time within injury categories generally are not statistically significant; in a few instances in which changes over the entire time period are statistically significant that statistical significance is attributable to a sharp change in a single year.

Figure 3.8
Changes in the Probability of Plaintiff Award by Injury Type, 1993–2001

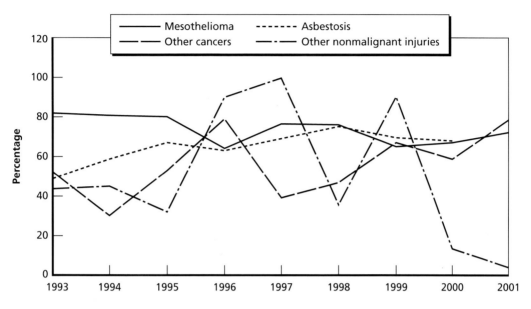

RAND *MG162-3.8*

Figure 3.9
Average Jury Awards by Injury Type

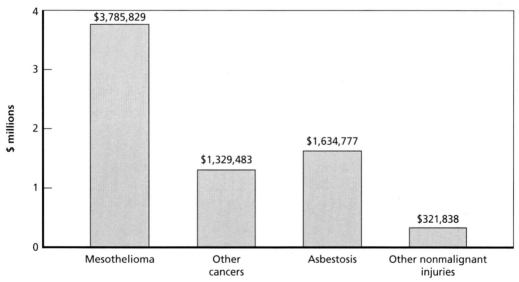

RAND *MG162-3.9*

Figure 3.10
Trends in Average Jury Awards by Injury Type

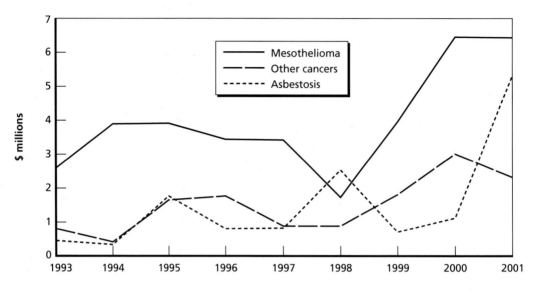

RAND *MG162-3.10*

asbestosis claims were consolidated, far more than any asbestosis award ever before delivered. That same year, two Texas juries awarded asbestosis plaintiffs $7.5 million and $18 million.

As a result of the differences in average jury awards by injury type, although plaintiffs with noncancerous diseases accounted for the largest number of plaintiff verdicts, mesothelioma plaintiffs obtained the largest proportion of dollars awarded. As Figure 3.11 illustrates, 60 percent of all dollars awarded by juries went to mesothelioma plaintiffs, who accounted for only 30 percent of all plaintiff verdicts. In contrast, plaintiffs with diseases other than cancer or asbestosis, who accounted for 20 percent of plaintiff verdicts, got 5 percent of the total dollars awarded.

In every year but 1998, the majority of dollars awarded went to mesothelioma plaintiffs. The share of dollars awarded to plaintiffs with other injuries varied over time, but the appearance of trends (e.g., a decline in the share of dollars for mesothelioma plaintiffs and an increase in the share for asbestosis plaintiffs) is attributable to verdicts in just a few years (see Figure 3.12).[76]

---

[76] A statistically significant trend over the entire period for mesothelioma (coeff = −.024, p = .060) becomes statistically not significant when 1998 and 2001 are excluded (coeff = −.018, p = .226); a statistically significant trend for asbestosis (coeff = .031, p = .029) becomes statistically not significant when 1998 and 2001 are excluded (coeff = .017, p = .137).

Figure 3.11
Distribution of Dollars Awarded in Plaintiff Verdicts by Injury Type

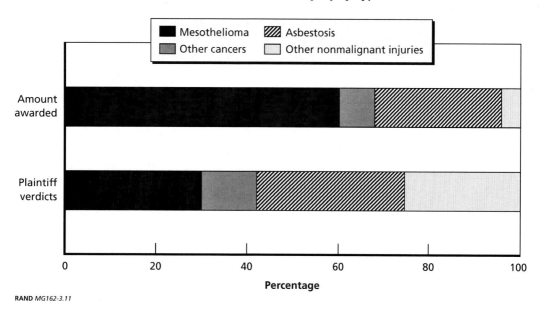

Figure 3.12
Distribution of Total Dollars Awarded by Juries over Time by Injury Type

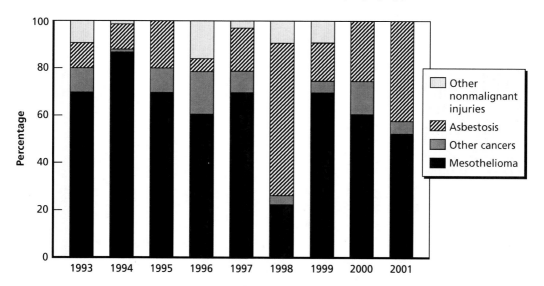

Outcomes of Consolidated Trials

As discussed previously, close to 80 percent of plaintiffs whose cases reached trial during the study period had their claims grouped together with others and tried to a single jury. (Recall that this 80 percent figure does not account fully for plaintiffs whose claims may have been decided in part by a jury who found liability in the first phase of a consolidated trial after having heard evidence for a different set of plaintiffs chosen to represent all of the consolidated claims.) Using our jury verdict database, we were able to investigate whether the outcomes of claims that are grouped are systematically different from the outcomes of claims tried individually. We examined differences between claims tried individually and in smaller (two to five claims) and larger (six or more claims) groups, and between homogeneous and heterogeneous injury groups (for example, all asbestosis claims, compared with groups with a mix of asbestosis and mesothelioma claims). We note where we found statistically significant differences but caution readers that the differences observed may be the result of unobserved differences between claims assigned to different trial treatments, rather than the effect of trial organization itself.

During the study period, there was little difference in the probability of winning for plaintiffs whose claims were tried individually, compared with all those whose claims were tried in groups (see Figure 3.13).[77] But plaintiffs whose claims were tried individually were less likely to win than plaintiffs whose claims were tried in small groups,[78] and plaintiffs whose claims were tried in small groups were more likely to win than plaintiffs whose claims were tried in large groups.[79]

However, mesothelioma victims, on average, received higher awards when their claims were tried individually than when they were tried in groups (see Figure 3.14).[80] Asbestosis plaintiffs received higher awards, on average, when their cases were tried in large groups rather than small groups,[81] but received lower awards, on average, when they were tried in small groups rather than individually.[82] (The difference in average awards for asbestosis plaintiffs in smaller and larger groups results from the two large awards to asbestosis plaintiffs whose cases were tried in Texas in 1998 and in Mississippi in 2001 in groups of six and 18 claims, respectively.)

---

[77] coeff =.026, p = .391.

[78] coeff = −.067, p = .054.

[79] coeff = .142, p = .000.

[80] coeff = 1285244, p = .046.

[81] coeff = −1467458, p = .004.

[82] coeff = −1187478, p = .001.

Figure 3.13
Probability of Plaintiff Success by Injury Type and Trial Organization

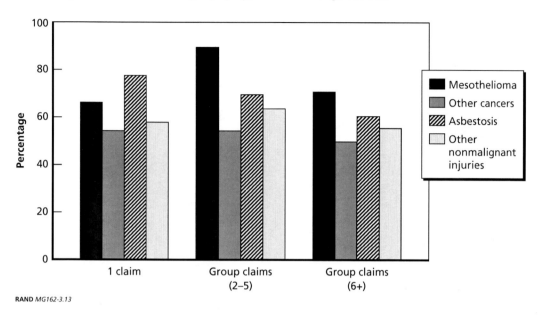

RAND *MG162-3.13*

Figure 3.14
Average Jury Awards by Injury Type and Trial Organization

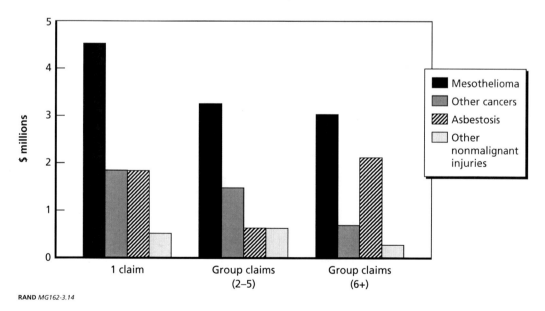

RAND *MG162-3.14*

Early in the period studied, when claims were grouped together for trial, they were likely to include a mix of injuries. In the last three years of the period studied, when claims were grouped for trial, they were more likely to be homogeneous with regard to injury (see Figure 3.15).

Plaintiffs whose claims were grouped with plaintiffs with similar injuries (i.e., in homogeneous groups) on average had a higher probability of winning than plaintiffs whose claims were grouped with plaintiffs with different injuries (i.e., in heterogeneous groups) (see Figure 3.16).[83] There is no evidence that mesothelioma plaintiffs' chances of winning varied depending on the nature of the claim groupings,[84] but asbestosis plaintiffs whose claims were tried in homogeneous groups had a higher probability of winning.[85]

On average, plaintiffs whose claims were grouped for trial obtained higher awards when the groupings were homogeneous, rather than heterogeneous.[86] But this observed difference appears to be attributable to the effect of grouping on mesothelioma plaintiffs, who received substantially less when their claims were tried in

Figure 3.15
Distribution of Claims by Single Plaintiff Versus Homogeneous and Heterogeneous Injury Groups, 1993–2001

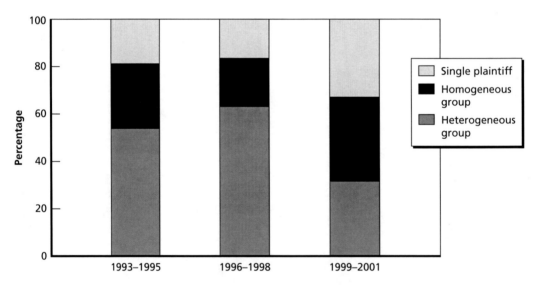

RAND *MG162-3.15*

---

[83] coeff = −.099, p = .001.

[84] coeff = −.068, p = .207.

[85] coeff = −.249, p = 000.

[86] coeff = −1467925, p = .000.

Figure 3.16
Probability of Plaintiff Success by Injury Type and by Single Plaintiff Versus Homogeneous and Heterogeneous Injury Groups

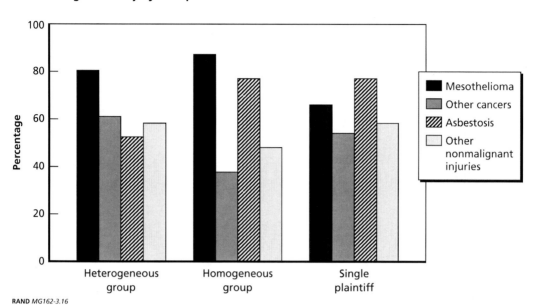

RAND MG162-3.16

heterogeneous groups.[87] In other injury categories, differences in the average award between homogeneous and heterogeneous groups are not statistically significant (see Figure 3.17).

Choice of Forum and Venue

"Forum shopping" is a term frequently used to refer to parties' strategic efforts to find the most attractive jurisdiction and venue in which to pursue or defend their cases. Although forum shopping is officially frowned upon (Algero, 1999), the U.S. legal system offers litigants considerable flexibility with regard to forum selection, and lawyers who fail to choose a forum wisely may be susceptible to charges of malpractice. Depending on how they structure the litigation, plaintiffs may be able to choose between federal and state courts, among different state courts, and among different venues within a state. Plaintiffs in civil litigation get to take the first step by

---

[87] coeff = −2208466, p = .000.

Figure 3.17
Average Jury Verdicts by Injury Type and by Single Plaintiff Versus Homogeneous and Heterogeneous Injury Groups

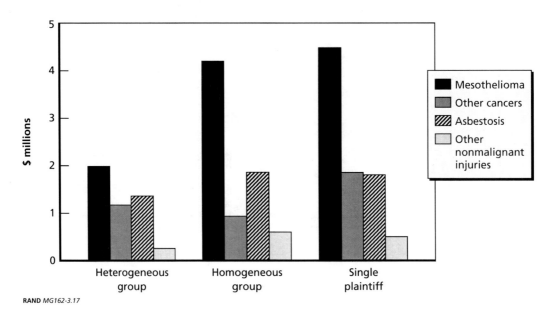

RAND *MG162-3.17*

filing their suit in a particular jurisdiction and venue within that jurisdiction. Civil defendants may contest the plaintiff's choice and, if successful, may remove the lawsuit to another jurisdiction, or sometimes, another venue.[88]

The federal judiciary seeks to constrain forum shopping by applying the same procedural rules in all federal courts. But in diversity cases (private suits between parties from different states), federal courts apply substantive state law including state doctrine on choice of law in situations in which several different states' laws may be implicated. These state laws differ in ways that can determine outcomes of product liability cases such as asbestos lawsuits, even when brought in federal courts.

As in the federal system, state courts are supposed to apply uniform procedural rules statewide. Most states model their procedural rules upon the federal rules, but there are important differences between federal and state rules and among state rules. Because states' substantive law and procedural rules differ, and because, in reality, informal practices differ across and within state and federal courts, the U.S. system of federalism provides strong incentives for plaintiffs to structure their lawsuits in ways that allow them to file in favorable forums, and for defendants to seek ways of veto-

---

[88] The U.S. Supreme Court has held that "there is ordinarily a strong presumption in favor of the plaintiff's choice of forum, which may be overcome only when the private and public interest factors clearly point towards trial in [an] alternative forum." *Piper Aircraft Co. v. Reyno,* 454 U.S. 235 (1981).

ing these choices and moving cases to jurisdictions that they believe will be more favorable to them.[89]

Shift from Federal to State Courts

In the early years of asbestos litigation, cases were divided more or less evenly between federal and state courts and were generally concentrated in locales in which there were heavy concentrations of workers who had been exposed to asbestos: California, Pennsylvania, Maryland, New Jersey, and Illinois (Hensler et al., 1985). In the late 1980s, filings began to move away from federal courts. As shown in Figure 3.18, 41 percent of all claims were filed in federal courts in 1988. But after the JPMDL transferred all federal asbestos cases to Judge Charles Weiner in the Eastern District of Pennsylvania for pretrial processing, many plaintiff attorneys became wary of filing in federal court, knowing that their new cases as well would be transferred to Judge Weiner,[90] whose rulings many plaintiff attorneys perceived as antithetical to their clients' interests. By proceeding in state courts, plaintiff attorneys retained control over their cases and preserved the option of pursuing the litigation in more plaintiff-friendly jurisdictions. Ten years later, only about 13 percent of claims were being filed in federal courts. While the proportion of cases filed in federal courts declined, filings in state courts soared. Over time, litigation moved to the Gulf States (e.g., Texas, Mississippi), where shipyard workers and workers in petrochemical facilities had a high probability of asbestos exposure.

Distribution of Claims by Jurisdiction and Venue

Throughout the history of asbestos litigation, a small number of jurisdictions has accounted for the bulk of the litigation, but the areas of concentration have changed somewhat over time (see Table 3.3).

From 1970 to 1987, four states accounted for 61 percent of asbestos claimants who filed in state courts: California, Illinois, New Jersey, and Pennsylvania. By the late 1990s, however, filings of asbestos claims in these states accounted for only 8 percent of the total. Between 1998 and 2000, five other states captured 66 percent of filings: Texas, Mississippi, New York, Ohio, and West Virginia. These states had accounted for only 9 percent of the claims filed before 1988. Only two states that have been important in the litigation, Maryland and Florida, have had a relatively stable proportion of the filings.

---

[89] In bankruptcy, where defendants (debtors) select the filing jurisdiction, analysts have detected signs of forum shopping as well (Eisenberg and LoPucki, 1999).

[90] Under 28 U.S.C. §1407, new filings are regarded as "tag along" cases and are automatically transferred to the transferee judge after filing.

Figure 3.18
Percentage of New Cases Filed in Federal Courts

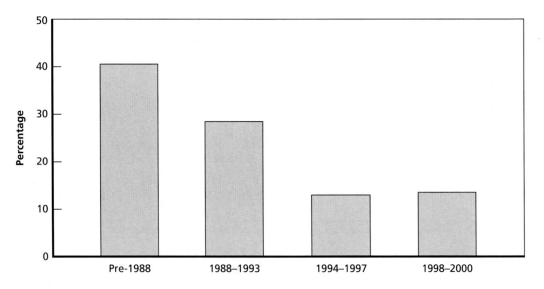

RAND MG162-3.18

Table 3.3
Percentage of Claims Filed in State Courts by State

	Time Period			
	1970–1987	1988–1992	1993–1997	1998–2000
California	31	5	2	2
Florida	3	4	5	4
Illinois	6	4	1	1
Maryland	8	9	3	7
Mississippi	1	9	5	18
New Jersey	7	6	2	1
New York	2	4	5	12
Ohio	1	5	3	12
Pennsylvania	17	11	3	3
Texas	3	15	44	19
West Virginia	3	12	11	5

NOTE: Includes all states with at least 2 percent of filings during any time period.

Some of the states and venues in which asbestos filings have been concentrated are areas with high levels of civil litigation generally. In 2000, New York and California led the nation in absolute numbers of civil case filings, with New Jersey in fourth place, and Texas following in eighth position (National Center for State Courts, 2001). Maryland led the nation in per capita civil case filings, with New Jersey and New York following in fifth and sixth places, respectively. But the concentration of asbestos filings across states and among venues within states primarily reflects the character and history of asbestos litigation, as well as the perceived advantages that different venues offer plaintiffs. New York, where many workers were exposed to asbestos in the Brooklyn Navy Yards, barred asbestos latent injury claims until 1988, when it amended its statute of limitations. After 1988, many asbestos claims were filed in New York state courts, explaining the increasing concentration of filings observed in that state. Many firms developed asbestos specialty practices because they were located in regions with high asbestos exposure. Not surprisingly, they tended to file cases in states and venues in these regions. This explains the concentration observed, for example, in Maryland and Texas.

The differences in procedural rules and practices (e.g., joinder, consolidation, inactive dockets, expedited dockets, and discovery rules) and in substantive law (e.g., criteria for legal injury, "two disease" rules) described earlier in this chapter also help to explain forum and venue choice. Whereas formal procedural rules and state substantive doctrine apply to all cases within a state, informal judicial management practices, which vary from court to court, may make some venues more attractive to plaintiffs or defendants. Case management and trial schedules may be viewed as conferring advantages on plaintiffs or defendants. Judges or juries in some jurisdictions are regarded as being more or less friendly to plaintiffs than judges or juries in other jurisdictions.

By the mid-1990s, three counties in Texas (Harris [Houston], Galveston, and Jefferson [Beaumont]) accounted for more than 25 percent of all new filings in all state courts across the country. In the late 1990s, two counties in Mississippi (Jefferson [Natchez] and Claiborne [Vicksburg]) joined the list of venues attracting large numbers of claims. In 1998–2000, close to 20,000 cases, more than 10 percent of the total filed over that period, were filed in these two counties (see Table 3.4).

Sharp changes in filing patterns over time more likely reflect changes in parties' strategies in relationship to changes in the (perceived) attractiveness (or lack thereof) of state substantive legal doctrine or procedural rules, judicial case management practices, and attitudes of judges and juries toward asbestos plaintiffs and defendants, than changes in the epidemiology of asbestos disease.

Distribution of Jury Trials

The concentration of claims in certain jurisdictions and venues is reflected in the distribution of jury trials by state and county. From 1993 to 2001, 65 percent of trials that resulted in verdicts were held in just five states: Pennsylvania, Texas, California,

Table 3.4
Distribution of State Court Filings by Venue

1970–1987			1988–1992		
State	Venue	%	State	Venue	%
CA	Los Angeles County	14.3	MS	19th Circuit Jackson County	8.4
CA	San Francisco County	7.6	WV	13th Circuit Kanawha County	7.8
PA	Philadelphia County	7.5	MD	8th Circuit Baltimore City	6.7
MD	8th Circuit Baltimore City	6.4	NJ	Middlesex County	4.5
CA	Alameda County	5.9	PA	Philadelphia County	3.9
NJ	Middlesex County	4.5	TX	Orange County	3.7
IL	3rd Circuit Madison County	3.8	TX	Morris County	3.6
PA	Cambria County	2.7	NY	New York County	3.5
PA	Allegheny County	2.4	CA	Los Angeles County	2.5
WA	King County	2.4	OH	Summit County	2.5
			TX	Harris County	2.3
			IL	3rd Circuit Madison County	2.1
			FL	4th Circuit Duval County	2.0

1993–1997			1998–2000		
State	Venue	%	State	Venue	%
TX	Harris County	11.0	OH	Cuyahoga County	11.7
TX	Galveston County	9.9	MS	6th Circuit Jefferson County	8.8
TX	Jefferson County	6.8	NY	New York County	8.0
NY	New York County	4.7	MD	8th Circuit Baltimore City	6.8
WV	17th Circuit Monongalia County	4.3	MS	9th Circuit Claiborne County	3.9
WV	13th Circuit Kanawha County	3.5	NY	Erie County	3.5
MD	8th Circuit Baltimore City	3.0	WV	2nd Circuit Marshall County	2.6
TX	Morris County	2.5	TX	Jefferson County	2.3
WV	2nd Circuit Marshall County	2.4			
MI	10th Circuit Saginaw County	2.3			
OH	Cuyahoga County	2.3			
LA	Civil District Orleans Parish	2.2			
TX	Brazoria County	2.1			

NOTE: Includes all courts with at least 2 percent of state court filings in any period.

Louisiana, and Maryland (see Figure 3.19). These states also had a slightly higher ratio of plaintiffs to trials: 75 percent of plaintiffs whose claims went to verdict presented their case in one of these five venues.

The distribution of trials has changed over time, mirroring changes in the distribution of filings. Pennsylvania at one time accounted for 50 percent of plaintiffs whose claims reached verdict; more recently, the proportion of plaintiffs whose claims reached verdict in Pennsylvania dropped to less than 20 percent. In the three most-recent years for which we have data, Texas and Maryland together accounted

Figure 3.19
Distribution of Trials and Claims by State

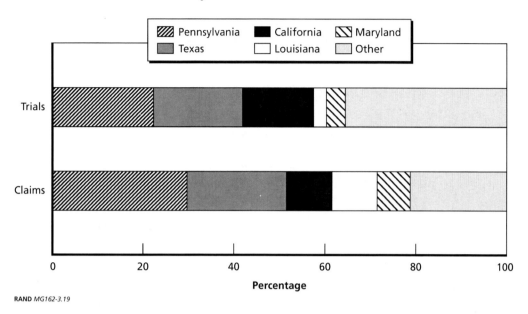

RAND *MG162-3.19*

Figure 3.20
Distribution of Claims Tried to Verdict by State and Year

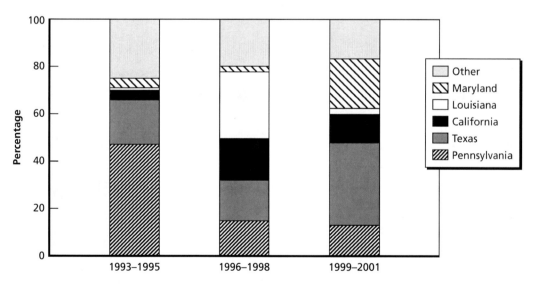

RAND *MG162-3.20*

for the largest share of claims tried to verdict (see Figure 3.20). But the share of verdicts in a single state may be misleading as an indicator of general patterns: Louisiana is among the top five states for trial verdicts because of the single verdict in a case brought by 129 plaintiffs in 1996, reflecting the potential for a single consolidated trial to shape the profile of asbestos litigation in any year.

Bankruptcy Litigation

Since the early 1980s, asbestos litigation in federal and state courts has played out against a background of parallel litigation in the bankruptcy courts, which has influenced the primary litigation against non-bankrupt defendants and, in turn, has been shaped by that litigation. When the Manville Corporation filed for Chapter 11 reorganization in 1982, it temporarily disrupted asbestos litigation patterns, as plaintiffs and non-bankrupt defendants alike sought to prevent the stay of litigation against Manville, which had until then been the lead defendant in the litigation (Hensler et al., 1985). The difficulties attendant on estimating the financial exposure of the Manville Bankruptcy Trust (discussed further in Chapter Six) highlighted for non-bankrupt defendants the difficulties of estimating their own future liabilities. The Manville bankruptcy reorganization at first provided cautionary lessons on the use of bankruptcy to resolve asbestos claims. But after Congress amended the bankruptcy statute to facilitate the creation of post-bankruptcy trusts to resolve asbestos injury claims, many looked to the Manville Trust as a model for aggregating claims and capping corporate liability exposure due to asbestos even for those corporations that were not at the time facing bankruptcy themselves (Glater, 2000, p. C4).

As the early Chapter 11 reorganizations were approved by the courts and the trusts that were established by the reorganizations began to pay claims, the ability to collect compensation through a streamlined administrative process may have been a factor in attracting new plaintiff law firms to asbestos litigation (see Table 3.1) and also may have helped fund ongoing litigation outside the bankruptcy courts. Although the trusts paid only modest sums to each claimant, the total fees available to law firms for representing large numbers of claimants on their trust filings could be substantial.[91] When increasing asbestos claims rates encouraged scores of defendants to file Chapter 11 petitions (discussed in Chapter Six), the resulting stays in litigation against these defendants drove plaintiff attorneys to press peripheral non-bankruptcy defendants to shoulder a larger share of asbestos claims value and to widen their search for other corporations that might be held liable for the costs of asbestos exposure and disease. In addition, the surge of filings for Chapter 11 reorganization in early 2003 may have provided another incentive for some asbestos plaintiff law firms to seek representation of large numbers of asbestos claimants: Under Section 524(g) of the bankruptcy code, a proposed reorganization plan must obtain support from 75 percent of current asbestos claimants to win court approval, meaning that law

---

[91] For a discussion of the economics of mass filings of small-value cases, see McGovern (2002).

firms that represent large numbers of claimants will wield the most power over the reorganization negotiations (Parloff, 2004).

As bankruptcy proceedings have expanded to include most of the original lead defendants in asbestos litigation and scores of other companies besides (see Chapter Six), the dynamics of these proceedings have come increasingly to mirror the dynamics of the primary litigation in federal and state courts. Borrowing from case management practices in trial courts, district courts have consolidated multiple bankruptcy reorganizations and assigned mass tort "specialist" judges to preside over them.[92] Parties have sought to transfer[93] related claims to bankruptcy courts in the hope of achieving an attractive global resolution of those claims.[94] In the USG Corporation bankruptcy, Judge Alfred Wolin ordered that claimants with cancer would have their claims processed before claimants with non-cancer injuries, essentially establishing an expedited docket. Judge Wolin also appointed special masters and mediators to work with bankruptcy parties to achieve consensual reorganization plans, just as Judge Tom Lambros and Judge Robert Parker (among others) had earlier appointed special masters and mediators to work with parties in the trial courts.[95] And seemingly borrowing a page from the controversial "futures" settlements that were rejected by the U.S. Supreme Court in *Amchem* and *Ortiz*, lawyers have sought to fashion resolutions of bankruptcy claims against a number of major corporations that offer attractive settlements of current claims in exchange for support for reorganization plans that will determine payments of other claimants far into the future (Plevin et al., 2003; Parloff, 2004).

---

[92] See "3rd Circuit Judge Orders 5 Bankruptcies . . ." (2001) (announcing the decision of Chief Judge Edward Becker to assign multiple bankruptcies to Judge Alfred Wolin of the District Court of New Jersey). Judge Wolin appointed two bankruptcy court judges to assist in managing the reorganizations. Subsequently, Judge Wolin was removed from three of the cases by the Third Circuit Court of Appeals and then retired from the bench, handing over supervision of the two remaining cases. See Freudenheim (2004).

[93] *In re USG Corp.*, No. 01-2094, Mem. Op. and Order (Bankr. Del. Feb. 19, 2003). Judge Wolin was subsequently removed from this case. See Freudenheim (2004).

[94] See "Consolidated Bankruptcy Judge Transfers . . ." (2001) (reporting motion by General Motors, Ford, and Daimler-Chrysler to transfer asbestos lawsuits against them to bankruptcy court, under the court's authority to handle "related cases"). The "friction defendants," who also included other automobile and automobile product manufacturers, reportedly hoped to achieve a nationwide dismissal of claims against them as a result of hearings (required by the U.S. Supreme Court's decision in *Daubert v. Merrell Dow Pharms.*, 516 U.S. 869 [1995]) at which they planned to challenge the scientific evidence underlying the claims. Ultimately, the claims against the auto manufacturers were remanded to the state courts in which they have been filed. See "Federal Judge Denies Big 3 . . ." (2002); Berke (2002); *In re Federal-Mogul Global, Inc.*, 300 F.3d 368 (2002).

[95] See "Judge Wolin Appoints Consultants . . . " (2002) (reporting appointment of five consultants to serve as special masters). The special masters included David Gross, whose firm defended the Manville Corporation prior to its 1982 filing for Chapter 11 reorganization, and Francis McGovern, who served as special master to Judges Lambros and Parker in their asbestos case management activities described earlier in this chapter. McGovern was also appointed to serve as mediator in the Federal-Mogul, Babcock & Wilcox, and Owens-Corning bankruptcy proceedings. See "Delaware Bankruptcy Judge Appoints Mediator . . ." (2002) and "Owens Corning Files Motion . . ." (2002).

Some have argued that bankruptcy trusts, including those established as the result of "prepackaged" bankruptcies (discussed in Chapter Six), will provide swifter, less expensive, and more certain compensation for asbestos injury victims, while allowing society to realize the value of a defendant corporation's activities. Others contend that reorganization plans that provide payments far into the future to large numbers of functionally unimpaired claimants—in some instances, after substantial assets have been committed to pay current functionally unimpaired claimants—threaten the ability of trusts to conserve resources for seriously injured claimants who will come forward in the future. Others question whether proposed bankruptcy trust plans that rely on insurance assets whose availability is in some instances itself in contention will prove solvent. Whether and to what extent bankruptcy litigation will solve the central issues of asbestos litigation—providing adequate compensation to the seriously injured, achieving efficient and fair resolution of asbestos claims, predicting future claiming patterns, estimating future claim values, and regulating conflicts of interest—is currently unclear.

CHAPTER FOUR

Claimants and Defendants

In this chapter, we estimate the total number of claimants and defendants involved in asbestos litigation between the mid-1970s, after *Borel v. Fibreboard*, and 2002. We also describe trends in the types of injury claims and the industries represented by defendants named in the litigation. Although we cannot disclose the names of asbestos defendants, we can identify the proportion of defendants from various industries and the changes in that proportion over time.

Asbestos Claimants

Approach to Estimating Total Number

It is not easy to answer the most basic questions about asbestos litigation, such as how many claimants and defendants have been involved in the litigation. There is no national registry of asbestos claimants. Some claims are not filed formally in court as lawsuits. Federal courts report the number of asbestos lawsuits filed, but in recent years most lawsuits have been filed in state courts, which do not routinely identify and report annual asbestos lawsuit filings. Privately held information about asbestos litigation is regarded as highly sensitive by those who hold it, because information about historical trends in asbestos litigation may have significance for current and future settlement negotiations and outcomes and for other business and law firm transactions. Hence, most private parties are willing to share data only under confidentiality agreements on a not-for-attribution basis.

The only way to estimate the total number of claimants in these circumstances was to obtain confidential data from many participants in the litigation. In each instance, we specified the data we sought and conducted sufficient investigation (for example, comparing information from multiple sources) to assure ourselves that the data provided to us were reliable. We used only data that we confirmed with other data or with other participants in the litigation.

We compared lists of claimants provided by defendants and personal injury trusts established subsequent to Chapter 11 reorganization and deleted redundant entries to identify the number of unique individuals who had filed asbestos personal injury claims by the end of 2002. In making these comparisons, we deleted claimants on each list for which we did not have adequate information to determine whether those claimants were also included on any of the other lists. We also recognized that claimants occasionally filed a suit naming several defendants and then, at a later date, added defendants or filed a claim with a trust or against other defendants. We counted each claimant once, in the year in which they initially filed a claim, regardless of whether they subsequently filed additional claims. In all, we identified about 710,000 unique individuals who had brought an asbestos claim by the end of 2002, the end of our main field research study period.

We then examined the observations we had deleted because the information we needed to identify those claimants was missing. We suspect that the large majority of the claimants on any one list for whom we lacked adequate information to determine if they were also on another list did in fact appear on another list. However, some of the claimants we deleted from one list because of inadequate identification information may not have been represented on any of our other lists and therefore are not included in the 710,000-claimants estimate. We assumed that the probability that a claimant with missing information on one list was also on another list equaled the probability that a claimant on the first list for whom we had complete information was also on some other list. Applying these probabilities to the observations left out of the comparisons because of missing information, we estimated that our data included approximately 20,000 additional individuals who had filed asbestos personal injury claims by the end of 2002.

We had intended to examine the distribution of injuries claimed by asbestos claimants. However, we discovered that defendants do not generally agree on a classification scheme for nonmalignant injuries. For example, one defendant who provided information to us classified all nonmalignant claims into five categories. Another defendant divided them into 28 different categories, none of which matched any of the five categories used by the first defendant. Further, several defendants told us that they had changed the systems they used to classify nonmalignant claims over time. In these cases, we cannot even consistently classify nonmalignant claims by categories over time for the same defendant, let alone merge that defendant's claims data with the data provided by other defendants and trusts. Thus, in the subsequent discussion, while we are able to distinguish among mesothelioma claimants, other-cancer claimants, and nonmalignant claimants, we have not been able to break down nonmalignant claimants into finer categories.

Results

Approximately 730,000 People Had Filed an Asbestos Claim Through 2002. Table 4.1 shows the number of individuals identified in our data that filed an asbestos personal injury claim, broken out by the year of the filing and the category of the

Table 4.1
Number of Claimants by Claimed Injury

Year	Claimed Injury			
	Mesothelioma	Other Cancer	Nonmalignant	Total
Before 1980	238	467	3,431	4,136
1980	222	528	3,415	4,165
1981	264	587	3,881	4,732
1982	291	604	3,984	4,879
1983	324	657	3,579	4,560
1984	423	879	4,822	6,124
1985	519	1,202	7,681	9,402
1986	660	1,964	12,675	15,299
1987	972	2,997	17,087	21,056
1988	1,266	3,292	24,713	29,271
1989	2,411	6,376	45,151	53,938
1990	1,275	2,386	21,357	25,018
1991	979	2,451	19,322	22,752
1992	971	2,569	26,343	29,883
1993	817	2,151	23,005	25,973
1994	1,207	2,536	20,702	24,445
1995	1,306	3,624	43,283	48,213
1996	1,312	2,887	43,824	48,023
1997	1,347	3,132	28,978	33,457
1998	1,387	2,828	38,539	42,754
1999	1,520	2,863	40,815	45,198
2000	1,776	2,623	52,055	56,454
2001	1,893	3,639	89,308	94,840
2002	1,856	3,148	50,112	55,116

claimed injury. The data presented in Table 4.1 do not include the approximately 20,000 individuals who we estimate had filed asbestos personal injury claims by the end of 2002 but for whom we lacked the information necessary to determine whether they were included on more than one of our lists. We had no way to estimate either the year in which they filed a claim or their claimed injury.

We conclude that approximately 730,000 individuals brought an asbestos-related personal injury claim by 2002, including the 710,000 claimants included in Table 4.1 and the estimated 20,000 claimants we omitted because of missing information. We believe this number is probably an underestimate. It is possible that some individuals brought asbestos claims but did not name any of the defendants from whom we had obtained data and therefore were not included on any of the lists of claimants that defendants made available to us. Because the entities that provided these lists include defendants that have been prominent in asbestos litigation, we believe there are few claimants who did not name any of those defendants. Nonetheless, there are likely to be some claimants who are not included on any of the various lists of clients provided to us.

The sharp surge in claimants filing asbestos claims in 1988 and 1989 probably reflects the impact of the establishment of the Manville Trust in 1988. Claims against the Johns Manville Corp. were stayed when the corporation filed for Chapter 11 bankruptcy in 1982. It appears that many potential claimants postponed filing claims until the Trust was established.

The Number of Claims Filed Annually Has Increased Sharply in the Past Few Years. As shown in Table 4.1, the annual number of individuals filing asbestos injury claims has grown sharply over time, particularly in recent years. The early 1980s typically saw about 5,000 claims per year. In the late 1980s and early 1990s, the annual rate of new claims grew to roughly 25,000 claims per year. By the mid- to late 1990s, roughly 50,000 claims per year were being filed.

This surge in the annual number of filings has been reflected in the filings experienced by individual defendants. Figure 4.1 shows the number of claims filed each year over the 1990s against five major defendants, including a bankruptcy trust, two defendants who have entered bankruptcy, and two non-bankrupt corporations. (We include only five defendants on the chart so as not to obscure the details of each defendant's experience.) Each of these defendants has a particular posture in the litigation, so we would not expect their experiences to be identical. Nor would we expect their experiences to be representative of all defendants. However, in dozens of interviews we conducted with participants on all sides of the litigation, there has been near universal agreement that these defendants' experiences are broadly representative of the patterns of asbestos claim filings over the 1990s.

The sharp year-to-year changes in the annual number of filings against each of these defendants reflect events in the litigation in general or in the circumstances of a particular defendant. The general pattern, however, is the same for all of them: Over the past decade, the number of claims filed annually against each of these defendants has increased substantially. Four of them were each receiving 15,000 to 20,000 claims per year at the beginning of the 1990s. That number grew throughout the decade until, by 2000, it had grown to roughly 50,000 claims per year. The bottom line in Figure 4.1 shows one defendant that appeared to have the litigation under control in the early 1990s, when actually the annual number of claims against it was drifting downward. But even that defendant experienced a sharp increase in claims toward the end of the decade.

Whether these trends will continue into the future is an open question. But it is clear from our interviews with participants in the litigation that recent changes in filing rates have played an important role in shaping the future expectations of attorneys, parties to the litigation, policymakers, and business analysts.

Figure 4.1
Annual Number of Claims Against Five Major Defendants, 1991–2000

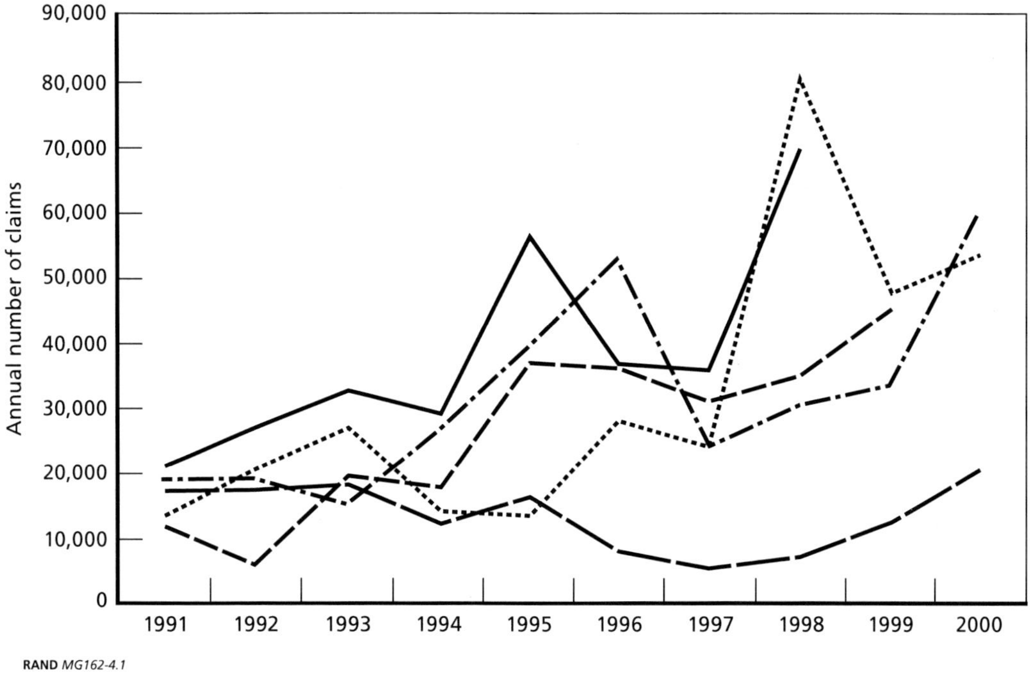

RAND *MG162-4.1*

Claimants with Nonmalignant Injuries Account for Most of the Growth in Claims. Claims for nonmalignant injuries grew sharply through the late 1990s and early 2000s. Almost all the growth in the asbestos caseload can be attributed to the growth in the number of these claims, which include claims from people with little or no current functional impairment. Many of the participants we interviewed, including those involved on behalf of both plaintiffs and defendants, cited the rapid growth in the annual number of claims for nonmalignant injuries as the most important recent trend in the litigation.

Figure 4.2 shows the trends in the annual numbers of new claimants alleging each type of injury relative to the number of new claimants who had alleged that type of injury before 1980. It is clear that throughout the 1980s, claims for mesothelioma, other cancers, and nonmalignant injuries grew at approximately the same rate. The lines in Figure 4.2, which show the relative annual numbers of new claimants alleging each type of injury, are almost exactly the same. Even the 1988–1989 spike in new claimants reflects the same relative changes for each injury type.

However, beginning in the early 1990s, the annual number of new claimants alleging a nonmalignant injury has grown much faster than the annual number of

Figure 4.2
Trends in the Number of Claims by Type of Injury

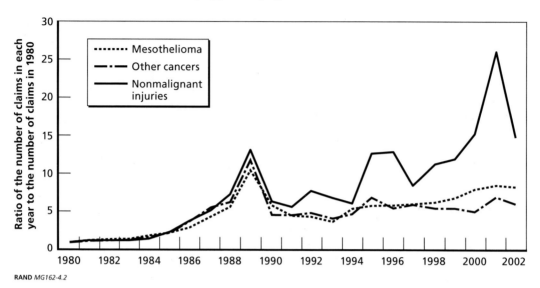

RAND *MG162-4.2*

new claimants alleging some form of cancer. The growth in the annual number of claims is almost entirely due to increases in the numbers of nonmalignant claims entering the system.

The Number of Claimants with Mesothelioma Has Been Increasing in Recent Years. Figure 4.2 also reveals a recent upward trend in the number of mesothelioma claims filed annually. Leaving aside the 1989 spike in claims, through the late 1980s and early 1990s, the number of mesothelioma claims filed each year was about five times the number of such claims filed before 1980. Beginning in 1994, however, the annual number of mesothelioma claims filed grew each year until, by 2002, it had approximately doubled from the corresponding early 1990s numbers.

Although the annual number of mesothelioma claims grew over the decade, the absolute number of these claims is very small compared with the absolute number of nonmalignant claims. Hence, the growth in the annual number of mesothelioma claims accounted for only a very small part of the growth in the total number of claims entering the system each year. Nonetheless, because these are the most serious—and consequently most costly—injuries, some of the attorneys we interviewed cited the growth in the annual number of mesothelioma claims as the most important change in the litigation in the late 1990s and early 2000s.

Claims for other cancers grew during the first half of the 1990s, then gradually declined. The annual number of claims for cancers other than mesothelioma ended the decade at a level roughly 10 percent greater than had been experienced at the outset of the decade.

Claimants with Nonmalignant Conditions Are a Growing Proportion of All Claimants. The rapid growth in the annual number of claims filed for nonmalignant conditions has profoundly affected the overall distribution of claims entering the system. As Figure 4.3 shows, nonmalignant claims accounted for roughly 80 percent of all claims entering the system through the mid-1980s. The fraction of claims that asserted nonmalignant conditions grew through the late 1980s and early 1990s, rising to more than 90 percent of annual claims in the late 1990s and early 2000s.

Although the annual number of mesothelioma claims has been increasing in recent years, the number of all claims has been increasing much faster. Therefore, mesothelioma claims are decreasing as a proportion of the whole. They accounted for 6–7 percent of all claims in the 1970s and early 1980s, but fell as a percentage of total claims in the mid-1980s, accounting for roughly 4–5 percent of claims through most of the 1980s. In the late 1980s, the mesothelioma share of the claims entering the system each year fell further, to roughly 3 percent of all claims, and remained at that level through the early 2000s.

Claims for other cancers exhibit a similar pattern. They accounted for 11–14 percent of annual total claims through the 1970s and most of the 1980s. The other-cancer share of claims declined through the 1990s to about 5 percent of the total in the early 2000s.

Some Evidence Suggests That Most Nonmalignant Claimants Are Currently Unimpaired. The fraction of claimants with nonmalignant diseases that are functionally unimpaired at the time they file a claim is a source of sharp controversy. It is difficult to determine this fraction or to examine trends in the distribution of claims by injury severity because there is no database in which claimants' medical data are consistently and reliably entered over time. The only information on severity of

Figure 4.3
Annual Distribution of Claims by Type of Injury

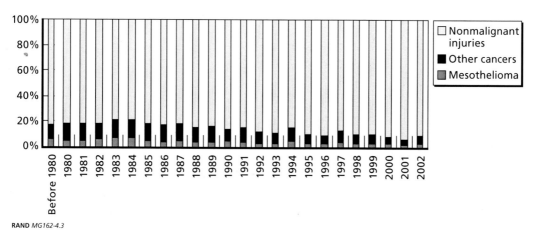

injury, including the existence of impairment, comes from limited studies in which an analyst draws a sample of individual claims from defendants' files and reviews the medical information provided by the claimants to determine whether the information in the file offers evidence that the claimant was impaired.

In 1995, the Manville Trust implemented an audit program in which independent B Readers (physicians who read X-rays with B Readings) reviewed the X-rays from a random sample of claimants.[1] The Trust operates under the supervision of federal district court judge Jack B. Weinstein. The B Readers were selected in consultation with the plaintiffs' bar; none of the B Readers employed in the audit had testified on behalf of an asbestos defendant. The X-ray review process was designed to give the benefit of any doubt to the claimant. Two B Readers reviewed each claim in the sample. A claim was downgraded only if both B Readers independently determined that they saw no indication of even low-level, sub-diagnostic X-ray evidence of interstitial fibrosis. According to an affidavit filed with the court, ". . . of the X-rays the Trust actually received, approximately 50% failed independent B-reader review."[2]

Several more-recent studies have found fractions of unimpaired claimants ranging from two-thirds to up to 90 percent of all current claimants (Edley and Weiler, 1993; Bernick et al., 2001a; Rourke, 2001; Chambers, 2002). Because most of these studies were commissioned by defendants, and because the issue of impairment is central to the asbestos litigation controversy, their findings are hotly contested.

Based on the available data, we conclude that a large and growing proportion of the claims entering the system in recent years was submitted by individuals who had not at the time of the claim filing suffered an injury that had as yet affected their ability to perform the activities of daily living.

Claims Filed by Workers Exposed to Asbestos in Nontraditional Industries Are Increasing. Although people have been exposed to asbestos in various ways and, hence, claims arise from various sources, most claims are based on exposure to asbestos in the workplace. In the early years of asbestos litigation following *Borel*, most claimants came from industries in which workers physically manipulated asbestos or products containing asbestos and typically inhaled large amounts of asbestos fibers on an everyday basis. Nicholson et al. (1982) focused on the industries in which occupational exposure to asbestos was substantial: asbestos mining, manufacture, or installation; shipyards; railroad and automobile maintenance; construction; chemicals; and

---

[1] According to the Centers for Disease Control (see http://www.cdc.gov/niosh/pamphlet.html), "NIOSH B-reader approval is granted to physicians who demonstrate proficiency in the classification of chest X-rays for the pneumoconioses using the International Labour Office (ILO) Classification System."

[2] Affidavit of Patricia G. Houser, *In re Manville Personal Injury Settlement Trust Medical Audit Procedures Litigation,* 98 Civ. 5693, March 13, 1999, p. 9.

utilities. Because workers in these industries were so heavily exposed to asbestos and, consequently, accounted for the large majority of claimants in the early days of the litigation, these industries are often termed the "traditional" industries.

More recently, however, there has been rapid growth in the numbers of claims brought by people working outside the traditional industries where they typically did not handle asbestos but asbestos was present in the workplace atmosphere. For example, in the early 2000s, workers in the textile industry brought large numbers of claims (Claims Resolution Management Corporation, 2001). Textile workers sometimes work with machines run by motors with gaskets that contain asbestos or in facilities ventilated by ducts lined with asbestos. Those workers may have inhaled asbestos fibers released into the air, but they are not likely to have inhaled as much as shipyard workers—who worked in enclosed, tight quarters, in an atmosphere thick with asbestos fibers—or asbestos installers.

Table 4.2 compares trends in claiming from individuals who were exposed to asbestos in traditional and nontraditional industries. As the table shows, the rate of increase in claims from workers in nontraditional industries is such that there are now about as many of those claims filed annually as there are claims from workers in traditional industries. The growth in claims from workers in nontraditional industries is an example of how unpredictable asbestos litigation has become. Earlier projections of the magnitude of the litigation, based on Nicholson et al. (1982), did not take into account these claims.

The increasing number of claims filed by workers in nontraditional industries occurred during the same period that we observed an increase in the fraction of claims filed by workers with nondisabling, nonmalignant asbestos injuries.

Table 4.2
Claims from Workers in Nontraditional Versus Traditional Industries

	Number of Claims			% Increase	
	1999	2000	2001	1999–2000	2000–2001
Traditional	16,997	31,496	43,397	85	54
Nontraditional[a]	11,420	23,582	40,453	107	71

SOURCE: Claims Resolution Management Corporation, 2001.
[a]Food and beverage, textiles, paper, glass, iron/steel/nonferrous metals, durable (metal) goods, and other industries.

Asbestos Defendants

Approach to Estimating Total Number

Most asbestos claims name dozens of defendants, amplifying the effects of the litigation beyond what is observed in a more ordinary tort lawsuit against one or a few defendants. Moreover, as the litigation has continued and, in particular, as mounting bankruptcies have stayed litigation against defendants who formerly provided a substantial share of the compensation obtained by claimants (see Chapter Three), more defendants have been drawn into the litigation. A number of defendants, insurers, plaintiff and defense attorneys, and courts provided us, usually on a confidential basis, lists of entities that they knew had been named as defendants on asbestos product liability claims. Almost all of these defendants were businesses. Many are large corporations with thousands of employees and billions in annual revenues. Others are firms with as few as 20 employees and just a few million dollars in annual revenues. The lists also included a small number of government agencies and nonprofit entities.

When we merged these lists, the resulting list of defendants totaled 10,463 entities. We observed that some of the entities on the merged list were subsidiaries or branches of defendants rather than independent companies. We also observed some cases in which it appeared that a defendant's name had been misspelled on a list so the same defendant essentially appeared twice on the merged list. To develop a valid list of defendants that included only independent entities, we set out to verify the existence of the defendants on the merged list. At the same time, we identified the two-digit Standard Industrial Classification (SIC) code classification[3] for each of the companies we could verify, using the contemporary (2003) editions of InfoUSA[4] and Dun and Bradstreet's Hoover's Online.

We started the verification process as soon as we received the first lists of defendants. When it became clear that the number of defendants on the merged list was building into the thousands, we realized that it would take more time and resources than were available to us to verify all the entries on the entire merged list. When we stopped looking up every company on the merged list, we had verified almost 2,000 entities on InfoUSA and Hoover's. But we did not know whether the defendants on the lists we had obtained at the beginning of the process, when we began checking every defendant on a list provided to us, were representative of the entire population of defendants. Accordingly, we decided to draw a random sample of 500 defendants

---

[3] The U.S. Department of Commerce uses the SIC system to categorize economic activity for statistical purposes. The system is hierarchical. All types of economic activity are divided into a small number of very broad categories with narrower subdivisions. Every entity engaged in any type of economic activity in the United States is assigned an SIC code according to its primary activity.

[4] InfoUSA is a subscription database sold only to libraries, educational institutions, and government agencies.

from the merged list and to base our estimates of the number and type of defendants primarily on the random sample. We drew this sample from the entire merged list of defendants, including both those we had already looked up and those on the merged list that we had not yet verified.

Results

At least 8,400 Entities Have Been Named as Asbestos Defendants Through 2002. We were able to identify 401 of the 500 defendants in the random sample. This implies that the number of unique defendants is about 8,391. We calculated the 95 percent confidence interval using the binomial approximation to the normal distribution. The result suggests that we can be 95 percent confident that the number of unique defendants is at least 8,025 and no more than 8,756. Accordingly, we estimated that about 8,400 firms have been named as defendants on asbestos personal injury claims.

This number is probably an underestimate. Because we collected lists of defendants through the end of 2002, our merged list did not include any entities named after 2002 as defendants on an asbestos claim for the first time. The sources we used to verify firms do not list firms that did not exist in 2002, even though they may have existed at some prior date. Thus, we would not have found firms that were named as defendants at some time before 2002 and subsequently ceased doing business under the names they had when they were named as a defendant. It is likely that some firms named as defendants before 2002 had been liquidated, were acquired by or had merged with another firm, or simply changed their name before 2002. Finally, in some cases, the name of the defendant was incomplete, and it was impossible to identify the particular entity against which the claim was brought.[5]

Approach to Analyzing Distribution of Defendants Across Industries

We estimated the percentage of defendants in each two-digit SIC category based on our random sample. We assumed that the 99 companies we could not identify were randomly distributed among SIC categories. This random distribution is not verifiable, because we do not know whether the companies we could not classify were disproportionately drawn from particular SIC codes. As such, we used a LaPlace estimator of proportion:

---

[5] We had no way to determine the number of asbestos defendants that were not included on any of the lists provided to us. Those defendants would include both defendants that were named for the first time after 2002 and those that had not come to the attention of the individuals who provided us with lists of defendants. Also, our estimate does not include defendants that *did* appear on a list provided to us but that we could not identify. Such defendants would include both those that had liquidated or changed their names prior to 2002 and those whose names were misspelled on the lists provided to us. In sum, our estimate of 8,400 asbestos defendants probably underestimates the true number of entities that have been named as defendants on an asbestos claim.

$$p_i = (n_i + 0.5) / (n+1)$$

where i indexes SIC codes. Without the 0.5 in the numerator and the 1 in the denominator, this would be a proportion. Using the LaPlace correction provides a moderate amount of smoothing. The estimated proportions were then rescaled such that they sum to 100 percent. We constructed 99 percent confidence limits for the estimates using the binomial approximation to the normal distribution based on the random sample.

In the initial stage of this analysis, when we were looking up the defendants on the full merged list, we identified and verified about 2,000 defendants. These defendants included a few whose primary industry was not included in the list of industries for the 401 defendants we identified in the random sample. Because the defendants we identified in the initial stage of the analysis were not drawn from a random sample, we could not simply combine the list of defendants from the random sample and the list of defendants from the initial stage of the analysis. However, if a defendant identified in the initial stage of the analysis fell into industry X, we know that industry X included at least one asbestos defendant even though no defendant among the 401 from the random sample was included in that industry. Rather than discard the information we obtained from the initial stage of the analysis, we used the classifications based on that stage of the analysis as lower limits. For example, if the initial stage of the analysis classified 100 defendants into industry X, then we know that the lower limit for industry X is 100/10,463 = 1 percent. It turned out that the lower limits often fell within the usual confidence intervals rather than below the lower limit. For example, for industry X, the confidence interval might have been [0.6–2.0], but we know that the lower limit had to be at least 1 percent for industry X. We, therefore, reconstructed the confidence intervals to ensure that the lower limit (e.g., 1 percent) is less than or equal to the lower confidence interval limit (e.g., 0.6 percent).

We computed the lower limit as the maximum of the lower limit and the lower confidence limit. In the above example, the minimum is max(0.6 percent, 1 percent) = 1 percent. We then adjusted the upper limit to reflect the change of the lower limit. We treated this as a truncated normal distribution where the truncation occurs at the lower limit. We compute the upper confidence limit to correspond to the 99th percentile of the non-truncated probability mass function. Computationally, this can be accomplished by adjusting the confidence level on the untruncated normal distribution as follows:

New level = $1 - [(1 - \text{old level}) (1 - \Phi(\text{lower limit}))]$

where $\Phi()$ refers to the cumulative distribution function of the normal distribution, lower limit is the percentage that is already classified to this category based on the initial stage of the analysis, and old level is the usual confidence level. Here, we use a usual confidence level of 0.99. This new confidence level is used only to adjust the upper confidence limit.

To carry the example further, we need to make more assumptions. We know that the (mean) estimate is the midpoint of the confidence interval (0.6,2.0), thus the estimate is 1.3 percent. Further, assume the standard deviation is 0.35. Then

$$\Phi(\text{lower limit}) = \Phi((1.0 - 1.4)/0.35) = 0.127$$

Accordingly, the new level is 0.9987. Finally, the upper confidence limit needs to be computed based on normal theory in the usual way. Because the new level is higher than the old level (0.99), the upper confidence limit will be larger than before. Since the lower limit is also larger than before, this is exactly the desired effect.

To illustrate these calculations with another value, suppose there is no lower limit (i.e., the lower limit equals minus infinity), then the new level turns out to be the old level (as it should) because $\Phi(-\text{infinity}) = 0$.

In summary, the confidence limits were revised because the lower confidence limit often was lower than the lower limit. After the lower limit was adjusted, the upper limit also needed adjustment.

Throughout, we chose a larger confidence limit than is usually used in analyses such as these (99 percent versus 95 percent), because we construct confidence limits for a large number of categories. The larger the number of categories, the more likely it is that one of the confidence intervals does not contain the true percentage.

Results

Defendants Are Distributed Across Most Industries. Asbestos litigation has spread well beyond the asbestos-related manufacturing and installation industries where it first began to touch almost every form of economic activity that takes place in the United States. We found that 75 out of a total of 83 different industries in the SIC system at the two-digit level included at least one firm that had been named as an asbestos litigation defendant.

Table 4.3 presents our estimates of the fraction of asbestos litigation defendants in each two-digit SIC industry. It also presents the confidence intervals for these estimates.

It should be noted that some entities pursue business activities in multiple industries. Hence, a claim against an entity may have been based on activities outside its principal business activity. Therefore, these data indicate the spread of the litigation in terms of the distribution of entities named as defendants across SIC codes and do not necessarily indicate the range of economic activities that have given rise to asbestos claims.

Table 4.3
Distribution of Defendants by SIC Two-Digit Industry Code

SIC Code	Industry	Defendants (%)	Confidence Limits (%) Lower 99%	Upper 99%
1	Agricultural Production Crops	3.4	3.4	3.6
7	Agricultural Services	0.3	0.1	0.9
9	Fishing, Hunting, and Trapping	0.1	0.0	0.4
10	Metal Mining	0.1	0.0	0.4
12	Coal Mining	0.1	0.1	0.5
13	Oil and Gas Extraction	1.7	0.4	3.0
14	Mining and Quarrying of Nonmetallic Minerals, Except Fuels	1.3	0.4	2.5
15	Building Construction General Contractors and Operative Builders	4.3	2.2	6.4
16	Heavy Construction Other Than Building Construction Contractors	1.1	1.1	1.2
17	Construction Special Trade Contractors	9.9	6.8	12.9
20	Food and Kindred Products	2.9	2.9	3.3
21	Tobacco Products	0.4	0.4	0.6
22	Textile Mill Products	0.3	0.0	0.9
23	Apparel and Other Finished Products Made from Fabrics and Similar Materials	0.3	0.2	0.9
24	Lumber and Wood Products, Except Furniture	0.9	0.1	1.9
25	Furniture and Fixtures	0.5	0.2	1.3
26	Paper and Allied Products	0.5	0.0	1.2
27	Printing, Publishing, and Allied Industries	0.3	0.2	0.9
28	Chemicals and Allied Products	4.3	2.2	6.4
29	Petroleum Refining and Related Industries	1.3	1.3	1.9
30	Rubber and Miscellaneous Plastics Products	1.5	0.4	2.8
31	Leather and Leather Products	0.7	0.7	0.8
32	Stone, Clay, Glass, and Concrete Products	4.3	2.2	6.4
33	Primary Metal Industries	1.5	1.3	2.8
34	Fabricated Metal Products, Except Machinery and Transportation Equipment	4.9	2.7	7.1
35	Industrial and Commercial Machinery and Computer Equipment	4.3	2.2	6.4
36	Electronic and Other Electrical Equipment and Components, Except Computer Equipment	1.4	1.4	2.4
37	Transportation Equipment	1.5	0.5	2.8
38	Measuring, Analyzing, and Controlling Instruments; Photographic, Medical, and Optical Goods; Watches and Clocks	0.9	0.9	1.2
39	Miscellaneous Manufacturing Industries	0.3	0.3	0.9
40	Railroad Transportation	1.1	0.1	2.2
41	Local and Suburban Transit and Interurban Highway Passenger Transportation	0.3	0.3	0.9
42	Motor Freight Transportation and Warehousing	0.3	0.0	0.9
44	Water Transportation	8.9	6.0	11.8
45	Transportation by Air	1.5	1.5	1.6
47	Transportation Services	0.1	0.1	0.5
48	Communications	0.3	0.1	0.9
49	Electric, Gas, and Sanitary Services	1.3	0.1	2.5
50	Wholesale Trade-Durable Goods	9.5	6.5	12.5
51	Wholesale Trade-Non-Durable Goods	3.6	3.6	4.3

Table 4.3—Continued

SIC Code	Industry	Defendants (%)	Confidence Limits (%) Lower 99%	Upper 99%
52	Building Materials, Hardware, Garden Supply, and Mobile Home Dealers	1.9	0.7	3.3
53	General Merchandise Stores	0.4	0.4	1.0
54	Food Stores	0.3	0.1	0.9
55	Automotive Dealers and Gasoline Service Stations	0.5	0.0	1.2
56	Apparel and Accessory Stores	0.5	0.3	1.3
57	Home Furniture, Furnishings, and Equipment Stores	0.5	0.0	1.2
58	Eating and Drinking Places	0.1	0.1	0.5
59	Miscellaneous Retail	0.5	0.1	1.2
60	Depository Institutions	0.3	0.1	0.9
61	Non-Depository Credit Institutions	0.1	0.1	0.5
62	Security and Commodity Brokers, Dealers, Exchanges, and Services	0.3	0.0	0.9
63	Insurance Carriers	0.5	0.0	1.2
64	Insurance Agents, Brokers, and Service	0.7	0.2	1.6
65	Real Estate	1.3	0.3	2.5
67	Holding and Other Investment Offices	0.9	0.5	1.9
70	Hotels, Rooming Houses, Camps, and Other Lodging Places	0.5	0.4	1.3
72	Personal Services	0.3	0.2	0.9
73	Business Services	1.5	0.2	2.8
75	Automotive Repair, Services, and Parking	0.3	0.3	0.9
76	Miscellaneous Repair Services	0.3	0.1	0.9
78	Motion Pictures	0.2	0.2	0.5
79	Amusement and Recreation Services	0.3	0.0	0.9
80	Health Services	0.1	0.1	0.5
81	Legal Services	0.3	0.3	0.6
82	Educational Services	0.5	0.1	1.2
83	Social Services	0.3	0.3	0.9
84	Museums, Art Galleries, and Botanical and Zoological Gardens	0.1	0.0	0.5
86	Membership Organizations	0.3	0.0	0.9
87	Engineering, Accounting, Research, Management, and Related Services	2.1	0.6	3.6
89	Services Not Elsewhere Classified	0.6	0.6	0.7
91	Executive, Legislative, and General Government, Except Finance	0.5	0.0	1.2
92	Justice, Public Order, and Safety	0.1	0.1	0.5
94	Administration of Human Resource Programs	0.1	0.0	0.5
96	Administration of Economic Programs	0.3	0.0	0.9
99	Nonclassifiable Establishments	0.5	0.0	1.2

Litigation Is Concentrated in Eight Industries. Although asbestos litigation is widespread throughout the economy, it is spread very unevenly across industries, with only a handful of defendants in some industries and hundreds of defendants in others. Three industries, Construction Special Trade Contractors (SIC code 17), Water Transportation (44), and Wholesale Trade-Durable Goods (50), each contain about 10 percent of all defendants. Five other industry classifications, Building Construction General Contractors and Operative Builders (15), Chemicals and Allied Products (28), Stone, Clay, Glass, and Concrete Products (32), Fabricated Metal Products, Except Machinery and Transportation Equipment (34), and Industrial and Commercial Machinery and Computer Equipment (35), each represent from 4 to 5 percent of the total. The remaining industries each contain smaller percentages of the defendants.

It Was Not Possible to Identify How Often a Single Defendant Has Been Named. Our data were not sufficient to estimate the number of claimants that had named any particular defendant or the defendants in any particular industry group. Most of those who provided lists of defendants to us had not attempted to count the number of times any particular defendant had been named. And, even in those instances in which someone was able to provide data on the number of times that they knew a particular defendant had been named, we had no way to determine the fraction of claims against that defendant included in their data.

Plaintiff attorneys, for example, know the defendants named on the claims they had filed. But the list of defendants they named on claims filed on behalf of claimants who were exposed to asbestos under one set of circumstances (e.g., site, duration, occupation, etc.) would generally differ from the list of defendants they named on claims filed on behalf of claimants exposed to asbestos under a different set of circumstances. While several plaintiff attorneys could provide the names of defendants to us, they generally did not have counts of the number of times they had named any particular defendant readily available. And they generally had no data on how often other plaintiff attorneys had named any of those defendants.

Similarly, defendants or defense attorneys know the names of the co-defendants on claims against them or their clients. But, because the list of co-defendants named on some claims can differ from the list of co-defendants on other claims, defendants generally did not have counts of the number of times any particular co-defendant had been named. Here, too, even if defendants or defense attorneys had maintained counts of the number of times a defendant had been named on claims against them or their clients, they still had no idea of how often that defendant had been named on claims on which they themselves had not been named.

In sum, we can identify those entities that have been named as a defendant on at least one asbestos claim. But we have no data on, or estimates of, how often any of those entities has been named on all claims combined. Consequently, while we can identify the range of industry groups that include at least one entity that has been named as a defendant on an asbestos claim, we cannot distinguish among industry groups that include entities named on large numbers of claims and industry groups that include entities named very infrequently.

The distribution of defendants across industries (see Table 4.3) suggests the groups for which it is likely that entities within those groups have generally experienced substantial numbers of claims. Water Transportation (SIC 44), for example, includes between 6.0 percent and 11.8 percent of all defendants. This means that roughly 500 to 1,000 firms in that industry have been named on at least one asbestos claim. It seems very unlikely that so many different firms in the same industry would have been named on an asbestos claim unless the activities undertaken in that industry had led to substantial asbestos exposures which, in turn, suggests that a substantial number of claims have been filed against firms in that industry. Some of these firms may have seen very few claims, but it seems likely that if that many firms from the same industry have been named, some, or perhaps most, of them would have been named frequently.

Conversely, between 0.1 percent and 0.5 percent of the entities in the Health Services (SIC 80) industry had been named on an asbestos claim. This means that roughly eight to 40 Health Services firms have been named on at least one asbestos claim. It seems very unlikely that so few entities in the same industry would have been named on an asbestos claim unless substantial asbestos exposure is infrequent in that industry and, consequently, few entities in that industry see a substantial number of claims. One, or a few, of these firms may have seen a number of claims. But it seems likely that if that few firms have been named at all, most of them would have been named infrequently.

In sum, asbestos litigation has spread across the U.S. economy in the sense that at least one firm in each of 75 different industries has been named as a defendant on a claim. However, the concentration of the litigation is very uneven, with only a handful of defendants in some industries and hundreds of defendants in others. Three industries each contain about 10 percent of all defendants, five others each include about 4 to 5 percent of defendants, and the remaining industries each contain smaller percentages of the defendants. While we do not have estimates of the numbers of claims that name the defendants in each industry, it seems reasonable that the distribution of claims is roughly similar to the distribution of defendants. That is, it is likely that the entities in eight industries have generally seen substantial numbers of claims while the entities in the other 67 industries have each generally seen comparatively few claims.

There could, of course, be exceptions. There may be entities in the heavily impacted industries that have seen few claims, and there may be entities in the industries that include relatively few defendants that have been the target of large numbers of claims. However, it seems likely that while the litigation has spread across the U.S. economy, the litigation is still highly concentrated in certain industries in the sense that entities in the heavily impacted industries have probably been named relatively often while the entities in the less heavily impacted industries have been named only infrequently.

CHAPTER FIVE

Costs and Compensation

In this chapter, we estimate the total amount of money spent on asbestos personal injury claims by defendants and insurers. We then estimate how much of the money spent on asbestos litigation was consumed by transactions costs and how much ended up in claimants' pockets. The components of those costs are illustrated in Figure 5.1.

Total spending refers to the net amount defendants and insurers combined spent on asbestos litigation. This sum is the amount defendants spent after being reimbursed from insurers and the amount insurers spent after being reimbursed by reinsurers. Total spending is broken down into defense transaction costs and the gross compensation paid to claimants. *Defense transaction costs* include the costs defendants and insurers incurred in all asbestos-related litigation, including litigation with other defendants and insurers. *Gross compensation* consists of claimants' legal fees and expenses and the claimants' net compensation. We discuss each of these components in this chapter, beginning with total spending. For each component, we first describe our approach to estimation and then present our findings. At the end of the chapter, we discuss estimates of future expenditures on asbestos litigation.

Total Spending

Approach to Estimation

There are no publicly available data on total spending on asbestos litigation, on the fraction of that amount that goes to transaction costs, or on the net compensation to claimants. We obtained confidential data and the results of proprietary studies from a variety of sources and used these data to estimate total spending on asbestos litigation from the inception of the litigation in the 1960s through 2002.

Our first step in estimating total spending was to estimate the number of claims closed each year through 2002, by type of claim (mesothelioma, other cancer, or nonmalignant injury). We used the methods described in Chapter Four to estimate the number of claimants who initially filed an asbestos claim in each year through 2002. Specifically, we compared the lists of claimants provided to us by defendants

Figure 5.1
Components of Asbestos Litigation Costs and Compensation

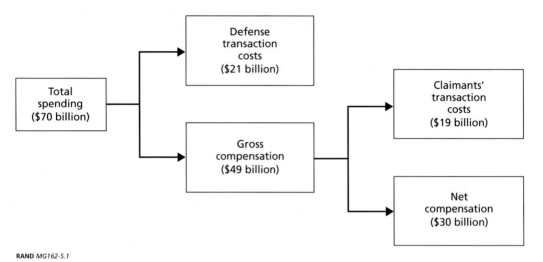

RAND *MG162-5.1*

NOTE: Dollar figures are approximate.

and personal injury bankruptcy trusts to identify the number of unique individuals who had filed an asbestos personal injury claim in each year through the end of 2002. As we described earlier, in making these comparisons, we deleted the claimants on each list for whom we did not have adequate information to determine whether that claimant was also included on any of the other lists. We also recognized that claimants occasionally filed a claim naming several defendants and then, at a later date, added defendants or filed a separate claim with a personal injury bankruptcy trust or against other defendants. We counted each claimant once, in the year in which claimants initially filed a claim, regardless of whether they subsequently filed additional claims.

We then calculated the distribution of time-to-disposition for all defendants combined for each type of claim. The defendants and personal injury bankruptcy trusts who provided these data to us generally told us they believe they do not systematically settle claims faster, or slower, on average, than other defendants. In our interviews with other participants in the litigation, we asked if they could suggest defendants or personal injury bankruptcy trusts whom they thought were particularly quick, or slow, to settle claims. While a variety of entities were discussed in these conversations, the defendants and trusts in our database were not often mentioned. We assume that the distributions of time-to-disposition for the defendants and trusts that provided information to us are representative of the distribution of average time-to-disposition by type of claim for all defendants and personal injury bankruptcy trusts.

We assume that, on average, the share of the total claim value (assessed at the time of settlement) paid by a defendant is not related to how long, from the time of filing, it takes for that defendant to settle the claim. Thus, if a defendant would pay, on average, X percent of the value of a particular claim if it settled that claim N years after it was filed, it would, on average, pay X percent of the value of that claim if it happened to settle that claim sooner, or later, than N years after the claim was filed. Then, the average share of the total value of a given claim paid by the defendants who settle that claim in any given year is independent of the year in which those defendants settle the claim. We multiplied the estimated number of claimants who filed each type of claim in each year by the distribution of time-to-disposition for that type of claim. The resulting numbers are estimates of the average percentage of the value of the claims of each type filed in each year that defendants paid in settlements in each subsequent year.

For example, on average, defendants settle about 6 percent of the claims brought against them within one year of when the claims are filed. Thus, we assume that, on average, a claimant will settle with about 6 percent of the defendants the claimant named within one year of when he or she brought the claims. We also assume that defendants' payments to claimants are independent of when they settle any particular claim. So, on average, the payments made to a claimant in any given year are proportional to the fraction of the defendants named by that claimant that settle with that claimant in that year. Under these assumptions, the payments a claimant receives within one year of when he or she files the claim will, on average, add up to about 6 percent of the value of the type of claim he or she alleged in that year. Similarly, defendants settle about 16 percent of the claims brought against them one to two years after the claims are filed. We assume that claimants will, on average, settle with about 16 percent of the defendants they name one to two years after they bring their claims and will receive from those defendants payments that will, on average, add up to about 16 percent of the value of claims for their alleged type of injury in that year. And this pattern of claims payments continues over future years.

The share any particular defendant or group of defendants pays on claims may vary over time in response to changes in the environment (e.g., a defendant's bankruptcy). We are assuming that claimants and their attorneys respond to changes in the environment (e.g., bankruptcy filings) by seeking larger settlements from viable defendants, naming larger numbers of defendants, and bringing new defendants into the litigation. In sum, we assume that, on average, a claimant receives the same share of the total value of his or her type of claim in any given year after filing his or her claim. The specific group of defendants that compensate any particular claimant at any particular time may differ from what the group would have been had the claim been filed at a different time.

We then obtained three independent estimates of what total spending on a claim of each type would have been, on average, in 2000, if all the defendants named on the claim had settled in that year. First, we interviewed defense attorneys, who represented several of the defendants who provided data to us, to obtain their estimates of the share of the total value of each type of claim that the defendants they represented had paid, on average, in 2000. Because we knew what the defendants had paid, on average, in 2000 on claims of each type, we could use the attorneys' estimates of defendants' shares to estimate each attorney's implicit estimate of total spending on each type of claim by his or her defendant. Many of the defense attorneys we interviewed were not able to offer estimates of the shares of total spending their clients had paid. We averaged the estimates from attorneys who could provide them in order to estimate the average total value of each type of claim in 2000.

Second, analysts at Tillinghast-Towers Perrin, a leading actuarial consulting firm, had conducted an analysis similar to ours to estimate the average total amount spent for each type of claim in the year 2000. Tillinghast-Towers Perrin provides actuarial services to a large number of clients regarding their asbestos liabilities. In the course of this work, Tillinghast gained access to extensive data on its clients' spending on each type of claim. Tillinghast reviewed the settlement amounts, by injury type and year, that were paid by the asbestos defendants it represented and estimated the defendants' shares of total claimant awards to develop estimates of the total value of claims by injury type (inclusive of plaintiff attorney fees). Tillinghast interviewed its clients' legal staffs and the defense counsel who represented those clients to verify what those clients paid on claims of various types and their estimates of their share of the total value of each claim that they paid. We then used that information to estimate the total value of each type of claim. Tillinghast shared its results with us on a confidential basis. Its estimates were generally similar to ours.

Third, a research corporation with extensive experience in asbestos analysis had conducted a similar analysis to estimate the average total amount spent for each type of claim in 1998 and 1999. It had worked with a substantial number of defendants to estimate the share of the total value of each type of claim that each of those defendants typically paid and, consequently, the total value of each type of claim. The corporation also shared its results with us on a confidential basis.[1] Its estimates for some types of claims differed from those we had obtained ourselves and that Tillinghast-Towers Perrin had provided to us.

Because of the differences in the estimates we obtained from the two outside sources, we performed the analysis of total spending on asbestos personal injury claims twice, first using the Tillinghast-Towers Perrin estimates and then using the research corporation's estimates. Because our estimates were similar to those obtained by Tillinghast-Towers Perrin, and because Tillinghast had access to a greater amount of data than we did, we did not perform a third analysis using our estimates.

---

[1] Our confidentiality agreement with this research corporation prohibits our disclosing its identity.

We then estimated what total spending on a claim of each type would have been, on average, in each year, if all the defendants named on the claim had settled in that year. We began with Kakalik et al.'s (1983) estimates of the average amount spent per claim by all defendants and insurers combined in 1981 by type of claim. We then estimated the corresponding average spending per claim by all defendants and insurers combined in either 2000 (when using the Tillinghast estimates) or 1998–1999 (when using the research corporation estimates) by type of claim. We computed the average annual rate of increase in total spending per claim for each type of claim over the 1981–2000 (Tillinghast) or 1998–1999 (research corporation) period. We assumed that the total amount spent per claim, by type of claim, grew at this annual average rate from 1981 through either 2000 or 1998–1999 and computed the resulting average amount spent per claim by type of claim and year. We have no reason to believe that the average total amount spent on each type of claim grew smoothly over that period. Average total spending per claim undoubtedly grew more rapidly in some years than in others. However, the average of the estimates of spending by year we developed by smooth exponential interpolation between 1981 and 2000 or 1998–1999 should be close to the average of the true values over that period.

We extrapolated the 1982–2000, or 1982 through 1998–1999, trends in total spending per claim by type of claim to 2001 and 2002. In doing so, we may have overestimated spending per claim in those years. A substantial number of major defendants filed for bankruptcy between 2000 and the summer of 2002. (See Chapter Six for a discussion of these filings.) Because claims against these defendants are barred pending their reorganization, claimants lost access to several defendants who had until then been substantial sources of compensation. Plaintiff attorneys whom we interviewed told us that they attempt to make up for their inability to obtain compensation from these defendants by demanding larger amounts in compensation from the surviving defendants and by bringing new defendants into the litigation (see Chapter Three). Defense counsel confirmed the reports of these plaintiff attorneys. While these actions may have closed some of the gaps opened by the disappearance of the major defendants who petitioned to file for reorganization under Chapter 11, it is quite possible that compensation by type of claim did not grow as rapidly in 2001 and 2002 than it had in other years. If so, our estimate of the amounts spent per claim in 2001 and 2002 will overstate the true amounts.

We multiplied our estimate of the number of claims, by type of claim, filed in each year over the period 1982–2002 by the corresponding estimates of the distribution of time-to-disposition and each of the estimates of average spending per claim by type and year. The results are estimates of the total amount paid out by defendants and insurers on each type of claim in each year over the period 1983–2002. We added these estimates to the Kakalik et al. (1983) estimate of total spending on asbestos litigation through 1982 to obtain estimates of the total amount spent on asbestos litigation through 2002.

Results

Total Spending on Asbestos Claims Through 2002 Was About $70 Billion. Tables 5.1a and 5.1b present alternative estimates of annual total amounts spent on asbestos litigation by all defendants and insurers combined, defense and claimants' transaction costs, and claimants' gross and net compensation through 2002. We used the Tillinghast-Towers Perrin estimates of the average total amount spent on a claim of each type in 2000 in calculating the estimates presented in Table 5.1a. We used the corresponding estimates of the average total amount spent on a claim of each type in 1998–1999 by the research corporation in calculating the estimates presented in Table 5.1b.

The two sets of estimates are remarkably similar. They each imply that approximately $70 billion has been spent on asbestos litigation through 2002. Analysts at Milliman USA, another leading actuarial consulting firm, have independently

Table 5.1a
Estimates of Asbestos Litigation Compensation ($ millions) Through 2002 (Using Tillinghast-Towers Perrin Estimates of Year-2000 Claim Values)

Year	Total Spending by All Defendants and Insurers	Defense Transaction Costs	Gross Compensation	Claimants Transaction Costs	Net Compensation
1982 and earlier	549	203	346	135	211
1983	306	101	205	80	125
1984	376	204	172	67	105
1985	479	212	267	104	163
1986	658	391	267	104	163
1987	950	400	550	215	336
1988	1,370	540	830	324	506
1989	2,055	550	1,504	587	918
1990	2,859	1,325	1,534	598	935
1991	3,169	1,588	1,581	616	964
1992	3,373	1,391	1,983	773	1,209
1993	3,475	1,766	1,708	666	1,042
1994	3,560	1,020	2,540	991	1,550
1995	3,956	1,277	2,679	1,045	1,634
1996	4,511	1,510	3,001	1,171	1,831
1997	4,934	1,635	3,299	1,286	2,012
1998	5,330	1,731	3,599	1,404	2,195
1999	5,775	1,141	4,635	1,808	2,827
2000	6,314	1,209	5,106	1,991	3,114
2001	7,480	1,496	5,984	2,334	3,650
2002	8,907	1,781	7,126	2,779	4,347

Table 5.1b
Estimates of Asbestos Litigation Compensation ($ millions) Through 2002 (Using an
Independent Research Firm's Estimates of Claim Values in 1998–1999)

Year	Total Spending by All Defendants and Insurers	Defense Transaction Costs	Gross Compensation	Claimants Transaction Costs	Net Compensation
1982 and earlier	549	203	346	135	211
1983	303	100	203	79	124
1984	372	201	170	66	104
1985	473	210	264	103	161
1986	649	385	263	103	161
1987	933	392	541	211	330
1988	1,341	528	813	317	496
1989	2,009	538	1,471	574	897
1990	2,804	1,300	1,504	587	918
1991	3,123	1,565	1,558	608	950
1992	3,330	1,373	1,957	763	1,194
1993	3,425	1,741	1,684	657	1,027
1994	3,512	1,006	2,506	977	1,529
1995	3,917	1,264	2,653	1,035	1,618
1996	4,447	1,488	2,959	1,154	1,805
1997	4,872	1,615	3,257	1,270	1,987
1998	5,300	1,721	3,579	1,396	2,183
1999	5,790	1,143	4,647	1,812	2,834
2000	6,418	1,228	5,190	2,024	3,166
2001	7,597	1,519	6,078	2,370	3,707
2002	8,995	1,799	7,196	2,807	4,390

developed estimates of the total costs of asbestos litigation through 2000. Milliman provides actuarial services to a substantial number of defendants and insurers who are involved in asbestos litigation. In the course of their work, Milliman analysts have access to a large volume of data on asbestos payments to date. Using these data, Milliman estimated that about $50 billion was spent on asbestos claims through 2000 (Bhagavatula, 2002). Each of our sets of estimates of total spending on asbestos claims through 2000 implies that the total spending was about $54 billion. Thus, our estimate is similar to that of a well-respected organization with extensive access to data and substantial experience in analyzing asbestos litigation. We also discussed our estimate of total spending on asbestos claims with representatives of several major insurance and reinsurance companies. None of those we interviewed expressed strong reservations about our results. Some thought we might be somewhat high; others thought we were somewhat low. But none thought our estimate was very far off.

U.S. insurance companies are required to list their cumulative net paid losses, including loss adjustment expenses, in their annual statements. A. M. Best has collected and collated these data. A. M. Best reported that U.S. insurers had spent about

$21.6 billion on asbestos claims through 2000 (Altonji et al., 2001). Thus, through 2000, U.S. insurers accounted for about 40 percent of the total amount spent on asbestos personal injury claims.

Based on conversations with both U.S. and foreign insurance companies, we believe foreign insurers spent $8 billion to $12 billion through 2000, more than half of which has been assumed by the London market. Milliman estimates that foreign insurers have spent $8 billion on asbestos litigation to date (Bhagavatula, 2002). Foreign insurers accounted for 15 to 22 percent of the expenditures on asbestos litigation through 2000.

Subtracting the amounts U.S. and foreign insurers have spent on asbestos litigation from our estimate of $54 billion in total expenditures through 2000 implies that U.S. defendants spent between $20 billion and $24 billion on asbestos litigation through 2000, roughly 40 percent of the total spending. Milliman estimates that U.S. defendants' uninsured losses through 2000 were $20 billion (Bhagavatula, 2002). Table 5.2 summarizes our estimates of the distribution of total spending on asbestos litigation through 2000.

Nontraditional Defendants Now Account for More Than Half of Asbestos Expenditures. As we noted in Chapter Four, asbestos litigation has spread beyond the asbestos-related manufacturing and installation industries where it first began. Nontraditional defendants and their insurers are also paying an increasing share of the costs to resolve asbestos injury claims. A confidential study of asbestos costs that was shared with us reports that in the early 1980s traditional defendants accounted for about three-quarters of expenditures. In contrast, according to this report, by the late 1990s nontraditional defendants accounted for about 60 percent of asbestos expenditures. This study was performed for a private client by a respected analyst who has had extensive experience in the asbestos litigation area and whose work was cited to us by both plaintiff and defense attorneys. We discussed both the study's analysis and the data on which it was based with the analyst and determined that the work was analytically sound.

Given the number of major defendants that have filed for bankruptcy since 1998, it seems likely that the nontraditional defendants' share of total spending on asbestos injury claims has grown into the 2000s and is substantially higher today than it was in the late 1990s.

Table 5.2
Distribution of Total Spending on Asbestos Litigation Through 2000

Expenditure Source	Amount
U.S. insurers	$22 billion
Insurers outside the United States	$8–$12 billion
Defendants	$20–$24 billion

Defense Transaction Costs

Approach to Estimation

We obtained aggregate annual data on indemnity payments and defense costs for a large number of defendants. These data were available for some defendants from the early 1980s. In other cases, we were able to obtain data only for the past few years. When we sought these data, defendants were generally able to provide these data through 2001. In all, the data include more than 60,000 defendant-year observations. Because the data comprised annual average indemnity payments and defense costs, we had to assume the ratio of defense transaction costs to indemnity did not vary by type of claim. However, the widespread practice of settling claims in blocks, which frequently include different types of claims (see Chapter Three), effectively eliminates differences in the ratio of defense transaction costs to indemnity by type of claim. Accordingly, we used the observations we had for any given year to compute the weighted average ratio of defense transaction costs to total spending for those observations for that year. We then multiplied the ratio for each year and the corresponding estimates of total spending by type of claim to estimate defense transaction costs by year for each type of claim.

We subtracted the estimate of defense transaction costs in each year from the corresponding estimate of total spending per claim, by type of claim, to estimate claimants' gross compensation by claim type and year.

Results

Defense Transaction Costs Account for About 31 Percent of Total Spending. An earlier RAND study (Kakalik et al., 1983) concluded that, in the 1970s and early 1980s, defendants' and insurers' legal fees and expenses consumed about 37 cents of every dollar spent on asbestos litigation. Table 5.3 presents our estimates of defendants' and insurers' legal fees and expenses as a percentage of total spending each year since 1982 for all defendants combined for whom we had data. It also shows the mean and standard deviations of the observations we had for each year through 2001. We assume that defense transaction costs accounted for the same share of total spending in 2002 as they had in 2001.

We multiplied our estimates of the share of total spending consumed by defense legal fees and expenses in each year by each of our estimates of total spending in each year from Tables 5.1a and 5.1b. Each of our sets of estimates implies that defense legal fees and expenses consumed more than $21 billion, about 31 percent of the funds spent by defendants and insurers on asbestos personal injury claims through 2002.

The defense transaction costs associated with asbestos litigation generally accounted for well over 40 percent of total spending in the 1980s and early 1990s. The

Table 5.3
Defense Costs as a Percentage of Total Spending, 1983–2001

Year	Average Defense Costs, All Observations Combined (%)	Average Defendant's Defense Costs (%)	Standard Deviation of Average Defendant's Defense Costs (%)
1983	33	86	35
1984	54	57	43
1985	44	70	44
1986	59	56	41
1987	42	67	41
1988	39	71	38
1989	27	67	41
1990	46	69	45
1991	50	72	37
1992	41	72	40
1993	51	69	39
1994	29	71	41
1995	32	74	38
1996	33	73	38
1997	33	70	43
1998	32	65	37
1999	20	69	40
2000	19	70	39
2001	20	74	38

asbestos litigation environment in the 1980s was highly adversarial: Defendants disputed among themselves regarding responsibility for the asbestos at a site; defendants and insurers disputed over a host of coverage issues; and plaintiffs, defendants, and insurers vigorously disputed issues of causality, illness, and other such matters. Defense transaction costs averaged about 44 percent of total asbestos spending in the 1980s and early 1990s.

Many of these issues were essentially worked out in the late 1980s and early 1990s in the form of formal judicial decisions, agreements among defendants and insurers regarding joint defense efforts and coverage issues, and agreements between some plaintiff attorneys and defendants to settle claims according to a schedule of payments by claim type. These arrangements led to reduced defense litigation costs. Defense transaction costs averaged about 25 percent of total asbestos spending from the mid-1990s through the early 2000s. (See Table 5.3.)

Defense Transaction Costs Are Likely to Increase in the Future. Virtually all of our interview respondents discussed what they saw as new instabilities in asbestos litigation after the failure of the *Amchem* settlement (see Chapter Three). Many interviewees noted that the Center for Claims Resolution (CCR), a consortium of about 20 non-bankrupt corporations that were coordinating their defense of asbestos claims and the leading example of asbestos defendant cooperation, has ceased settling claims against its members. At the same time, interviewees told us, many defendants' agreements with plaintiff law firms were under reconsideration or being renegotiated. In particular, as an increasing number of major defendants have filed for bankruptcy and ceased paying asbestos claims pending their reorganization, plaintiff attorneys are seeking greater compensation from the defendants who remain in the litigation. Many of those defendants, in turn, are reluctant to pay greater compensation for a given type of claim than they had been paying in the past. Also, we have been told that many defendants are moving away from block settlements of large groups of claims and looking in more detail at individual claims. Plaintiff firms were said to be pursuing more-adversarial strategies. And a number of those we interviewed believe that as the litigation expands to defendants who had not been involved in the litigation before, there will be new insurance coverage battles.

No one we interviewed offered us qualitative or quantitative information about changes in transaction costs resulting from these new sources of instability. But all of these factors have significant potential to influence defense transaction costs, and it seems likely that those costs will increase, at least temporarily, as a result. Because some of these issues may take several years to resolve, such a period of higher costs could be relatively long.

Transaction Costs of a Bankruptcy Trust Are Considerably Lower. Once a bankrupt corporation is reorganized and a trust is established to assume its liabilities, claims processing procedures are largely administrative rather than adversarial. This should lead to dramatically lower transaction costs, as was the case of the Manville Trust.

From 1994 to 2000, the Manville Trust reported annual average operating expenses (not including special expenses associated with tobacco litigation) of about $10 million, about 5 percent of the total dollars it paid out to asbestos claimants plus expenses during this period. The Manville Trust also requires that attorneys representing claimants who file claims against it charge a fee of no more than 25 percent of the amount paid to the asbestos claimant. Our interviewees reported that attorneys generally adhere to that requirement.

Assuming that these expense ratios are correct, people who file claims against the Manville Trust receive about 70 percent of the total dollars spent by the Trust. However, it must be noted that the funds available to the Trust are limited. The money may be paid much more efficiently in this way, but the amount paid to any particular claimant is much less than would have been paid in litigation, given what other claimants are being paid for the same kinds of claims. Moreover, while some other trusts limit attorneys' fees, others do not.

Gross Compensation

Approach to Estimation

To estimate claimants' gross compensation, we multiplied our estimates of total spending on each type of asbestos claim in each year by one minus our estimates of the fraction of total spending that went to defense transaction costs in that year.

Results

Gross Compensation Is About 69 Percent of Total Spending. We estimate that the sum of indemnity payments to claimants through 2002 equaled almost $49 billion, about 69 percent of total spending on asbestos litigation through that date. Gross compensation to claimants accounted for about 56 percent of the funds spent through the 1980s and early 1990s. The drop in defense transaction costs as a share of total spending in the mid- to late 1990s resulted in an increase, to about 75 percent, in the share of total spending going to claimants, gross of their transaction costs.

The confidential analysis mentioned above also provided estimates of the total indemnity paid to asbestos claimants in each of four time periods through 1997. That study's estimates and our corresponding estimates from Tables 5.1a and 5.1b are shown in Table 5.4. Here, too, a well-respected analyst with extensive access to data and substantial experience in the asbestos litigation area arrived at estimates that are very similar to ours.

Table 5.5 shows our estimates of the distribution of claimants, by type of claim, who brought claims in each of the time periods of interest and the gross compensation paid to claimants by type of claim and time period. For purposes of comparison, the table also shows the only available comparative data: the distribution of claims brought against the Manville Trust in 1995–2000, the distribution of gross compensation paid by the Manville Trust over that time period, and Tillinghast Towers-Perrin estimates of the distribution of gross compensation paid, by type of claim, in 1991–2000.

Table 5.4
Gross Compensation Paid on Asbestos Personal Injury Claims

Years	Estimates ($ millions)		
	From Table 5.1a	From Table 5.1b	From Analyst's Confidential Study
1982 and earlier	346	346	267
1983–1987	1,461	1,441	1,447
1988–1992	7,431	7,304	6,309
1993–1997	13,228	13,059	14,721
Total	22,467	22,149	22,744

Table 5.5
Estimated Distribution of Claimants and Gross Compensation by Type of Claim

	Distribution of Claimants		
	Type of Claim		
	Mesothelioma (%)	Other Cancer (%)	Nonmalignancy (%)
RAND Estimates			
1982 and earlier	6	12	82
1983–1987	5	14	81
1988–1992	4	11	85
1993–1997	3	8	89
1998–2002	3	5	92
Manville Trust, 1995–2000	4	8	88

	Distribution of Gross Compensation		
	Type of Claim		
	Mesothelioma (%)	Other Cancer (%)	Nonmalignancy (%)
Table 5.1a Estimates			
1982 and earlier	18	15	67
1983–1987	21	19	60
1988–1992	20	21	59
1993–1997	20	21	60
1998–2002	20	20	61
Table 5.1b Estimates			
1982 and earlier	18	15	67
1983–1987	25	18	57
1988–1992	28	20	52
1993–1997	32	18	49
1998–2002	38	16	47
Manville Trust, 1995–2000	20	16	64
Tillinghast Towers-Perrin Estimates, 1991–2000	17	18	65

We estimate that mesothelioma claimants accounted for about 6 percent of total claims and about 18 percent of the gross compensation paid all claimants combined in the early days of the litigation. The fraction of claimants who filed claims for mesothelioma steadily declined over time until, by the early 2000s, only about 3 percent of claimants were filing mesothelioma claims. However, the amount paid in compensation on the average mesothelioma claim grew more rapidly over time than did the average amounts paid in compensation for other types of claims. Based on the Table 5.1a estimates, mesothelioma claimants' share of gross compensation has remained at about 20 percent since the early 1980s. The alternative estimates, in Table 5.1b, assume even more rapid growth in the average amounts paid in gross compensation on mesothelioma claims and, consequently, imply that the share of gross compensation that went to mesothelioma claims grew over time, reaching about 38 percent of gross compensation in the late 1990s and early 2000s.

The trends in claims for other cancers are very similar to those for mesothelioma. Other cancer claimants accounted for 12 to 14 percent of all claimants through the 1980s. The share of claimants who brought claims for other cancers steadily declined through the 1990s until, by the early 2000s, other cancer claimants accounted for only about 5 percent of claimants. However, the fraction of gross compensation that went to other cancer claimants remained roughly the same, about 20 percent of total spending, according to the Table 5.1a estimates, and roughly 18 percent of total spending, according to the Table 5.1b estimates, throughout the 1980s and 1990s.

As we discussed earlier, the fraction of claimants who brought nonmalignant injury claims grew steadily throughout the 1980s and 1990s. Nonmalignant injury claimants received about 60 percent of gross compensation over the entire period, according to the Table 5.1a estimates. The Table 5.1b estimates imply that the growth in the share of gross compensation going to malignant injury claimants resulted in a decline in the share of gross compensation going to nonmalignant injury claimants, from about two-thirds in the early 1980s to a little less than half in recent years.

The Claims Resolution Management Corporation recently published the distribution of the Manville Trust's claims payments by type of claim from 1995 through 2001 (Austern, 2002). Manville's experience over those seven years, as shown in Table 5.5, closely resembles the estimates we obtained using the Tillinghast Towers-Perrin estimates of total spending per claim by type of claim. Mesothelioma claims accounted for about 4 percent of the total claims paid by the Trust over that period and about 20 percent of the gross compensation paid by the Trust.

About 8 percent of the Trust's claims over this period were for cancers other than mesothelioma; those claimants received about 16 percent of the Trust's compensation payments. Nonmalignant claims accounted for about 88 percent of claims and 64 percent of the gross compensation.

At a meeting of casualty actuaries in May 2001, analysts from Tillinghast-Towers Perrin presented estimates of the relative average compensation provided to claimants across the country for mesothelioma claims, all other cancer claims, and all nonmalignant injury claims, respectively, combined from 1991 to 2000 (Angelina and Biggs, 2001). Those analysts estimated that, on average, over the 1991–2000 period, mesothelioma claimants recovered about twice as much as did claimants for lung cancers and other cancers and about seven times as much as did nonmalignant injury claimants.

We used our data to estimate the distribution of claimants by type for the period covered by the Tillinghast-Towers Perrin estimate. We then applied the Tillinghast-Towers Perrin estimates of the relative compensation provided to different types of claimants to the distribution of claimants by type in order to estimate how the total gross compensation provided to asbestos claimants over the 1991–2000 period was divided among the different types of claims. Those results are also presented in Table 5.5. Here, too, the results implied by the independent estimates obtained by experts with a great amount of experience in asbestos litigation are generally similar to ours.

Average Compensation for Mesothelioma Has Increased Sharply. The amounts that individual defendants paid claimants for all types of claims declined through the 1980s. Average payments per defendant for other cancer claims and nonmalignant claims bottomed out in the early 1990s and have changed little over the past decade, whereas the average amounts that a defendant paid to mesothelioma claimants grew dramatically through the 1990s.

Figure 5.2 shows the ratio of the average amount that the defendants who provided data to us paid in compensation for each type of claim in each year to what they paid in compensation for that type of claim in 1982. The total amount any claimant received depended on the number of defendants who paid compensation to that claimant.

Figure 5.2
Average Compensation Paid by Major Defendants by Claimed Injury, Relative to 1982

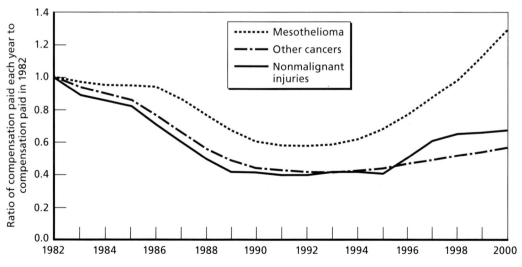

The results illustrated in Figure 5.2 were confirmed in our interviews with participants in the litigation, including both plaintiff and defense attorneys. They told us that the ratio between mesothelioma and other injury claims for non-bankrupt defendants has widened considerably in the past few years. Moreover, some interviewees said that settlement values have increased substantially in certain jurisdictions, and suggested that filing patterns have shifted over time because of this trend. Taken together, these results and comments suggest that the relative shares of total expenditures paid for the different types of claims shown in Table 5.5 could change substantially in the future.

Bankruptcies Erode Compensation. Bankruptcy has had a decided effect on compensation patterns. During the bankruptcy process, claimants are not paid. And after a corporation emerges from bankruptcy reorganized and with a trust established, significantly fewer dollars are available for current claims, and thus claimants are paid less. Because illness from asbestos exposure is characterized by long latency periods, it is likely that claimants will continue to come forward years into the future. The trusts are required to provide for future claimants and, consequently, the trusts are generally concerned about being sure there will be money for future claimants. The fact that many of the trusts pay only pennies on the dollar is one of the reasons why asbestos litigation is spreading to greater numbers of defendants. If claimants cannot get adequate compensation from the defendants who have filed for bankruptcy, they must look for greater compensation from other defendants or pursue additional defendants or both.

The costs of bankruptcy for current claimants can be easily inferred from the experience of the bankruptcy trusts over the years. These plans establish the amount due a claimant—termed the "full liquidated value" of a claim—for each type of claim. However, over time, trusts typically pay lower than liquidated value on current claims in order to preserve funds for paying future claims. In the next chapter, we detail the claims payment histories of the early personal injury bankruptcy trusts.

Claimants' Transaction Costs

Approach to Estimation

Kakalik et al. (1984) found that claimants' attorney fees and other legal expenses averaged about 39 percent of claimants' gross compensation. Claimants' contingency fees to attorneys averaged 34 percent on claims settled before trial and 39 percent on claims that went to trial. Overall, contingency fees averaged 34 percent of gross compensation. Other expenses averaged approximately 5 percent of gross compensation on settled claims and about 6 percent of gross compensation on tried claims. Overall, claimants' other legal expenses averaged 5 percent of gross compensation. Claimants' total legal expenses including both their lawyers' fees and other expenses averaged 39 percent of gross compensation.

We interviewed a number of individuals involved in asbestos litigation from a variety of perspectives, including some of the nation's leading asbestos plaintiff attorneys. None of the people we interviewed said they had seen any evidence that claimants' attorney contingent fee rates had been reduced to reflect changes in the litigation. Plaintiff attorneys may have recognized savings from routinization of the litigation (e.g., the widespread use of administrative payment schedules). However, none of those we interviewed suggested that any of these savings have been passed on to claimants. Similarly, the people we interviewed generally said that they had not observed any reduction in claimants' other legal expenses. Therefore, the estimates presented in Tables 5.1a and 5.1b assume that claimants' attorney contingency fee rates and other legal expenses continued to average 39 percent of gross recoveries through 2002. We multiplied the annual estimates of claimants' gross compensation by 39 percent to estimate claimants' transaction costs by type of claim and year.

Results

Claimants' Transaction Costs Account for 27 Percent of Total Spending. We estimate that claimants' legal fees and expenses added up to about $19 billion, 27 percent of total spending on asbestos personal injury claims through 2002. The drop in the share of total spending consumed by defense transaction costs and the consequent increase in the share of total spending going to gross compensation have resulted in an increase in the share of total spending going to claimants' transaction costs, from about 22 percent in the 1980s and early 1990s to about 29 percent in the mid- to late 1990s.

Although the people we interviewed generally agreed that claimants' total legal costs—the sum of their attorneys' legal fees and other costs, as a percentage of their recovery—had not, on average, changed over the past two decades, we thought it was still possible that legal costs had declined over time. Attorneys and experts in relevant areas have developed extensive knowledge and information on the issues that generally arise in contesting an asbestos claim and can presumably develop the evidence and expert opinions necessary to support a claim at less expense. To explore the implications of this possibility, we reestimated claimants' transaction costs and net compensation assuming that claimants' other legal costs declined at a constant annual average rate from 5 percent of compensation in 1982 to 0 percent in 2000.

Table 5.6 shows the estimates of claimants' transaction costs and, consequently, their net compensation when we assume that claimants' other legal expenses, as a percentage of gross compensation, steadily declined from 5 percent in 1982 to 0 percent in 2000. Under this assumption, claimants' legal fees and expenses added up to about $17 billion—24 percent of total spending on asbestos personal injury claims—through 2002. The share of total spending going to claimants' transaction costs increased from about 21 percent in the 1980s and early 1990s to about 26 percent in the mid- to late 1990s.

Claimants' Net Compensation

Approach to Estimation

We estimated claimants' net compensation by subtracting the estimates of claimants' transaction costs from the estimates of claimants' gross compensation.

Results

Claimants Net Compensation Is About 42 Percent of Total Spending on Asbestos Litigation. We estimate that claimants' net compensation through 2002 equaled about $30 billion, about 42 percent of total spending on asbestos litigation through that year.

Table 5.6
Modified Estimates of Claimants' Transaction Costs and Net Compensation ($ millions), Assuming Other Legal Expenses Declined to Zero in 2000

Year	Modified Table 5.1a Estimates		Modified Table 5.1b Estimates	
	Claimants' Transaction Costs	Net Compensation	Claimants' Transaction Costs	Net Compensation
1982 and earlier	135	211	135	211
1983	79	126	79	124
1984	66	106	65	105
1985	102	165	101	163
1986	101	166	100	164
1987	207	343	203	337
1988	310	520	303	509
1989	557	947	545	926
1990	564	970	553	951
1991	577	1,004	569	989
1992	718	1,264	709	1,248
1993	614	1,094	605	1,079
1994	906	1,634	894	1,612
1995	948	1,731	939	1,714
1996	1,054	1,948	1,039	1,920
1997	1,149	2,150	1,135	2,123
1998	1,244	2,355	1,237	2,342
1999	1,589	3,046	1,593	3,054
2000	1,736	3,370	1,765	3,425
2001	2,034	3,949	2,066	4,011
2002	2,423	4,703	2,447	4,750

On average, in the 1980s and early 1990s, about 34 percent of the total dollars spent on asbestos litigation was recovered by claimants after they paid legal fees and expenses. Claimants' net compensation grew as a fraction of total asbestos litigation expenditures in the mid- and late 1990s and early 2000s, averaging about 46 percent of total asbestos spending. Overall, the estimates presented in Tables 5.1a and 5.1b imply that about 42 percent of the funds expended on asbestos litigation have ended up in claimants' pockets.

Based on the data in Table 5.6, if claimants' other legal expenses, as a percentage of gross compensation, steadily declined from 5 percent in 1982 to 0 percent in 2000, claimants' net compensation through 2002 would have totaled about $32 billion, about 45 percent of total spending on asbestos litigation through that date.

In the future, it seems likely that many asbestos claimants will recover a share of their compensation from personal injury trusts established as a result of Chapter 11 reorganizations (see Chapter Six). If these trusts impose limits on attorney fees (e.g., if they require attorneys to charge no more than 25 percent of compensation received), or if attorneys choose to reduce their contingency fees for compensation obtained from personal injury trusts, the share of total dollars spent on asbestos litigation recovered by claimants may increase.

Future Compensation and Costs

The history of asbestos litigation has been characterized by failures to forecast its magnitude, scope, and evolution with any accuracy. For example, in 1982, respected analysts were predicting that the future costs of asbestos litigation could reach $38 billion (Kakalik et al., 1983). Among the participants in the litigation whom we have interviewed to date—most of whom have been involved in the litigation for more than a decade—there is no agreement about whether the litigation is approaching its end or will continue to grow or change in character.

Analysts' projections of the numbers of future claims and the claims' likely costs also vary dramatically. Analysts at Tillinghast-Towers Perrin project an ultimate total of one million claims, costing defendants and insurers $200 billion (Angelina and Biggs, 2001). Analysts at Milliman project a total of 1.1 million claims, but they estimate that the total costs of asbestos personal injury claims will reach $265 billion (Bhagavatula at al., 2001).[2]

The Manville Trust commissioned a deliberately high-side estimate designed to set an upper boundary on how many claimants might come forward in the future. The estimate was three million total claimants, which means the process is only

---

[2] The Milliman analysts estimate that the ultimate costs of asbestos litigation will eventually total $275 billion, including $265 billion for personal injury claims and $10 billion for property damage claims.

about one-quarter finished (Austern, June 21, 2001). The Trust did not attempt to estimate what this high number of claimants would imply for the total costs of asbestos litigation.

Analysts' projections of who will ultimately bear these costs are equally disparate. As noted above, Tillinghast-Towers Perrin analysts have estimated that, if current trends continue, by the time the litigation has run its course, defendants and insurers will have spent about $200 billion, of which defendants will have paid about 39 percent (Angelina and Biggs, 2001). Milliman analysts have estimated that current trends imply that asbestos defendants will ultimately pay about 64 percent of the litigation's total costs which, they estimate, will add up to $265 billion. Based on these estimates, defendants' uninsured losses could ultimately range from $78 billion (Tillinghast-Towers Perrin) to $170 billion (Milliman).

The large variation in the projections of future claims and costs reflects recent changes in the litigation: sharp increases both in the numbers of claims filed and in the fraction of new claims submitted for nonmalignant conditions, particularly by unimpaired claimants, and rapid increases in the compensation paid to mesothelioma claimants. There has also been a dramatic increase in the number of firms filing for bankruptcy. Analysts differ in their assumptions about the implications of these changes for the future course of the litigation.

However, the differences among these projections and the question of which is more likely to be accurate is not the important issue. The projections vary, but they do agree that the litigation is far from over. It is possible that hundreds of thousands of claims—or perhaps more than two million—have yet to be made. We estimate that defendants and insurers have spent $70 billion through the end of 2002 to compensate the 730,000 claimants who have come forward. Regardless of the differences among the various projections, they all suggest that, at most, only about 70 percent of the final number of claimants have come forward and, possibly, only a fourth. Based on these projections, the future costs of asbestos litigation could total $130 billion to $195 billion.

CHAPTER SIX

Bankruptcies

The total costs of asbestos litigation up to the present and the prospect of future costs have led many firms to file for bankruptcy. We examined information from numerous sources to compile a list of firms (provided in Appendix D) that have filed for bankruptcy and that have incurred and/or were expected to incur substantial asbestos-related liabilities.

In this chapter, we first describe our approach to identifying asbestos-related bankruptcies, then present information on trends in bankruptcy filings and describe the trusts that have been established by those firms that have emerged from bankruptcy. We review the available literature on the effects of these bankruptcies on the U.S. economy, including job losses and revenue losses over the lifetime of workers who have been laid off. Finally, we note that the economic effects of asbestos litigation extend beyond the bankruptcies. For asbestos defendants, each dollar paid out in defense costs and damage awards or settlements reduces retained earnings. As a result, these firms have fewer internal dollars available to finance investment and to create new jobs. Of course, the dollars paid out by defendants become income to others, including asbestos plaintiff lawyers as well as asbestos claimants. The economic effects of these wealth transfers have not been studied.

Approach to Identifying Asbestos-Related Bankruptcies

Several individuals and organizations have compiled lists of asbestos-related bankruptcies. These lists are generally quite similar. However, no two of these lists are identical; each one of them includes or omits firms listed in each of the others. Three factors underlie most of the differences among the lists: First, some lists treat the bankruptcy of a parent company and one or more of its subsidiaries as a single event and list only one of them. Others list both the parent company and any subsidiaries that also filed for bankruptcy. Second, some lists show a company under its original name, even though the company changed its name or was bought by another company before petitioning to file for reorganization under Chapter 11 of the bankruptcy code, while other lists show the company by the name under which it filed for bankruptcy. Finally, those who compiled the lists sometimes arrived at differing conclusions as to whether asbestos played a substantial role in a company's decision to file for bankruptcy.

Rather than rely on any one of these lists, we compiled our own list of asbestos-related bankruptcies through the end of 2003 from a variety of sources, including

- *Mealey's Litigation Report: Asbestos* (Mealey Publications)
- *Mealey's Asbestos Bankruptcy Report* (Mealey Publications)
- *Asbestos Litigation Reporter* (Andrews Litigation Reporter)
- *COLUMMS—Asbestos* (HarrisMartin Publishing)
- a list of asbestos-related bankruptcies maintained by the American Academy of Actuaries
- a list of asbestos-related bankruptcies maintained by the American Insurance Association
- a list of asbestos-related bankruptcies maintained by Porter Novelli Issue Advocacy, a public affairs communications firm
- Plevin and Kalish (2001)
- searches of Lexis-Nexis, Westlaw, and a number of newspapers and magazines that regularly cover business and financial topics.

In addition to the sources listed above, we searched publicly available bankruptcy filings, 10-K forms filed with the SEC, and standard references to business entities (e.g., such as Standard & Poor's and Dun & Bradstreet) to identify related companies, companies that changed their names, and companies for which asbestos liabilities did not appear to be a significant contributor to their bankruptcy. A bankruptcy can involve a parent company and one or more of its subsidiaries. When we observed bankruptcy filings by a parent and one or more of its subsidiaries, or by multiple subsidiaries of the same parent, we treated those filings as a single bankruptcy event even if the filings occurred at substantially different times. Table D.1 in Appendix D lists a parent company and any of its subsidiaries as a single bankruptcy. (Appendix D also discusses some instances in which the bankruptcy of a parent and the bankruptcy of its subsidiaries have been treated as separate events.)

It was sometimes difficult to identify the distinct entities among the many names that appeared in our information sources on asbestos-related bankruptcies. Companies changed names and were bought and sold. In some cases, the company that filed for bankruptcy is not as familiar as its predecessor. For example, Asbestospray is a well-known defendant and others have included it on their lists of asbestos bankruptcies. However, Asbestospray was purchased by H&A Construction in 1972, and it was H&A Construction that filed for bankruptcy in 1983. Accordingly, we do not include Asbestospray on our list, but we do include H&A Construction.

We did not attempt to list every name change, but we do identify common aliases in Appendix D.

The decision to file a Chapter 11 petition is a difficult one for corporations. Often, a variety of factors—e.g., foreign competition, declining market conditions, increased costs of capital, or poor management—enter into that decision. There are asbestos defendant companies that have filed for bankruptcy for reasons unrelated to asbestos litigation. But most asbestos defendants who have filed a Chapter 11 petition claim that they did so primarily, or in large part, because of the direct and indirect effects[1] of their asbestos liability exposure. We examined the information contained in the various sources listed above and included a company that filed for bankruptcy on our list only if several different sources indicated that the firm had incurred and/or was expected to incur substantial asbestos liabilities, and there were no strong indications that the firm filed for bankruptcy for reasons entirely unrelated to asbestos liability. Because we had no independent means for judging whether asbestos litigation actually "caused" a bankruptcy, Table D.1 should be interpreted as a list of "asbestos defendants that have filed for bankruptcy" and not as a list of "companies driven into bankruptcy by asbestos."

Trends in Bankruptcy Filings

As of summer 2004, we had identified 73 corporate asbestos defendants[2] that had dissolved or filed for reorganization under Chapter 11: one in 1976, 20 in the 1980s, 15 in the 1990s, and at least 37 between January 2000 and summer 2004. Bankruptcy is more common today than in the past, with as many new petitions filed in the 2000s as were filed in the previous two decades combined. Table 6.1 shows the distribution of bankruptcy filings over time.

Several individuals involved in asbestos litigation told us that a number of asbestos defendants that are contemplating filing for bankruptcy have postponed action in

---

[1] The *direct effects* of liability comprise the costs of the litigation, including payments to claimants and their lawyers and payments to defense counsel. The *indirect effects* of liability include loss of share value—as the financial markets assess the cost of continuing asbestos liability exposure—and increasing costs of capital.

[2] We omitted one company, Huxley Development, which appears on many lists of asbestos-related bankruptcies. Huxley Development is an asbestos defendant named in more than 15 published opinions, most of which are at least 20 years old. Apparently Huxley Development was a U.S. broker that bought and sold asbestos (*Irving v. Owens-Corning Fiberglas Corp.*, 864 F.2d 383 [5th Cir. 1989]). However, we were never able to confirm that the company filed for bankruptcy, much less where and when it filed. We reviewed the bankruptcy court dockets available online but found nothing pertaining to Huxley Development.

Table 6.1
Asbestos-Related Bankruptcy
Filings, 1976–2004

Year	Number of Filings
1976	1
1982	3
1983	2
1984	1
1985	1
1986	4
1987	3
1988	3
1989	3
1990	2
1991	2
1992	2
1993	2
1994	0
1995	1
1996	1
1997	0
1998	3
1999	2
2000	7
2001	9
2002	11
2003	6
2004	4

the hope that the U.S. Congress will enact asbestos-related legislation that will alleviate their problems.[3] We have no way of knowing whether the reduction in the filing rate in 2003 and early 2004 reflects such decisions or reflects a shift in the pace of filings.

Personal Injury Trusts

When Johns-Manville filed for bankruptcy in 1982, it was the largest producer of asbestos products. Although Johns-Manville was not the first company to file for bankruptcy due to the pressure of asbestos litigation,[4] it created the model for re-

---

[3] Some companies' recent asbestos reorganization plans included provisions nullifying the plans if Congress passed legislation on asbestos litigation in 2004. See "Halliburton, Equitas Reach $575 Million Deal," 2004.

[4] UNR, also known as Union Asbestos and Rubber, filed for bankruptcy a month earlier and North American Asbestos had filed six years earlier.

solving asbestos personal injury litigation under the protection of bankruptcy.[5] The model includes a trust funded by a majority of the defendants' stock, plus other corporate assets including insurance coverage.[6] The trust is the only recourse for asbestos claimants, who are barred by injunction from pursuing a reorganized company.[7] The bar is known as a "channeling injunction" and has since been codified in the Bankruptcy Code at 11 U.S.C. §524(g). As noted by the presiding Johns-Manville bankruptcy judge, "All concerned recognized that the impetus for Manville's action was not a present inability to meet debts but rather the anticipation of massive personal injury liability in the future."[8] In light of this concern, the Manville reorganization plan established a trust to provide for an anticipated 50,000 to 100,000 future claims as well as the present claims, for a total estimated liability of about $2 billion. The trust was funded with assets valued at more than $3 billion, including 80 percent of the company's stock.

The Manville bankruptcy became the model for resolving asbestos personal injury claims through reorganization. As of the end of 2002, eight defendants who filed for reorganization under Chapter 11, including Johns-Manville, had confirmed their reorganization plans that arranged for compensation for personal injury through an asbestos personal injury trust funded under their plans. Data on these eight bankruptcies are presented in Table 6.2.

The duration from bankruptcy petition to confirmation of reorganization of these eight companies ranged from 2.5 to ten years. The National Gypsum bankruptcy lasted only 2.5 years, but the trust has been, and remains, troubled. Under the

Table 6.2
Petition and Confirmation Information on Completed Asbestos Bankruptcies

Debtor	Court	Petition Date	Date of Reorganization Plan Confirmation	Years in Bankruptcy
UNR	N.D. Ill.	07/19/82	06/01/89	7
Johns-Manville	S.D.N.Y.	08/26/82	10/28/88	6
Amatex	E.D. Penn.	11/02/82	04/26/90	8
Forty-Eight Insulations, Inc.	N.D. Ill.	04/17/85	05/16/95	10
Celotex	M.D. Fla.	10/12/90	03/04/97	6.5
National Gypsum	N.D. Tex.	10/31/90	03/09/93	2.5
EaglePicher, Inc.	S.D. Ohio	01/07/91	11/18/96	6
H. K. Porter	W.D. Penn.	06/14/91	06/26/98	7

[5] *In re Johns-Manville Corp.*, 68 B.R. 618 (Bankr. S.D.N.Y. 1986), decision affirmed in part, reversed in part, 78 B.R. 407 (S.D.N.Y. 1987), order affirmed, 843 F.2d 636 (2d Cir. 1988).

[6] 68 B.R. at 621; Hodara and Stark, 2001.

[7] 68 B.R. at 624.

[8] 68 B.R. at 624.

National Gypsum reorganization plan, a bankruptcy trust was to contribute funds to CCR. The National Gypsum reorganization plan further specified that if the value of the National Gypsum trust fell below $500 million, the trust would take over responsibility from CCR for paying claims against National Gypsum.[9] After the Supreme Court invalidated CCR's class-action settlement of all future claims against it (see Chapter Three),[10] National Gypsum withdrew from CCR and established the Asbestos Claims Management Center to pay claims against National Gypsum. The Center was unable to pay the claims presented to it, and the National Gypsum trust sought a declaratory judgment establishing that the reorganized company was not protected from liability that the trust was unable to compensate. The Fifth Circuit Court held that the reorganization did not protect the reorganized National Gypsum after the trust was depleted.[11] New National Gypsum then agreed to contribute an additional $347 million to the trust in April 2002 in order to fund the Asbestos Claims Management Center, but was unable to save the Center from bankruptcy. The Asbestos Claims Management Center filed for reorganization on August 19, 2002.

The National Gypsum bankruptcy preceded the codification of the channeling injunction (discussed above) and was designed to complement the CCR Class Action Settlement. It is unlikely that another reorganization will be subject to the insolvency of a personal injury trust.

The financial status and liability exposure varied among the eight defendants listed in Table 6.2; subsequently, the size and funding of the eight trusts also varied. Data on each reorganization trust are presented in Tables 6.3 and 6.4. The data were compiled from corporate annual statements, filings with the bankruptcy court, judicial opinions, and other publicly available records. Table 6.3 presents the estimated claim numbers and values, which were submitted by each defendant in support of its petition for a channeling injunction. Table 6.4 shows the initial value of the trust established by each of these defendants and the source of the funds provided to each trust.

The Trusts' Experience

The Manville Trust did not break new ground easily. Johns-Manville filed a Chapter 11 petition in 1982. Its reorganization plan created a trust that would pay future

---

[9] Nos. 390-37213-SAF-11, 390-37214-SAF-11, N.D. Tex.

[10] *Amchem Products Inc. v. Windsor,* 521 U.S. 591 (1997).

[11] *New National Gypsum Co. v. National Gypsum Settlement Trust,* 219 F.3d 478 (5th Cir. 2000).

Table 6.3
Estimated Numbers and Values of Claims Submitted by Defendant Debtors in Support of a Petition for a Channeling Injunction

Debtor	Present Claims		Future Claims		Total Claims	
	Number	Value ($ millions)	Number	Value ($millions)	Number	Value ($ millions)
UNR	17,000	$254	120,000	$1,796	137,000	$2,050
Johns-Manville	76,000	$1,352	15,500	NA	91,500	NA
Amatex	9,315	$15	60,000	$65	69,315	$80
Forty-Eight Insulations, Inc.	130,510	$333	40,736	$104	171,246	$437
Celotex	105,000	$1,380	814,000	$5,900	919,000	$7,280
National Gypsum	62,000	$127	157,500	$730	219,500	$857
EaglePicher, Inc.	149,403	$478	333,467	$2,025	482,870	$2,503
H.K. Porter	73,118	$345	485,775	$1,675	558,893	$2,020

NOTE: NA = not available.

Table 6.4
Value of Trusts and Sources of Funds

Debtor and Trust Value ($ millions)	Sources of Funding and Amounts ($millions)	
UNR $150.00	63% of company stock	$150.00
Johns-Manville $3,154.40	Cash	$155.40
	80% of company stock	$454.00
	Interest-bearing note	$50.00
	Bonds	$1,800.00
	Insurance proceeds	$695.00
	20% of company profit (1992 and later)	Unknown
Amatex $15.70	Insurance	$9.90
	Company deposit	$4.40
	Promissory note	$1.40
Forty-Eight Insulations, Inc. $56.29	Liquidated assets of company	$56.29
Celotex $1,130.84	100% of Celotex stock	$600.00
	100% of Jim Walter Corp. stock	$151.86
	Veil-piercing settlement	$150.48
National Gypsum $815.00	Undisputed insurance	$300.00
	Disputed insurance	$390.00
	Austin Company stock	$125.00
EaglePicher, Inc. $641.76	Cash	$75.38
	Tax refund	$67.00
	Divestiture notes	$29.55
	Sinking-fund debentures	$250.00
	97.4% of new stock	$219.83
H.K. Porter $92.00	Liquidated assets of company	$92.00

claimants the compensation due them from the Johns-Manville Corporation.[12] The amount due a claimant, or the liquidated value of the claim, was determined by an administrative schedule (termed a "matrix") established when the bankruptcy reorganization plan was approved. Under the reorganization plan, the trust was to compensate all future claimants for 100 percent of the liquidated value of their claims against Johns-Manville. The trust began to pay claims in 1988.

Within two years, the trust had paid out so much money that there were serious doubts about its future solvency (Smith, 1990). In 1990, Judge Jack Weinstein ordered the trust to cease payments to all but exigent cases, pending a review of its financial prospects. After extensive expert analyses, a new plan was drawn up under which the trust was to pay all claims against Manville that were expected to arise thereafter, but at the much reduced rate of one-tenth of litigation value.[13]

In 1995, a new reorganization plan was approved by Judge Weinstein.[14] Although appeals were pending, the trust resumed payments to claimants at a rate of 10 percent of the liquidated value of the claims. Payments continued at this rate for six years.

Claims filed with the Manville Trust soared in the last half of 2000 and into the first half of 2001. As a result, demands on the trust exceeded expectations and again threatened its long-term fiscal prospects. The trust commissioned several different projections of likely future claim filings. Various consultants, each of whom had extensive previous experience in the asbestos litigation arena, examined the trends in claims filings and the available epidemiological models on the incidence of asbestos injury and disease. In a letter to Manville Trust claimants, the trust's CEO noted that the consultants now predicted that the trust would receive 1.5 million additional claims and could possibly see as many as 2.5 million additional claims (Austern, June 21, 2001). In July 2001, after analyses of the recent filing trends, the CEO of the trust announced that, pending resolution of any controversy concerning the amount of the pro rata share, the trust would henceforth pay claims at the rate of five cents on the dollar (Austern, July 5, 2001). Analyses of filing trends in late 2001 and 2002 suggested that the funds expected to be available to the trust going forward would not be sufficient to pay all future claims even at the reduced level of 5 cents on the dollar, meaning that the trust would have to further reduce its payments. Although the prior reductions (to 10 percent and then to 5 percent of the liquidated value of

---

[12] *Matter of Johns-Manville Corp.,* 68 B.R. 618 [(Bankr. S.D.N.Y., 1986)], *aff'd in part, rev'd in part, Kane v. Johns-Manville Corp.,* 843 F.2d 636 (2nd Cir. 1988).

[13] *Findley v. Blinken,* 129 B.R. 710 (E.&S.D.N.Y. 1991) (approving a class action settlement), vacated 928 F.2d 721, modified 993 F.2d 7 (2nd Cir. 1993); *In re Johns-Manville Corporation,* 878 F. Supp. 472 (E.&S.D.N.Y. 1995).

[14] *In re Joint Eastern and Southern Districts Asbestos Litigation,* 878 F. Supp. 473 (E.D.N.Y. 1995), *aff'd in part, vacated in part,* 78 F.3d 764 (1996).

the claims) had reduced the amounts paid to all claimants, including the most seriously injured, the trust this time decided to adopt a sliding scale of reductions to its payment schedule, with the result that payments to less seriously injured claimants were reduced, while payments to more seriously injured claimants were maintained at the levels established in 2001.

The Manville Trust's experience has been replicated in the other trusts that were established to provide asbestos claimants with the compensation due them from a defendant who filed for bankruptcy. National Gypsum, as noted above, has also been relitigated due to an inability to fully compensate asbestos complainants. Facing an unexpected increase in claims, the UNR Asbestos Disease Claims Trust in November 2000 implemented a $100 filing fee for all claimants. It also lowered the cap on additional compensation paid to claimants who filed for independent review, and whose claims past muster, from 12.9 percent to 7.5 percent more than the amount specified in the compensation schedule for their category of claims.[15] (Claimants who simply accepted the amount of compensation specified in the compensation schedule without an additional review were not affected by the decrease in the award, although they were required to pay the filing fee.) In 2001, the EaglePicher and Celotex Trusts reduced payments to claimants to 15.5 percent and 10 percent, respectively, of the liquidated claim value (Claims Resolution Management Corporation, 2001, p. 26).

Disputed Reorganizations: Raymark Industries and Celotex

The reorganization of two companies that filed for bankruptcy in the wake of asbestos claims was complicated by extensive litigation involving pre-petition transactions with related entities. In both cases, it was alleged that the transactions were intended to shield corporate assets from asbestos litigation.

The first example concerns Raymark Industries and Raytech Corporation. Raymark Industries, the successor of Raybestos-Manhattan, was already in severe financial trouble in the mid-1980s. Raymark created a new subsidiary, Raytech Corporation, in June 1986. After a series of complex transactions, Raytech owned the only two remaining profitable divisions of Raymark and had none of the Raymark Industries' asbestos liability.[16] Raymark was named the debtor in an involuntary Chapter 11 petition filed in Pennsylvania in September 1988.[17] Raytech was held to be Raymark's "successor in liability" in December 1988.[18]

---

[15] "UNR Trust Lowers Payment Percentage . . . ," 2000.

[16] *Schmoll v. AC&S*, 703 F. Supp. 868, 869-873 (1988).

[17] *In re Raymark Industries*, No. 88-21315 (E.D. Pa. 1988).

[18] *Schmoll v. AC&S*, 703 F. Supp. 868, 869 (1988), *affirmed*, 977 F.2d 499 (9th Cir. 1992).

Raytech subsequently filed for bankruptcy in Connecticut and attempted to relitigate the successor liability issue in the new forum.[19] Raytech then sought a declaration that such liability was limited. Raytech's unlimited liability was finally resolved in February 1998.[20] Two months later, Raymark Industries filed a voluntary petition for bankruptcy in Utah.[21] The case was transferred to Connecticut.[22] The Connecticut court noted the following:

> The joint administration of these cases is more than merely appropriate and just—it is necessary to prevent the decisions in Schmoll, White, and Raytech, which imposed unlimited successor liability on Raytech, from being vitiated. The predicate for each of those decisions was the finding that a sophisticated corporate restructuring scheme was designed with the improper purpose of escaping asbestos related liability . . . .[23]

The bankruptcy of Raytech in 1989 is listed in Table D.1, but not the involuntary bankruptcy of Raymark in 1988, because the Raytech bankruptcy was essentially a continuation of the Raymark bankruptcy, which had ended without compensation of the asbestos claimants. Neither did we list the filing of Raymark in 1998, following the reasoning of the bankruptcy court quoted above. In 2002, the Raymark-Raytech bankruptcy was in the final stages of creating a personal injury trust.

In a similar case, asbestos claimants who were exposed to Celotex products pursued claims against Hillsborough Holdings Corp., the new parent of Jim Walter Industries, a former parent of Celotex. Hillsborough filed for bankruptcy in December 1989—almost a year before Celotex's bankruptcy petition was filed.[24] The Hillsborough reorganization plan, confirmed in March 1995, included a settlement of $375 million for a class of asbestos tort creditor-claimants who sought to "pierce the corporate veil" and establish rights to Hillsborough's assets. The funds were held for the Celotex bankruptcy court to distribute to claimants through the Celotex personal injury trust.[25] The settlement agreement was approved even though preliminary litigation in the bankruptcy and trial courts suggested that the claimants would not be successful in their attempt to pierce the corporate veil of Hillsborough and collect

---

[19] *In re Raytech Corporation*, No. 89-00293 (D. Conn. 1989).

[20] *Raytech Corp. v. White*, 54 F.3d 187 (3d Cir. 1995), *cert. denied*, 516 U.S. 914 (1995), holding that Raytech was collaterally estopped from relitigating the question of successor liability; *Raytech Corp. v. Official Committee of Unsecured Creditors*, 217 B.R. 679 (Bankr. D. Ct. 1998), holding that Raytech's liability for Raymark was unlimited.

[21] *In re Raymark Corporation*, No. 98-24212 (D. Utah, filed 4/15/1998).

[22] *In re Raytech Corp.*, 222 B.R. 19 (Bankr. D. Ct. 1998).

[23] 222 B.R. 19 at 25.

[24] *In re Hillsborough Holdings Corp.*, 176 B.R. 223 (Bankr. M.D. Fla. 1994).

[25] "Hillsborough Holdings Reorganization Plan . . . ," 1994, p. 19.

compensation from Hillsborough for their exposure to Celotex's products. Judge Parskay wrote:

> Notwithstanding the Debtors' probability of success on the merits, the Debtors have sound business reasons for eliminating the threat of future litigations. The court believes it prudent to approve the [settlement and plan] to avoid the crippling effect that continuance of the litigations of Settlement Claims would likely have on the Debtor's businesses ("Hillsborough Holdings Reorganization Plan . . . ," 1994, p. 19).

In Table D.1, we did not list Hillsborough Holdings as a separate bankruptcy, having included the settlement under the umbrella of the Celotex bankruptcy. Table D.1 also omits the bankruptcies of Celotex subsidiaries Carey Canada, Panacon, Phillip Carey Company, and Smith & Kanzler.

Recent Bankruptcies

In 2000, the annual rate of asbestos-related bankruptcy filings increased sharply and continued to increase through 2002. Seven companies filed for bankruptcy in 2000, ten filed in 2001, and 12 filed in 2002. The rate of filings fell in 2003 and the first half of 2004; only six asbestos defendants filed for bankruptcy in 2003, and four asbestos defendants filed through summer 2004. However, as mentioned above, many observers of asbestos litigation have suggested that the possibility of federal legislation has led some defendants who would have filed for bankruptcy to hold off doing so in the hope that federal legislation would obviate the need for them to do so. If that is true, federal inactivity in this area could lead to additional bankruptcy filings.

Of the 29 companies that filed for bankruptcy between January 2000 and December 2002, six were valued at more than $1 billion: W. R. Grace, Owens Corning, Kaiser Aluminum, U.S. Gypsum Company (USG), Armstrong World Industries, and Federal-Mogul Corporation. All six are publicly traded. We compiled relevant litigation and financial data for these six companies from SEC and bankruptcy filings (see Table 6.5).

Economic Effects of Bankruptcies

Transaction Costs

Previous research on the legal, accounting, and other transaction costs of bankruptcy reorganization (Franks and Touros, 1989; Weiss, 1990; White, 1996) shows that the cost of reorganization is equal to about 3 percent of a firm's book value or about

Table 6.5
Financial Data for Bankruptcies Exceeding $1 Billion (dollar amounts in $ millions)

	Armstrong World Industries	Federal-Mogul	Kaiser Aluminum	Owens Corning	USG	W. R. Grace
Number of Employees	18,900	50,000	7,800	20,000	13,700	6,300
Bankruptcy filing date	12/6/00	10/1/01	2/12/02	10/5/00	6/25/01	4/2/01
Court	D. Delaware	D. Delaware	D. Delaware	D. Delaware	D. Delaware	D. Delaware
Case number	00-04471	01-10578	02-10429	00-03837	01-02094	01-01139
Assets	$4,164	$10,150	$3,364	$6,494	$3,200	$2,493
Liabilities	$3,297	$8,860	$3,100	$5,710	$2,740	$2,570
Asbestos liability	$484	$1,818	$621	$685	$1,185	$1,003
Available insurance	$236	$771	$501	$59	$76	$369
Prepetition claims	$173,000	$365,000	$112,000	$36,000	$100,000	$124,000
Reorganization cost	$12	$51	NA	$111	$12	$16

6 percent of a firm's market value. But, to date, no one has studied the costs of asbestos bankruptcy reorganization. The bankruptcies that have been studied involved large publicly traded corporations comparable in size to large asbestos defendant corporations. But reorganization costs for asbestos defendants may be higher than the 3 (or 6) percent of a firm's book (or market) value reported in these earlier studies because none of the bankruptcies in those studies included massive numbers of tort creditors.

Various other bankruptcy-related costs also impinge on a firm's ability to do business. Bankruptcy disrupts relations with suppliers and customers. It also impairs, or entirely eliminates, access to credit. And bankruptcy distracts senior managers, diverting their attention from the firm's business activities to bankruptcy-related activities.

Time to Resolution

We collected information on the length of time from bankruptcy petition to confirmation of the reorganization plan for 11 major asbestos defendant bankruptcies. The average length of time from petition to confirmation for these 11 bankruptcies is six years, but three bankruptcies (National Gypsum, Keene Corporation, and Rock Wool Manufacturing Company) took only three years and one (Forty-Eight Insulations, Inc.) took ten years. However, these numbers do not accurately portray the length of time it has taken some corporations to move from bankruptcy petition to *paying claimants.*

Johns-Manville filed its petition in 1982, which was finally approved six years later, in 1988.[26] Payments began then but were suspended in 1990 (Smith, 1990) and did not resume again until 1995, 13 years after Manville's initial filing.[27] The Amatex reorganization plan was confirmed eight years after filing of the petition, but the Amatex Trust did not become operational until six years after that, or 14 years from the time the petition was first filed.

Prepackaged Bankruptcy

In an effort to reduce the time and costs associated with the bankruptcy litigation process, asbestos plaintiff lawyers and debtors have increasingly adopted a strategy of negotiating reorganization plans *before* filing for reorganization under Chapter 11, an approach known as "prepackaged bankruptcy." In brief, before formally petitioning to file for reorganization, the debtor approaches asbestos plaintiff attorneys who currently represent large numbers of plaintiffs (and who, by inference, will represent large numbers of future claimants as well) and attempts to negotiate a plan that will secure the support of enough current tort creditors (i.e., plaintiffs and their attorneys) to gain approval from the bankruptcy court when the reorganization plan is filed. Bankruptcy law requires that all creditors vote on proposed reorganization plans, with half of the creditors by number who collectively have claims for at least two-thirds of the dollar value of claims outstanding required for approval. Under 11 U.S.C. §534(g), to secure a channeling injunction, asbestos reorganization plans must obtain a super-majority of 75 percent of all creditors.[28] Hence, if the debtor can secure agreement from attorneys representing 75 percent of current claimants (who will vote on behalf of their clients), the debtor is likely to be able to substantially reduce the time that would normally be required to negotiate a reorganization plan after filing a petition.[29]

Using a prepackaged bankruptcy approach, plaintiff attorneys and debtors anticipate reducing the time from petition to approval to as little as three to six months,

---

[26] *Matter of Johns-Manville Corp.,* 68 B.R. 618 (Bankr. S.D.N.Y. 1986), *aff'd in part, rev'd in part, Kane v. Johns-Manville Corp.,* 843 F.2d 636 (2nd Cir. 1988).

[27] *In re Joint Eastern and Southern Districts Asbestos Litigation,* 878 F. Supp. 473 (E.D.N.Y. 1995), aff'd in part, vacated in part, 78 F.3d 764 (1996).

[28] Future claimants, by definition, cannot vote on a proposed reorganization plan because they are not creditors. Bankruptcy judges typically appoint a "futures representative" to negotiate on behalf of future claimants' interests. In prepackaged bankruptcies, debtors have appointed "futures representatives" to participate in the negotiations on the reorganization plan. See Plevin et al., 2003 (reporting that David Austern, the General Counsel for the Manville Trust, was appointed by Combustion Engineering as the futures representative in the Combustion Engineering prepackaged bankruptcy).

[29] See, e.g., "Congoleum Files Prepackaged Chapter 11 Petition . . . " (2004), which reported that Congoleum announced in December 2003 that it had "received the requisite number of votes to approve its prepackaged bankruptcy plan" and had filed a petition for Chapter 11 reorganization. Congoleum's plan was sent to asbestos tort creditors in October 2003, two months before it filed for reorganization.

with comparable savings in bankruptcy litigation costs. For example, in July 2004, U.S. Bankruptcy Judge Robert McGuire and U.S. Judge Lynn Hughes of the Southern District of Texas confirmed a prepackaged bankruptcy plan for Utex Industries that had been filed with Utex's petition for Chapter 11 reorganization in March of 2004, just four months earlier.[30]

Through 2004, at least ten asbestos defendants have used a prepackaged bankruptcy strategy (see Table 6.6). The first corporation to use the prepackaged strategy was Fuller-Austin, which filed its Chapter 11 petition in 1998 (Plevin et al., 2003); all of the other prepackaged bankruptcies have been filed since 2001.

How prepackaged bankruptcies actually affect the time and expense required to resolve bankruptcy litigation is uncertain. In at least some of the bankruptcies listed in Table 6.6, debtors began negotiating prepackaged bankruptcies at least a year before finally filing their reorganization plans.[31] Moreover, some prepackaged bankruptcies have been challenged by creditors or insurers whose assets were relied on to fund the proposed trusts (Plevin et al., 2003; Parloff, 2004). When time and costs associated with resolving these issues are accounted for, adopting a prepackaged bankruptcy strategy may not in fact yield much savings. For example, a report of

Table 6.6
Prepackaged Bankruptcy Filings

Debtor	Date of Filing
Fuller-Austin Insulation, Inc.	1998
Western Asbestos	2002
J.T. Thorpe Co.	2002
Shook & Fletcher Insulation Co.	2002
AC&S, Inc.	2002
Dresser Industries (DII)/Kellogg, Brown & Root (KBR) (Halliburton subsidiary)	2003
Combustion Engineering/ABB	2003
Congoleum Corporation	2004
Utex Industries, Inc.	2004
Quigley Co. (subsidiary of Pfizer, Inc.)	2004

[30] See "Utex Industries Files Prepackaged Bankruptcy Plan . . ." (2004).

[31] For example, the first reports that Dresser (DII) and KBR were seeking a prepackaged bankruptcy appeared in December 2002, and the first report that Congoleum had adopted a similar strategy appeared in January 2003. Dresser (DII) filed its petition for reorganization in December 2003 ("Halliburton, Equitas Reach $575 Million Deal, " 2004). Congoleum filed its petition for reorganization in January 2004 ("Congoleum Files Prepackaged Chapter 11 Petition . . . ," 2004).

proceedings related to a challenge to Congoleum's prepackaged bankruptcy reorganization plan lists 24 law firms representing 19 interested parties.[32]

Costs to Workers

Bankruptcy can impose costs on the filing firm's labor force. First, there is likely to be a reduction in the size of the firm's labor force. Workers who lose their jobs because of their employer's bankruptcy may incur a period of unemployment and, when they find a new job, are likely to earn lower wages. Further, both workers who lose their jobs because of their employer's bankruptcy and those who retain their jobs despite the bankruptcy incur financial losses to the extent that their pension plan holds shares of their employer's stock.

Stiglitz et al. (2002) estimated the magnitude of these costs for workers employed by asbestos defendants who filed for bankruptcy through September 2002. They developed a list of 61 asbestos-defendant bankruptcies through September 2002 and succeeded in collecting time-series employment data for 31 of them. Stiglitz et al. observed that the 31 firms include the largest firms among the 61 bankruptcies and likely account for about 90 percent of the total employment of all bankrupt asbestos firms combined. They compared the change in employment in these firms over the five years preceding their bankruptcy filing to the change in employment over that period for other firms in the same industry at the four-digit SIC code level.

Stiglitz et al. estimated that the 31 firms for which they had time-series employment data had lost about 52,000 more jobs than they would have if the firms' employment level had changed at the same rate as the employment level in the firms' respective industries as a whole. Assuming that the other bankrupt firms for which time-series employment data could not be obtained had incurred job losses, relative to job losses in their respective industries, at the same rates as had the firms for which data could be obtained, Stiglitz et al. estimated that bankruptcies of asbestos defendants cost a total of about 60,000 jobs.

Most of the workers displaced by asbestos bankruptcies will eventually find other jobs. However, they will generally suffer a period of unemployment and, when they do find a new job, they will likely earn lower wages at that new job. Assuming that the average displaced worker has 20 years to retirement and discounting their future wages to the present at a 5 percent annual rate, Stiglitz et al. (2002, p. 29) estimated that the present value of the displaced workers' wage losses adds up to between $1.4 billion and $3.0 billion.

A significant fraction of employees' pension plans includes stock in their companies. The bankruptcy of an asbestos defendant consequently can result in losses to

---

[32] "Bankruptcy Judge Lifts Stay . . ." (2004). Prepackaged bankruptcies have also been the subject of charges of conflict of interest and denials of due process to certain creditors and other interested parties.

the defendant's employee pension plans. Stiglitz et al. estimated the impact of asbestos-related bankruptcies on the value of employees' pension plans by estimating the change in stock prices due to asbestos liabilities and calculating the effects of those changes on workers' retirement assets. They obtained time-series data on stock prices for 13 asbestos defendants who filed for bankruptcy prior to September 2002. They compared trends in the price of stock in each of these defendant companies for the five years prior to the companies' bankruptcy filing and up to five years after the filing to corresponding trends in stock market prices for a control group of companies, weighted for market capitalization, that produced similar products and faced similar market conditions during the comparison period. Each of the companies' stock significantly underperformed that of the control group.

Using SEC data to estimate the fraction of each firms' employee pension plan assets held in company stock, Stiglitz et al. (2002, p. 33) concluded that the average employee of those firms lost more than $8,000 in pension assets when compared with what the pension plan assets would have been worth if the companies' stock had performed as did the company stock of the control group firms. The total losses in assets, Stiglitz et al. concluded, amounted to more than $350 million.

Broader Economic Effects

Bankruptcy is not the only economic effect of asbestos litigation. Defendants that have not filed for bankruptcy have nonetheless incurred asbestos litigation costs, including both their defense costs and the indemnity payments they made to claimants. These costs have consumed some of their resources and, in some cases, a significant fraction of their resources.

To finance investments in new plants and equipment, most firms first use their retained earnings. Only when firms have more good investment opportunities than they can finance from retained earnings do they turn to external sources of finance, such as loans or new equity issues. For asbestos defendants, each dollar paid out in defense costs and damage awards or settlements reduces retained earnings. As a result, these firms have fewer internal dollars available to finance investment. They may respond by reducing their investment levels by either limiting their investments to what can be financed using retained earnings or, if they borrow externally, eliminating investments that are unattractive because of the higher cost of capital. For example, Fazzari et al. (1988) estimate that a $1 reduction in a firm's retained earnings will, on average, lead to a reduction of 42 cents in its investments.

Reductions in investment levels, in turn, can lead to reductions in the creation of new jobs. The average capital-to-labor ratio in U.S. durable goods manufacturing is roughly $78,000. (This estimate is based on the value of the capital stock in durable goods manufacturing—$861 billion in 1998—divided by the size of the labor force in durable goods industries—10,985,000 workers in 1999) (U.S. Department of the Census, 2000, Tables 684 and 888). These figures imply that, on average, one less job is created each time a firm reduces its investment levels by $78,000.

We can estimate the amount by which asbestos litigation costs reduce defendant firms' investments and, consequently, reduce the numbers of new jobs those firms create. However, the money paid to asbestos claimants and attorneys does not disappear. Some of the funds paid to claimants and their attorneys are likely saved. And some of these savings, in turn, will enter capital markets and become available to firms seeking investment funds. Thus, some of the funds removed from capital markets when retained earnings are used to compensate asbestos claimants return to those markets. Similarly, the number of jobs lost in the economy as a whole as a result of the adverse effect of asbestos litigation on defendants' investments could be at least partially offset by jobs created by firms that could afford to make investments only because claimants and their attorneys saved some of the funds they obtained from defendants. Because it seems unlikely that claimants and attorneys will save or invest all the funds they obtain from asbestos litigation, it would seem that asbestos litigation would result in some reduction in investments and job creation. But we lack the data needed to estimate the impact of the litigation on the economy as a whole.[33]

Nonetheless, bankruptcy per se is not the only effect of asbestos litigation costs on the financial condition of defendant firms and, consequently, the economy.

---

[33] In earlier work (Carroll et al., 2002), we estimated the reductions in investments by asbestos defendants and, consequently, the reductions in jobs they created. Because these estimates did not take into account the extent to which the adverse effect on defendants' investments from asbestos litigation costs could be at least partially offset by jobs created by other firms, the numbers we cited in that earlier report were upper-bound estimates of the effects of asbestos litigation on the economy. However, these estimates were often cited by others as estimates of the net effect of asbestos litigation on the economy. We have come to believe that the potential misunderstanding of these estimates outweighs their value; therefore, we do not include them in this report.

CHAPTER SEVEN

Implications for the Future

When the Rand Institute for Civil Justice conducted its first studies of asbestos litigation in the early 1980s the litigation was surging, the Manville Corporation had just petitioned for Chapter 11 reorganization, and lawyers and judges were struggling to adapt civil procedure rules to the new phenomena of "mass torts" (Kakalik et al., 1983; Kakalik et al., 1984; Hensler et al., 1985). By the early 1990s, many parties to the litigation, lawyers, and judges had established routine practices for dealing with the litigation. Although questions about litigation practices and case outcomes remained, the perception of an asbestos litigation crisis that had characterized the 1980s had been largely abated. Some observers anticipated that the courts would fashion a global resolution to asbestos litigation, similar to the comprehensive settlements that had been achieved in other mass tort litigation.

The late 1990s saw an unraveling of those expectations. The U.S. Supreme Court rejected efforts to resolve future asbestos litigation through class action settlements. Defendants' settlement programs foundered. New cases, including many claims from workers who had been exposed to asbestos but who were not functionally impaired at the time of filing, entered the system at a more rapid pace than they had previously. Payments to claimants with more serious injuries increased substantially, perhaps because these cases had been undervalued previously. Many more corporations sought the protection of Chapter 11 reorganization to address their asbestos exposure liability.

With rapid growth in asbestos filings and costs, and new claims projected to be filed for several more decades, concern mounted as to whether there would be funds available to pay claimants who would come forward in the future. The allocation of compensation between those with serious or fatal injuries and those with legally cognizable injuries but little or no current functional impairment became a flash point of controversy. The spread of litigation beyond the major asbestos manufacturers raised questions about whether responsibility for asbestos injuries was being properly attributed. A flood of corporate bankruptcies traced to current and future asbestos liability exposure raised concerns about the effects of asbestos litigation on the economy. Many of those engaged in the litigation and many observers asked: Are there alternative strategies for resolving asbestos litigation that would provide more adequate and fairer allocation of compensation dollars and more appropriate allocation of responsibility for payments, and achieve both ends more quickly and with lower direct and indirect costs than the current system?

Efforts to improve the resolution of asbestos litigation implicate strongly held views about the value of the tort system, which has traditionally been the primary vehicle in the United States for compensating victims of injurious behavior by others and an important tool for regulating corporate behavior. Those who believe that tort liability is the optimal system for resolving injury claims oppose substituting tort with a non-tort approach for resolving asbestos claims or modifying critical aspects of the tort system for asbestos plaintiffs. Even if some of these tort supporters might be persuaded that a different or modified system would be appropriate for resolving future *asbestos* claims, they still worry that adopting an alternate system for tort would set a precedent that would impair the rights of future *non-asbestos* injury victims.

Moreover, any effort to devise an alternative to tort for resolving asbestos claims must address the very same questions that have complicated resolution of the claims through tort: How many claims will come forward in the future? What will be the distribution of claims by severity of injury? What are the proper standards for allocating compensation among those with diverse injuries, ranging from nondisabling pleural scarring to fatal mesothelioma? How should the responsibility for paying for these injuries be allocated among those who manufactured or distributed asbestos products or operated workplaces in which asbestos was present?

For the past several years, plaintiff and defense attorneys, defendant corporations and insurers, labor unions, and the allies of all these groups have worked in various combinations and contexts to consider alternative strategies for resolving future asbestos claims. By the end of 2004, no proposal for comprehensively changing the asbestos litigation system had been able to garner sufficient support from the various stakeholders in the current system to be adopted into federal law, although some changes in substantive and procedural law affecting asbestos cases had been adopted by state legislatures and state court judges in certain jurisdictions. As this report went to press, the U.S. Senate had once again taken up the issue of asbestos litigation reform.

Evaluating the Tort System's Performance in Asbestos Litigation

Most of the factual data reported in this monograph are not disputed by participants in asbestos litigation. The sharp differences between and among plaintiff attorneys, defense counsel, defendant corporations, and insurers derive primarily from differences in assessments of the performance of the tort liability system and assessments of how well the tort system serves the interests of the various parties who have a stake in asbestos litigation.

Tort Objectives

Traditionally, the tort system in the United States has been viewed as having three objectives: compensation, deterrence, and individualized corrective justice (e.g., Schwartz, 1997; Keating, 2000). In theory, the system properly compensates injury victims for their losses, properly calibrates defendants' incentives to avoid injuring others, and provides a sense that "justice has been done" through individualized consideration of each plaintiff's and defendant's situation. Moreover, as a common law (rather than statutory) system, tort liability has proved remarkably adaptable to changing social, cultural, and technological trends. The commitment of tort law to "make victims whole," deter injurious behavior, and provide individuals with their "day in court," as well as its adaptability to change, is generally seen as the justification for the tort system's transaction costs, which are understood to be considerably higher than the costs associated with delivering benefits through administrative systems, such as workers' compensation and social insurance schemes (Fleming, 1984; Sugarman, 1985).

In practice, empirical studies conducted over the past several decades have shown that the tort system often falls short of its goals (Hensler et al., 1991; Kakalik and Pace, 1986; Shanley and Peterson, 1983). It is difficult for individuals with meritorious claims for minor injuries to find representation because their cases require a significant investment of time and expense and offer limited potential damages in return (Kritzer, 2002). Although plaintiffs with more substantial injuries and viable factual and legal claims are more likely to find legal representation, their compensation may be limited by a variety of factors, including the defendant's ability to pay and the plaintiff's and plaintiff attorney's risk aversion.

When cases are pursued to trial, juries may award damages that reflect the jurors' perceptions of defendants' resources in addition to their assessment of defendants' culpability, or they may make judgments about causation that are scientifically questionable, or they may take into account such extra-legal factors as the plaintiff's race (Chin and Peterson, 1985; Ostrom et al., 1992 and 1996; Diamond, Saks, and Landsman, 1998). Plaintiffs with the same injuries and economic losses receive widely varying amounts, depending on the skills and incentives of the attorneys representing them, the jurisdictions in which their cases are brought and, perhaps, their own "attractiveness" as potential trial witnesses.

Because many plaintiffs with meritorious claims do not find their way to court, and because many suits are settled without liability ever being formally established, and because the outcomes of suits that are filed are uncertain, the theoretical deterrence value of tort is, in practice, eroded. Depending on the circumstances, the tort system may under-deter or over-deter injurious practices (Garber, 1998).

Moreover, most litigants find little in the way of individualized treatment or procedure. Ordinary tort lawsuits, such as automobile accident cases, are routinely settled according to long-established formulae. Product injury and toxic exposure cases are typically handled in aggregative forms, with little involvement of individual plaintiffs (Hensler, 1998).

Notwithstanding these limitations on tort's performance, it has proved to be a remarkably adaptive system, with an ability to modify substantive legal doctrine and procedural rules to meet the challenges of new types of harms, changing cultural norms, and new forms of social and economic organization.

How Does Asbestos Litigation Measure Up?

Compensation. Ordinarily, only a small fraction of all those who are injured seek compensation from the courts (Hensler et al., 1991). Typically, the high costs of tort litigation screen out of the system the majority of claims for minor injuries and modest losses. In asbestos litigation, however, mass litigation strategies have effectively opened the courts to everyone who can prove exposure to asbestos and demonstrate a legally cognizable injury. As asbestos litigation has continued, an increasingly large fraction of those who have come forward and found representation are not currently functionally impaired, although they do meet the legal standard for a compensable injury in most jurisdictions.

Some participants in asbestos litigation and some observers as well view asbestos claimants' increased access to courts (in comparison with other tort victims) as a positive achievement, fulfilling—at least in this instance—the promise of tort law. Others argue that opening the system so widely jeopardizes the ability of the tort system to compensate all claimants who may have a claim in the future, some of whom will have serious or fatal injuries.

Because the typical asbestos claimant receives compensation from dozens or more defendants, the only source of information about adequacy of total compensation is the plaintiff attorney. To our knowledge, there is no published research comparing the total compensation received by asbestos plaintiffs with their economic loss, nor were we able to obtain such data for our study. It is certain that many of the asbestos personal injury trusts established as a result of Chapter 11 bankruptcy reorganizations pay only a small fraction of the agreed-upon value of plaintiffs' claims; there is no reason to believe that the bankruptcy reorganizations currently in process will yield vastly different outcomes. How these diminished payments resulting from bankruptcy will affect adequacy of compensation is uncertain, as shortfalls in compensation from bankrupt defendants may be met by increased compensation from corporations that are newly drawn into the litigation. Moreover, if asbestos personal injury trusts limit attorney fees, asbestos plaintiffs may receive a larger fraction of the dollars paid out by the reorganized defendant corporations. The experience to date is too slim and varied to determine whether such potential savings in transaction costs will be realized and passed on to asbestos plaintiffs. How limitations on attorney fees imposed by some bankruptcy personal injury trusts might affect claiming rates in bankruptcy is also uncertain; the modest limitations on attorney fees imposed by the Manville Trust do not seem to have diminished claiming rates, but severe restrictions on attorney fees might impair claimants' ability to bring claims against the trusts.

Deterrence. The historical case against asbestos manufacturers has been widely discussed in articles and books about the inception of the litigation (Brodeur, 1985; Castleman, 1996). Companies such as Johns-Manville (later renamed the Manville Corporation) were central to this history, as were some of the other asbestos product manufacturers that were the prime targets of litigation through the 1980s. As the litigation has spread to companies outside the asbestos and building products industries, the culpability of the defendants called upon to pay asbestos victims is more in dispute, although some corporations that became major targets of litigation in the 1990s found themselves in that position as the result of acquisitions of other corporations whose responsibility for widespread asbestos exposure is indisputable (Tweedale, 2000).

From a deterrence perspective, the issue is not whether asbestos victims should be able to receive compensation from *some* entity, but rather *which* entity can fairly be called upon to shoulder the financial burden. Requiring companies that played a relatively small role in exposing workers to asbestos to bear substantial costs of compensating for asbestos injuries not only raises fundamental questions of fairness but undercuts the deterrence objectives of the tort system. If business leaders believe that tort outcomes have little to do with their own behavior, then there is no reason for them to shape their behavior so as to minimize tort exposure.

Individualized Treatment. In principle, the tort system promises individualized justice to plaintiffs and defendants. Empirical research suggests that individualized treatment satisfies people's desire for procedural fairness, which in turn leads to trust in the justice system (Tyler, 1990). In practice, tort litigation often offers little individualized treatment in ordinary or mass litigation (Hensler, 1995 and 1998).

In asbestos litigation, individualized process is a myth. Most cases are settled, many according to standardized agreements negotiated by defendants and plaintiff attorneys to apply to what attorneys conventionally refer to as their "inventories" of cases. Under such agreements, all cases against some defendants may be settled for a flat fee, while cases against other defendants will be sorted into a "matrix" of claims, according to a few distinguishing characteristics, and paid the values associated with the different matrix cells. Bankruptcy personal injury trusts, which absent congressional action will pay an increasing share of asbestos compensation in the future, institutionalize this administrative compensation process for asbestos claims. A congressionally authorized administrative compensation program will likely follow suit.

Among the small numbers of asbestos claims that reach trial, a majority is tried in group form, along with a few or more like or unlike claims. Sometimes, more than a hundred claims may be tried together; sometimes, the trial of a few claims will decide critical outcomes for thousands more. Claims against multiple defendants, in arguably quite different circumstances, may also be tried together. Although consolidated trials are not unique to asbestos litigation, they do appear to be more prevalent, of a larger scale, and more complex in asbestos litigation than in other mass torts.

Adaptability. Whatever observers may think of the tort system's achievements or failures in asbestos litigation, few would disagree that the system has proved to be incredibly adaptive. State legislatures have changed statutes of limitation to address latent injury torts. Some states have adopted new definitions of injury to address asbestos lawsuits that do not claim any current impairment or functional disability. The federal judiciary has used its authority under 29 U.S.C. §1407 to collect all asbestos lawsuits filed in federal courts and transfer them to a single judge for pretrial purposes, and that judge has used his authority to settle or dismiss thousands of claims. Federal judges have attempted to resolve future asbestos claims through class action settlements, but these settlements were set aside by the U.S. Supreme Court. State judiciaries have adopted new rules for collecting asbestos claims within their states and assigning them to a single judge for pretrial and trial purposes. Federal and state court trial judges have devised special procedures, sometimes supported by sophisticated data analysis, to settle large groups of asbestos claims. State trial court judges have used a dizzying array of procedures to try asbestos claims in the aggregate. Federal and state trial judges have adopted new calendaring rules, deferring processing of lawsuits not claiming a current functional impairment and expediting claims of mesothelioma and other cancers (see Chapter Three).

While they reflect the adaptive ability of the courts, these mechanisms are not uniformly welcomed or celebrated. Whose interests are served by deferred dockets, consolidated trials, and other special practices for asbestos cases—and indeed, whether courts do or should have the power to adopt such special practices—is sharply disputed.

Is There a Better Way?

Since the inception of asbestos litigation in the 1970s, more than 15 bills have been introduced in the U.S. Congress proposing to change the nation's approach to resolving asbestos claims. As asbestos claims surged anew in the late 1990s and early 2000s, reform efforts proliferated, ultimately resulting in the most intensive effort to devise federal legislation to modify asbestos claims resolution to date. Unlike some previous reform efforts, the efforts in the 108th Congress attempted to build a broad coalition for asbestos reform, including plaintiff attorneys and labor union leaders as well as defendant corporations and insurers. Two competing strategies emerged from these reform efforts, neither of which was able to secure sufficient support for passage in the 108th Congress; both have been taken up again in the 109th Congress. In lieu of federal reform, critics of current asbestos litigation processes look either to state legislatures and courts or to bankruptcy proceedings and personal injury trusts to improve the resolution of asbestos claims in the future.

Congressional Efforts: (1) Medical Criteria

One reform strategy, supported by the American Bar Association (ABA) and asbestos plaintiff attorneys who specialize in representing mesothelioma and other cancer victims, seeks to limit compensation for asbestos disease to plaintiffs whose injuries meet certain specified medical criteria (Asbestos Claims Criteria and Compensation Act of 2003, S. 413).[1] In essence, this proposal would prevent people who are not currently functionally impaired and do not have an asbestos-related cancer from claiming compensation in the tort liability system, even if they have clinical evidence of asbestos exposure—e.g., pleural scarring—that under current state law in most jurisdictions would allow them to seek compensation. The statute of limitations for filing an asbestos injury claim would not apply to these claimants until they met the specified medical criteria. To its supporters, the medical criteria approach has the benefit of making arguably minimal changes in the tort liability system, leaving state tort doctrine and procedural rules to answer questions of how to deal with all those claims that met the medical criteria and remained within the litigation system.

Because it would eliminate many asbestos-exposed workers who are currently eligible for compensation from claiming compensation unless and until they met the specified criteria, the medical criteria proposal has been opposed by those who represent these workers, including many asbestos plaintiff attorneys and labor union leaders. Some defendant corporations and insurers also are reluctant to support the medical criteria proposal because they fear that the costs of compensating claimants with mesothelioma and other seriously injured claimants might become so high in the future that these corporations and insurers would not obtain the economic protection they are seeking. As we go to press, a new medical criteria bill has been proposed in Congress. Unlike previous proposals, it includes additional restrictions (beyond medical criteria) on access to compensation.

Congressional Efforts: (2) A Trust Fund

In 2004, with the success of the medical criteria proposal in doubt, many defendant corporations and insurers began to pursue an alternative strategy that would eliminate tort liability for asbestos claimants entirely and substitute an administrative

---

[1] On the ABA Commission proposal, see, for example, "ABA Delegates Set to Vote on Claims Standard Amid Opposition," 2003, and "ABA Votes to Adopt Medical Standards, Set to Lobby for Legislation," 2003. On congressional legislation incorporating the medical criteria approach, see "Bill Seeking Medical Standards in Line with AMA Introduced," 2003.

compensation program, funded by defendant corporations (including personal injury trusts established in Chapter 11 reorganizations) and insurers (Fair Act of 2004, S. 2290).[2]

The idea of substituting an administrative compensation system for tort liability is not new; most of the legislative initiatives addressing asbestos compensation in previous congresses proposed to substitute some sort of no-fault compensation program for tort. In the 108th Congress, supporters of the trust fund approach, in an effort to secure support for their proposal from labor union leaders and some asbestos plaintiff attorneys, did not propose to limit compensation wholly to cancer victims and those with severe respiratory impairment. As a result, some defendants and insurers became worried that eligibility for compensation from the trust fund would be so broad that the trust fund would be overwhelmed. As negotiations continued, the price tag for the proposed fund mounted to a level that some were unwilling to support.

Moreover, the trust fund proposal, unlike the medical criteria approach (which would have left each defendant to respond to the suits that remained within the tort system as it saw fit), requires that defendant corporations and insurers agree on a funding formula. Possible factors for determining funding include market share at key points in the history of asbestos use, historical patterns of asbestos compensation, and reserves set aside to pay asbestos claims. Deciding how bankruptcy personal injury trusts should be factored into the funding equation further complicates the decisionmaking process. Because defendants and insurers are differently positioned with regard to these factors, they were not able to reach agreement on a formula before the time for congressional action had expired.

The trust fund proposal also requires grappling with the question that has challenged designers of asbestos personal injury trusts in Chapter 11 proceedings, as well as those who have sought to negotiate long-term settlements of asbestos litigation outside of bankruptcy: How many more claimants will appear in the future? With the federal government unwilling to act as guarantor of the trust fund, payors' and claimants' representatives need to consider what might happen if the amount originally negotiated proves to be inadequate. As we go to press, the U.S. Senate is considering a new trust fund proposal that includes medical criteria for determining eligibility for compensation.

State Reform Efforts

With the success of congressional initiatives in doubt, by the end of 2004, reformers were turning their attention to the states. Medical criteria statutes were introduced into state legislatures in Louisiana, Ohio, and Texas. Legislation limiting successor

---

[2] On the 108th Congress's trust fund proposal, see "Hatch Introduces $108 Billion Asbestos Trust Fund Legislation," 2003; "Senate Judiciary Committee Issues Report on Trust Fund Legislation," 2003; and "The Fairness in Asbestos Reform Act—What Will It Do, Where Is It Now?" 2004.

liability, adopted previously by the Pennsylvania legislature, was adopted in Texas[3] as well. Venue rules that had invited large-scale consolidations in Mississippi were amended, and stricter venue rules were also adopted in Texas. An increasing number of courts were considering and adopting deferred dockets (see Chapter Three). Together, these changes may temper the rise in frequency of claiming for asbestos diseases. But such efforts are likely to leave in place a patchwork of tort doctrine and mass litigation procedural rules that promises continuing variation in asbestos outcomes for plaintiffs and defendants and does little to mitigate the high transaction costs of asbestos litigation.

Bankruptcy and Personal Injury Trusts

With an increasing number of corporations in Chapter 11 reorganization, some observers have suggested that the personal injury trusts that usually result from Chapter 11 bankruptcy reorganization offer the most promising means of resolving asbestos claims quickly and with lower transaction costs, particularly if the debtors and tort creditors negotiate "prepackaged bankruptcies" before a formal petition for Chapter 11 reorganization is filed. "Pre-packs" have the potential to substantially shorten the Chapter 11 process, which historically has averaged about six years for asbestos defendants. But some plans that have emerged from pre-pack processes have proved controversial, resulting in lengthy appellate processes and ancillary litigation. Moreover, some of these plans have been challenged on grounds of unfairness to certain classes of asbestos plaintiffs (see Chapter Three). Whether bankruptcy proceedings and personal injury trusts will significantly improve the resolution of asbestos claims is uncertain.

---

[3] See "Texas Legislature Passes Tort Reform Bill Limiting Successor Liability Damages," 2003.

Comparison of Projections of Asbestos-Related Diseases

This appendix provides further discussion of the early projections of asbestos-related diseases discussed in Chapter Two and displayed in Table 2.2. That table is reproduced here as Table A.1 for easy reference.

Of the 229,000 excess cancer deaths due to asbestos exposure from 1985 to 2009, Nicholson et al. (1982) predicted that 70,870 would be due to mesothelioma. As shown in Table A.1, Walker et al. (1983) projected 15,500 to 18,100 cases of asbestos-related mesothelioma among asbestos workers for the same period. Estimates of mesothelioma from other studies conducted at about the same time fall between these two sets of projections.

Figure A.1 compares experts' predictions of the incidence of death from mesothelioma over time. According to predictions by Nicholson et al. (1982), mesothelioma deaths among persons employed in selected industries and occupations would increase from 1,775 in the year 1982 to more than 3,000 in 2002, then decrease to less than 1,000 by 2027. The Walker et al. (1983) study estimated occupation-

Table A.1
Projections of Asbestos-Related Cancers Among Asbestos Workers, 1985–2009

Study	Mesothelioma	Lung Cancer	Gastrointestinal and Other Cancers	Total[a]
Higginson (1980)	25,000	37,500	—	62,500
Enterline (1981)	16,650	63,525	—	80,175
Peto et al. (1981)	20,925	79,515	—	100,440
McDonald and McDonald (1981)	22,870	123,750	—	146,620
Nicholson et al. (1982)	70,870	124,210	33,715	228,795
Walker et al. (1983)	15,500–18,100	23,885[b]	—	39,385–41,985
Lilienfeld et al. (1988)	21,500	76,700	33,000	131,200

SOURCE: Lilienfeld et al. (1988), Table 2 (with minor corrections).
NOTE: — = Not reported.
[a] "Total" includes only the types of cancer reported in the projections.
[b] From Table 8 in Manton (1983).

Figure A.1
Projections of Mesothelioma in the United States, 1982–2047

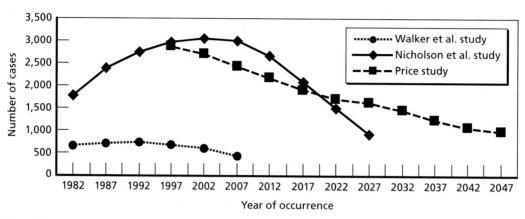

RAND *MG162-A.1*

related mesothelioma cases among asbestos workers to be about 640 in 1982, rising to a high of 720 in 1992 and decreasing to 420 in 2007. A more recent study by Price (1997) estimated about 2,850 mesothelioma cases in 1997 in the United States.

After 1997, Price predicted that the number of mesothelioma cases would decrease each year to about 975 by 2047. Based on his projections, the number of mesothelioma cases per year stabilizes at this level until 2067.

Despite the fact that mesothelioma is considered to be a signature disease for asbestos exposure, even more asbestos-related lung cancers than mesothelioma have been predicted to occur. Predictions of asbestos-related lung cancers occurring between 1985 and 2009 among asbestos workers vary; Walker et al. (1983) predicted 23,885 cases, whereas Nicholson et al. (1982) predicted 124,210 deaths. As with the mesothelioma estimates, the estimates of lung cancer by other projection studies in the 1970s and 1980s fall between these two predictions.

Figure A.2 compares experts' predictions of the incidence of lung cancer deaths due to asbestos exposure. The Nicholson study predicted more than 5,000 excess lung cancer deaths caused by occupational asbestos exposure would occur each year between 1982 and 1997, increasing to a maximum of 5,497 in 1992, then decreasing thereafter to 646 deaths in 2027. The Walker study estimated that 2,278 cases of lung cancer due to "plausible" asbestos exposure would occur in 1982, a figure that would decline rapidly to 284 by 2007. The Nicholson estimates range from twice as high as the Walker estimates (5,055 compared with 2,278 in 1982) to 13 times higher (3,921 compared with 284 in 2007).

Figure A.2
Projections of Asbestos-Related Lung Cancer in the United States, 1982–2047

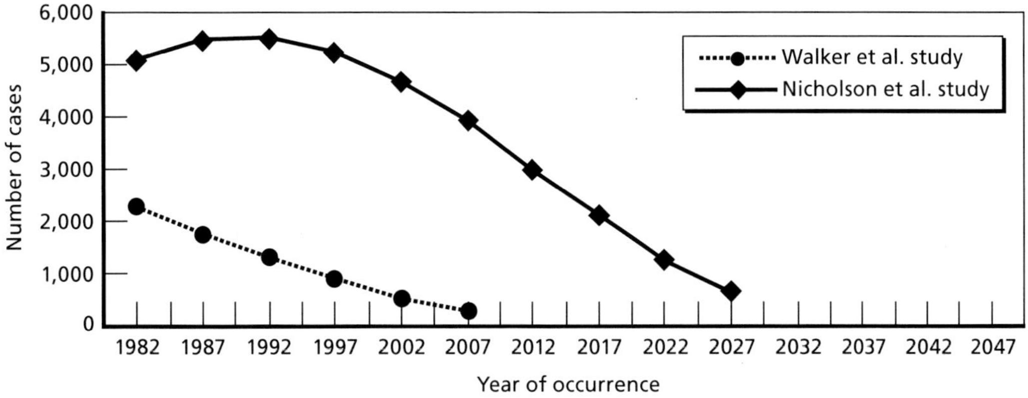

RAND *MG162-A.2*

Data on asbestosis cases or deaths are limited and unreliable because asbestosis generally is not fatal. Using data from the Walker study, Manton (1983) estimated that 2,774 excess deaths due to asbestosis would occur in 1982, decreasing to 734 in 2007 (not shown). The other studies cited in Table A.1 did not predict cases of asbestosis.

Based on a report by the National Institute for Occupational Safety and Health (NIOSH, 2004), the number of deaths among U.S. residents 15 years and older that were coded as caused by asbestosis increased from 77 in 1968 to 1,265 in 1999 (see Table A.2). The rapid increase in asbestosis deaths observed from 1968 to 1988 represents the delayed effects among workers exposed to asbestos during its peak use, starting in the mid-1940s. These figures represent deaths with asbestosis coded on the death certificate as either the underlying (i.e., main) or a contributing cause of death. According to the 2004 NIOSH report, asbestosis was coded as the main cause for about a third of these deaths throughout this time period. But the number of deaths underestimates the number of persons with asbestosis because asbestosis was often not listed on a death certificate as a cause of death even among persons having asbestosis at the time of their death because it is not always fatal.

Limitations of Projections

Although Nicholson et al. (1982) is the leading reference on projecting asbestos-related disease, the estimates from that study have two major limitations. First, the estimates might not include all workers who had significant exposure to asbestos between 1940 and 1979. Nicholson et al. restricted their worker cohorts to persons

Table A.2
Deaths Due to Asbestosis Among
U.S. Residents 15 Years of Age and
Older, 1968–1999

Year of Death	Number of Deaths
1968	77
1969	71
1970	87
1971	83
1972	138
1973	117
1974	114
1975	126
1976	143
1977	163
1978	240
1979	309
1980	339
1981	318
1982	428
1983	476
1984	445
1985	534
1986	702
1987	710
1988	769
1989	878
1990	948
1991	946
1992	959
1993	999
1994	1,060
1995	1,169
1996	1,176
1997	1,171
1998	1,221
1999	1,265

SOURCE: NIOSH, 2004.

NOTE: Includes all deaths with asbestosis recorded as either the underlying (i.e., main) cause or as a contributory cause.

working in specific industries and occupations who were most likely to be exposed to higher levels of asbestos. These industries include *primary manufacturing,* including asbestos products (such as friction products, pipe and sheet, asbestos textiles, floor tiles, roofing, and insulating and other building materials), gaskets, packing and sealing devices, and building paper and building board mills; *secondary manufacturing,* including heating equipment, boiler shops, industrial furnaces and ovens, and electric housewares and fans; *shipbuilding and repair*, and *construction*, including general contractors in residential and nonresidential building construction and in water, sewer, pipeline, communication, and power line construction. Nicholson et al. also identified workers in certain occupations who were at significant risk of asbestos exposure. Those workers included asbestos and insulation workers, automobile body repairers and mechanics, engine room personnel in the maritime industry, maintenance employees in chemical and petroleum manufacturing and in the railroad industry, stationary engineers, stationary firemen, and power station operators. In all, Nicholson et al. (1982) estimated that approximately 27.5 million workers in these industries and occupations had been exposed to asbestos from 1940 to 1979.

In recent years, workers from industries and occupations not included in Nicholson et al.'s analysis have begun to file claims for asbestos-related injury. The etiology of these injury claims is sharply disputed. Some litigators on both the plaintiff and defense sides argue that most workers in these industries have not actually suffered significant asbestos exposure or injury and they should not be compensated for asbestos-related injury. Other litigators argue that Nicholson et al. simply focused on the potential for asbestos exposure and asbestos-induced disease in high-risk industries and occupations and ignored the risk of exposure in other industries. We have not been able to find any epidemiological study that has systematically investigated asbestos exposure and the incidence of asbestos-induced disease that includes all industries and occupations in the United States.[1] Although some studies project cases of disease, not deaths (e.g., Walker et al. [1983], Price [1997], Price and Ware [2004]), no study has provided a reliable estimate of how many people are sick at a given point in time as a result of occupational exposure to asbestos.

A second limitation of the Nicholson et al. study is that the study's estimates do not include workers exposed to asbestos after 1979 who subsequently develop asbestos-related disease. The analysis is restricted to those working with asbestos between 1940 and 1979. Although regulations implemented during the 1960s and 1970s greatly reduced occupational exposure, U.S. industries continued to produce and process asbestos after 1979 (Agency for Toxic Substances and Disease Registry [ATSDR], 2001). The volume of asbestos produced by U.S. mines decreased from 299 million pounds in the late 1960s and early 1970s to 112 million pounds in 1987 and 37 million pounds in 1989. Production continued to decrease until it reached 13.2 million pounds in 1999. As of 2001, a total of 65 facilities in 27 states reported producing, processing, or using asbestos (ATSDR, 2001). Clearly, many workers have been exposed to asbestos since 1979.

---

[1] Some analysts have examined patterns of legal claiming by industry (Manville Personal Injury Settlement Trust, 2001).

Estimated Cases of Mesothelioma in the United States, 1985–2009

The total number of cases of mesothelioma that occurs in the United States each year is not available from public health reporting systems. This number, however, can be estimated using data from cancer registries throughout the country. The objectives of the analysis presented in this appendix are (1) to estimate the annual number of mesothelioma cases occurring in the United States from 1973 to 1998 using data from the National Cancer Institute's SEER program and (2) to estimate and compare the number of mesothelioma cases for 1985–2009 with the projections from the Nicholson et al. (1982) study.

Estimation Methods

The expected number of mesothelioma cases was estimated by multiplying cancer incidence rates from the SEER cancer registries by the number of persons in the United States for each year from 1973 to 1998. Age- (five-year categories) and gender-specific mesothelioma incidence rates were used to generate total cases for males, females, and both genders combined. The mesothelioma incidence rates and population counts for the United States were derived from SEER*Stat, a statistical analysis package available on the SEER Web site.[1] A single set of age- and gender-specific rates was generated for each year of the 26-year period (1973–1998) by combining rates for nine geographic areas. The nine SEER reporting areas include five states (Connecticut, Hawaii, Iowa, New Mexico, and Utah) and four metropolitan areas (Atlanta, Detroit, San Francisco–Oakland, and Seattle–Puget Sound).

In addition, we calculated the number of mesothelioma cases expected to occur in the United States from 1985 to 2009 by combining data from two sources. The estimated number of cases for 1985–1998 (based on the analysis described in the previous paragraph) and the estimated number of cases for 1999–2009 from Price (1997) were summed to yield a total for 1985–2009. We then compared this ex-

---

[1] As of this writing, the latest release of the SEER*Stat statistical software, SEER*Stat 5 (August 2004), is available at http://seer.cancer.gov/seerstat/.

pected number of mesothelioma cases for 1985–2009 with published estimates from Nicholson et al. (1982) for the same time period.

Results

Table B.1 and Figure B.1 show our estimates of the number of mesothelioma cases for males, females, and both genders combined for the United States for each year from 1973 to 1998. These numbers indicate that mesothelioma among males almost quadrupled during this period, from about 615 in 1973 to 2,437 in 1992. Although the number of mesothelioma cases among females was lower than that for males, mesothelioma among females also increased significantly, doubling from 287 in 1973

Table B.1
Estimated Cases of Mesothelioma in the United States, 1973–1998

Year of Occurrence	Males	Females	Total
1973	615.4	286.6	902.0
1974	871.6	322.2	1,193.7
1975	859.8	320.4	1,180.2
1976	918.5	385.9	1,304.4
1977	860.3	339.5	1,199.8
1978	1,223.9	269.1	1,493.0
1979	1,272.7	351.6	1,624.2
1980	1,637.3	423.8	2,061.1
1981	1,270.1	303.0	1,573.1
1982	1,300.0	463.5	1,763.5
1983	1,666.4	583.3	2,249.7
1984	1,856.9	452.4	2,309.3
1985	1,613.3	463.4	2,076.7
1986	1,544.3	551.6	2,095.8
1987	1,646.7	510.0	2,156.7
1988	1,761.0	487.2	2,248.2
1989	2,205.0	502.9	2,708.0
1990	2,075.6	621.3	2,696.9
1991	2,124.5	579.3	2,703.7
1992	2,436.7	553.9	2,990.6
1993	2,101.3	534.2	2,635.6
1994	2,293.6	595.1	2,888.7
1995	2,291.1	682.1	2,973.1
1996	2,284.2	659.1	2,943.2
1997	2,056.9	546.7	2,603.6
1998	2,208.8	557.0	2,765.9

NOTE: These numbers were estimated using mesothelioma incidence rates for nine SEER reporting areas for the indicated years.

Figure B.1
Estimated Incident Cases of Mesothelioma in the United States, 1973–1998

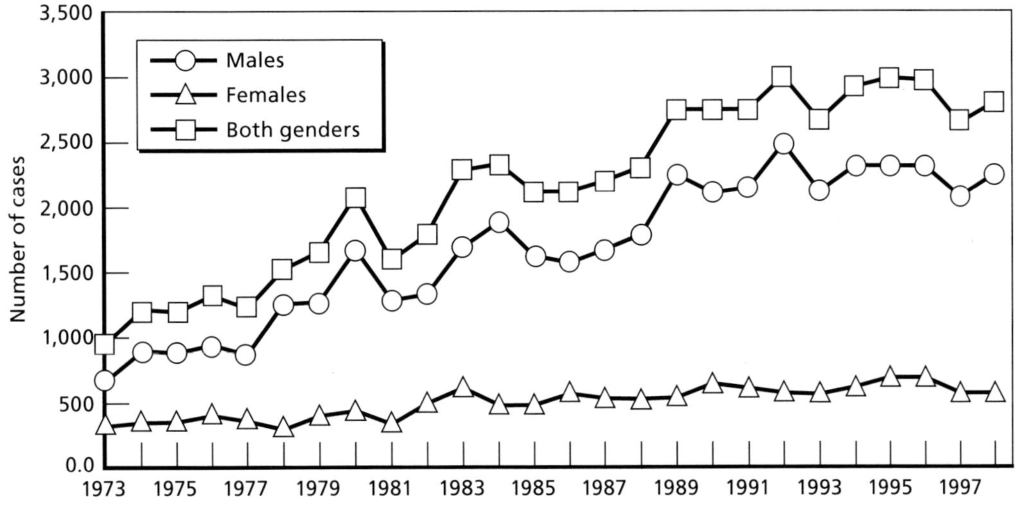

RAND *MG162-B.1*

to 557 in 1998. For both males and females, the number of cases was fairly stable from 1993 to 1998. In 1998, the last year for which SEER data were available at the time we conducted our analysis, an estimated 2,766 cases of mesothelioma were diagnosed in the United States among males and females combined, up from 902 in 1973, but down from a high of 2,991 in 1992.

Using the annual number of mesothelioma cases for 1985–1998 based on SEER incidence rates and the annual number of mesothelioma cases for 1999–2009 from the study by Price (1997), we estimated the number of cases of mesothelioma expected to occur between 1985 and 2009 among males and females in the United States to be 64,788 (see Table B.2).

Conclusion

Our estimates of the incidence of cases of mesothelioma in the United States for the years 1980, 1985, and 1990–1997 (see Table B.1) are the same as those in Stallard (2001), indicating that the data source and methods used in Table B.1 and the Stallard study are the same. We do not know, however, if our estimated number of mesothelioma cases (see Table B.1) is higher or lower than the true number of mesothelioma cases. The nine SEER reporting areas reflect the cancer experience of about 10 percent of the population of the United States. If the mesothelioma rates in these

Table B.2
Cases of Mesothelioma in the United States Based on SEER Incidence Rates and Study by Price (1997)

Year of Occurrence	Number of Cases Based on SEER Incidence Rates[a]	Number of Cases Estimated from Published Data[b]	Number of Cases[c]
1985	2,076.7	—	2,076.7
1986	2,095.8	—	2,095.8
1987	2,156.7	—	2,156.7
1988	2,248.2	—	2,248.2
1989	2,708.0	—	2,708.0
1990	2,696.9	—	2,696.9
1991	2,703.7	—	2,703.7
1992	2,990.6	2,070.0	2,990.6
1993	2,635.6	2,226.0	2,635.6
1994	2,888.7	2,382.0	2,888.7
1995	2,973.1	2,538.0	2,973.1
1996	2,943.2	2,694.0	2,943.2
1997	2,603.6	2,850.0	2,603.6
1998	2,765.9	2,818.0	2,765.9
1999	—	2,786.0	2,786.0
2000	—	2,754.0	2,754.0
2001	—	2,722.0	2,722.0
2002	—	2,690.0	2,690.0
2003	—	2,637.0	2,637.0
2004	—	2,584.0	2,584.0
2005	—	2,531.0	2,531.0
2006	—	2,478.0	2,478.0
2007	—	2,425.0	2,425.0
2008	—	2,373.0	2,373.0
2009	—	2,321.0	2,321.0
Total			64,787.7

NOTES: — = Data not available.

[a]See text and Table B.1.

[b]The numbers in the third column were estimated from Figure 4 of Price (1997).

[c]The fourth column represents the numbers from the second column for 1985–1998 and the numbers from the third column for 1999–2009.

nine areas are higher (or lower) than the mesothelioma rates in the rest of the United States, the estimated number of cancers will be higher (or lower) than the actual number of cancers. Walker et al. (1983) have suggested that mesothelioma rates from the SEER reporting areas might overestimate national rates because shipbuilding areas are overrepresented. Nicholson et al. (1982) suggested that the SEER rates might underestimate national rates because areas using asbestos in manufacturing and construction are underrepresented.

The number of mesothelioma cases expected to occur in the United States between 1985 and 2009 (64,788, as shown in Table B.2) is somewhat lower than the number of mesothelioma deaths estimated by Nicholson et al. (1982) (70,870, as shown in Table 2.2 in Chapter Two). There are differences between the methods used to generate the estimates. First, the numbers in Table B.2 are based on actual rates during the indicated years based on the general population living in the SEER reporting areas, whereas the Nicholson estimates are based on rates in a cohort of asbestos workers from epidemiologic studies conducted in the 1960s and 1970s. Second, the numbers in Table B.2 represent all mesothelioma cases occurring in the United States (which had a population of 270 million people in 1998), whereas the Nicholson estimates include only cases occurring among workers exposed to asbestos between 1940 and 1979 (about 27.5 million persons). If one assumes that almost all cases of mesothelioma in the United States between 1985 and 2009 have occurred (or will occur) within the worker cohorts exposed to asbestos identified by Nicholson et al. (1982), the numbers in Table B.2 validate Nicholson's estimates. If, on the other hand, one assumes that many cases of mesothelioma have occurred (or will occur) between 1985 and 2009 among persons not in Nicholson's asbestos-worker cohort, the numbers in Table B.2 indicate that Nicholson's estimates were too high.

Constructing the Jury Verdict Database

There is no national databank or tracking system for jury verdicts, including jury verdicts for asbestos cases. Therefore, we constructed our own database of verdicts for the years 1993–2001, using *Mealey's Litigation Report: Asbestos*, as a source of data for this study. *Mealey's*, a subscription service that is marketed to attorneys who require current and in-depth coverage of events related to asbestos litigation, relies on traditional news-gathering techniques, including sending reporters to the courtroom and obtaining information from the parties themselves. Because there is no nationwide system to track asbestos jury verdicts, it is impossible to test the inclusiveness of the *Mealey's* reporter. Several other researchers have used litigation reporters to conduct empirical analyses. In some instances, they were able to compare their data with public records, and they found that the litigation reporters identified a large majority of cases that reached verdict.[1]

We searched an electronic version of *Mealey's* for articles that included both the term "jury" and "verdict" and were published after January 1, 1993.[2] We screened these results by hand and removed articles that did not report on a specific jury verdict within the time period of interest. The dataset was limited to personal injury or wrongful death caused by asbestos exposure. As a result, we removed a few property damage cases and also a few verdicts that were only tangentially related to asbestos litigation, such as tobacco litigation and other toxic torts. In some instances, a single article reported on more than one trial. We created a separate entry for each trial to construct a database comprising all jury trials that reached verdict.

---

[1] Data for one reporter were found to be 84 percent inclusive of the jury verdicts in the public records, and data for another were more than 90 percent inclusive. Both reporters reported cases generally (rather than a specific category of cases, such as asbestos cases) but covered only certain counties. The investigators also found that the omissions were primarily low-value cases.

[2] The search was done in March 2002. Although we were constructing a database of verdicts for the years 1993–2001, we included reporters for the first few months of 2002 in the search to allow for any delay between a verdict and the publication date of the corresponding reporter article on that verdict.

Database Construction

From the litigation reporter information, we derived the following data fields:

- Article headline
- Publication month and year
- Verdict month and year
- Case name/number
- State where trial took place
- Court in which case was tried
- Verdict/award
- Verdict type (numerical code)
- Number of plaintiffs whose claims were tried together
- Whether trial was unitary or bifurcated.

These data fields constitute the trial-level database.

Because many trials include multiple claims tried together, we also constructed a plaintiff-level database, using the trial-level data as a starting point. We created a record for each plaintiff in each trial, according to the number of plaintiffs noted in the trial-level database. We derived the data for each plaintiff from the corresponding trials in the trial-level database and added a few new fields, including the following:

- Individual claim (numerical code)
- Individual verdict (numerical code)
- Individual award (if any)
- Individual or consolidated (group) trial
- If consolidated, whether grouped claims were homogeneous or mixed with regard to injury.

Because many asbestos trials do not proceed in a traditional single-claim, unitary form, we needed to develop rules to ensure that each plaintiff's claim was counted only once. Because our goal was to report verdict information, we also needed to develop rules to ensure that we counted only complete jury verdicts (i.e., decisions on liability and damages). To this end, we adopted the following rules:

- If the jury found for the defense in the liability phase, and the liability phase was the first phase of the trial, we coded the outcome of the claim as a defense verdict.

- If the jury found for the defense in the liability phase, but the liability phase was not the first phase of the trial, we coded the outcome of the claim as a defense verdict and discarded any damages awarded in earlier phases (because these damages decisions were set aside by the court as a result of the liability decision).
- If the jury found for the plaintiff in the liability phase of the trial, and the parties settled before the damages phase, we excluded the claim from our analyses.
- If damages were determined in the first phase of the trial, and the parties settled before the liability phase, we excluded the claim from our analyses.
- If the jury found for the plaintiff in the liability phase of the trial, and the liability phase was the first phase of the trial, but the damages phase had not taken place by the end of 2001, we excluded the claim from our analyses, since that claim did not reach a full verdict during our study period.
- If the jury calculated damages in the first phase of the trial, but the liability phase had not taken place by the end of 2001, we likewise excluded the claim from our analyses.
- If the jury found for the plaintiff in the liability phase and awarded damages in the damages phase before the end of 2001, we coded a single outcome for both phases, with "award" coded in the verdict field, the amount of the award entered in the appropriate field, and the date coded to reflect the completion of the second phase, regardless of the order in which the jury heard liability and damages.

We did not separate punitive and compensatory damages, nor did we separate compensatory damages into their respective parts, including loss of consortium, past medical expenses, future medical expenses, and so forth, because the reporter did not consistently report such information. For the same reason, we also did not code offsets for defendants who settled with the plaintiff, and did not further disaggregate the data by defendant, even if the jury verdict was mixed. If any one of the defendants was held liable and ordered to pay an award, we coded the outcome for both the trial and each plaintiff as an award for the plaintiff, although a defense verdict may have been entered for one or more defendants.

We did adjust for offsets in comparative negligence cases. This was an issue in only a few cases in which the plaintiff was a cigarette smoker, and the relevant state law required the jury to return separate findings for compensatory damages and the percentage of fault attributable to the plaintiff. In these cases, we coded the net award.

Major Asbestos Bankruptcies

We examined information from numerous sources to compile a list of major asbestos litigation defendants that have incurred and/or were expected to incur substantial asbestos-related liabilities and have filed for bankruptcy. Table D.1 presents our list of asbestos-related bankruptcy filings from 1982 through summer 2004. As we noted in Chapter Six, this list should be interpreted as asbestos defendants that have filed for bankruptcy, and not necessarily companies driven into bankruptcy by asbestos.

The table lists only one name for each corporate bankruptcy, regardless of the number of subsidiaries or related companies involved in the bankruptcy. Several names that frequently appear in discussions of asbestos-related bankruptcies are not included in the table for that reason. Below, we discuss some of the related companies and successor firms that were included in the bankruptcy proceedings of a company listed in Table D.1.

When Johns-Manville Corp. filed for bankruptcy (1982), it included Advocate Mines of Canada among its related companies. UNR Industries (1982 bankruptcy) included Union Asbestos and Rubber (Unarco) among its subsidiaries. The Chapter 11 petition for United States Lines (1986) included parent companies McLean Industries and First Colony Farms. National Gypsum's petition (1990) included parent company Aancor Holdings Inc. The Celotex petition (1990) included Carey Canada, Panacon, Phillip Carey Company, and Smith and Kanzler; we also included Hillsborough Holdings under the umbrella of the Celotex filing, although Hillsborough filed separately in 1989. Raymark Industries, the successor to Raybestos-Manhattan, and Raytech Corporation, a subsidiary of Raymark, filed for bankruptcy separately, but only Raytech is listed in Table D.1. H.K. Porter's filing (1991) included Southern Textile, formerly known as Southern Asbestos.

The bankruptcy of Harnischfeger Industries (1999) included subsidiaries Joy Technologies and Ecolaire. The Babcock & Wilcox bankruptcy (2000) included Americon, B&W Construction, and Diamond Power International. The Owens Corning bankruptcy (2000) included its subsidiary Fibreboard, while Armstrong

Table D.1
Largest Asbestos-Related Bankruptcies, 1982–2004

Company	Year	Federal District	Bankruptcy No.
A.P. Green Industries, Inc.	2002	W.D. Pa.	02-21639
A-Best Products Co.	2002	D.D. Del.	02-12734-JKF
AC&S, Inc.	2002	D.D. Del.	02-12687
Amatex	1982	E.D. Pa.	82-25220
American Shipbuilding Co.	1993	M.D. Fla.	93-11552-8B1
Armstrong World Industries	2000	D.D. Del.	00-04471
Artra Group, Inc.	2003	N.D. Ill.	02-21522
Asbestec Industries, Inc.	1988	S.D.N.Y.	88-02065
Atlas Corp.	1998	D. Col.	98-23331
Babcock & Wilcox Co.	2000	E.D. La.	00-558
Bethlehem Steel Corp.	2001	S.D.N.Y.	01-15288
Brunswick Fabrications	1988	E.D. Pa.	Unknown
Burns & Roe Enterprises, Inc.	2000	D.N.J.	00-41610
C.E. Thurston & Sons, Inc.	2003	E.D. Va.	03-75932-SCS
Cassiar Mining Corp.	1992	(Canada)	Not applicable
Celotex	1990	M.D. Fla.	90-10016-8B1
Chemetron Corp.	1988	W.D. Pa.	88-20452
Combustion Engineering	2003	D.D. Del.	03-10495
Congoleum Corp.	2003	D.N.J.	03-51524-KCF
DII	2003	W.D. Pa.	03-35593-JKF
Delaware Insulation	1989	D.D. Del.	89-00295
E.J. Bartells Co.	2000	W.D. Wash.	00-10390-KAO
EaglePicher Industries, Inc.	1991	S.D. Ohio	1-91-00100
Eastco Industrial Safety Corp.	2001	E.D.N.Y.	01-80367
Federal-Mogul Corp.	2001	D.D. Del.	01-10578
Flinkote Co.	2004	D.D. Del.	04-11300
Forty-Eight Insulations, Inc.	1985	N.D. Ill.	87 C 10594
Fuller-Austin Insulation, Inc.	1998	D.D. Del.	98-2038-JJF
Gatke Corp.	1987	N.D. Ind.	87-30308
G-I Holdings, Inc.	2001	D.N.J.	01-30135
H&A Construction Co.	1983	D. Mass.	83-10426
H.K. Porter	1991	W.D. Pa.	91-468WWB[PGH]
Harbison-Walker Refractories Co.	2002	W.D. Pa.	02-21627
Harnischfeger Industries, Inc.	1999	D.D. Del.	99-02171
Johns-Manville Corp.	1982	S.D.N.Y.	82 B 11656/76
JT Thorpe Co.	2002	S.D. Tex.	02-41487-H5-11
Kaiser Aluminum	2002	D.D. Del.	02-10429
Keene Corp.	1993	S.D.N.Y.	93-46090
Kentile Floors, Inc.	1992	S.D.N.Y.	92-46466-brl
Lone Star Steel Co.	1989	N.D. Tex.	89-33552
Lykes Brothers Steamship Co.	1995	M.D. Fla.	95-10465-8P1
M.H. Detrick Co.	1998	D. Ill.	98 B 01004
The Muralo Co., Inc.	2003	D.N.J.	03-26723-MS

Table D.1—Continued

Company	Year	Federal District	Bankruptcy No.
NARCO (North American Refractories Company)	2002	W.D. Pa.	02-20198
National Gypsum Co.	1990	N.D. Tex.	90-37213-SAF-11
Nicolet, Inc.	1987	E.D. Pa.	87-3574
North American Asbestos Corp.	1976	(State of Ill.)	Not applicable
Oglebay Norton Co.	2004	D.D. Del.	04-10558-JBR
Owens Corning	2000	D.D. Del.	00-03837
Pacor, Inc.	1986	E.D. Pa.	86-23251
Pittsburgh Corning Corp.	2000	W.D. Pa.	00-22876-JKF
Plibrico Co.	2002	N.D. Ill.	02-09952, 57
Porter-Hayden Co.	2002	D. Md.	02-54152
Prudential Lines, Inc.	1986	S.D.N.Y.	86-11773
Quigley Co.	2004	S.D.N.Y.	04-15739-PCB
Raytech Corp.	1989	E.D. Pa.	89-00293
Rock Wool Manufacturing Co.	1996	N.D. Ala.	96-08295-TBB
Rutland Fire Clay Co.	1999	D. Vt.	99-11390
Shook & Fletcher Insulation Co.	2002	N.D. Ala.	02-02771-BGC-11
Skinner Engine Co.	2001	W.D. Pa.	01-23987-MBM
Standard Insulations, Inc.	1986	W.D. Mo.	86-03413
Stone & Webster, Inc.	2000	D.D. Del.	00-02142
Swan Transportation Co.	2001	D.D. Del.	01-11690
Todd Shipyards Corp.	1987	D.N.J.	87-05005
U.S. Gypsum Co.	2001	D.D. Del.	01-02094
U.S. Mineral Products Corp.	2001	D.D. Del.	01-02471
United States Lines, Inc.	1986	S.D.N.Y.	86-12238
UNR Industries, Inc.	1982	N.D. Ill.	82-B9841
Utex Industries, Inc.	2004	S.D.Tex.	04-34427
W.R. Grace & Co.	2001	D.D. Del.	01-01139
Wallace and Gale Co.	1984	D. Md.	85-40092
Waterman Steamship Corp.	1983	New York	83-11732
Western Asbestos Co.	2002	N.D. Cal.	02-46284

World Industries' (2000) bankruptcy included Desseaux Corp. and Nitram Liquidators. The petition for U.S. Gypsum (2001) included its subsidiaries United States Gypsum Co., USG Interiors, L&W Supply Corp., and Beadex Manufacturing Co. The companies mentioned here are just some of the more well-known subsidiaries that were parties to bankruptcies; some bankruptcies included more than 100 subsidiaries.

Halliburton's DII (formerly Dresser Industries) subsidiary, which includes the KBR engineering and construction business, filed for Chapter 11 bankruptcy protection. DII is burdened with most of the company's asbestos liability. The filing for bankruptcy was part of an agreement with plaintiff attorneys that allowed Halliburton to keep control of its assets in return for a $4 billion payment into a Chapter 11 bankruptcy trust to settle all existing and future asbestos suits brought against Halliburton and its subsidiaries.

A few companies are known by more than one name. Pacor (1986) is also known by its full label, Philadelphia Asbestos Corporation. Artra Group, Inc. (2003) is also known as Synkoloid. U.S. Mineral Products (2001) is also known as Isolatek International. Standard Insulations (1986) had changed its name from Standard Asbestos.

Corporate mergers and acquisitions further complicate the situation. H&A Construction (1983) had acquired Asbestospray and Spraycraft, and Keene (1993) had acquired Baldwin Ehret Hill. Continental Products was the successor to North American Asbestos Co. (1976), and G-I Holdings (2001) is the successor to GAF, which is the successor by merger to Ruberoid.

Three subsidiaries of RHI Refractories Holding Co.—NARCO, A.P. Green Industries, and Harbison-Walker Refractories—each filed individually in 2002. Meanwhile, RHI Refractories remains outside the protection of Chapter 11.

The Muralo Company (2003) purchased the assets of Sylkanoid from Sylkanoid's parent, Artra Group, Inc., in 1981. As part of the purchase, Artra indemnified Muralo for product claims arising prior to 1981 and provided indemnity for all asbestos actions brought against Sylkanoid for a period of greater than 20 years. Over the next 20 years, the agreement held with Artra defending or settling every Sylkanoid asbestos action, most of which had been brought against "Sylkanoid, a Division of Muralo" (which was strictly incorrect, as all that Muralo had purchased were the assets of Sylkanoid). When Artra filed a Chapter 11 petition in 2003, Muralo and its affiliate, Norton and Son, were then named as defendants in a flood of asbestos filings that had their origin with Sylkanoid. Muralo and Norton then filed for bankruptcy on the basis that they had to reorganize themselves and formulate and implement a new strategy to challenge the asbestos claims against them and/or receive relief from Artra.

Finally, we omitted from the list in Table D.1 four companies—SGL Carbon, Huxley Development, Powhatan Mining, and Washington Group International—that appear on many lists of asbestos-related bankruptcies. We understand that SGL Carbon did file for Chapter 11 reorganization; however, the U.S. Court of Appeals dismissed its petition.[1] We have not been able to confirm that either Huxley Development or Powhatan Mining ever filed for bankruptcy, much less where and when they filed or whether asbestos litigation was a significant contributor to the decision to file—if, in fact, there was a filing. Washington Group International filed for Chapter 11 reorganization in 2001; however, there is no evidence that asbestos liabilities were an important contributor to its financial problems. We understand that

---

[1] 200 F.3d 154; 1999 U.S. App. LEXIS 34433; 1999-2 Trade Cas. (CCH) P72,739; Bankr. L. Rep. (CCH) P78,084; 43 Collier Bankr. Cas. 2d (MB) 668; 35 Bankr. Ct. Dec. 116.

Washington Group International had been named on some claims filed in federal courts and included in the multidistrict litigation (MDL) (see Chapter Three). Washington Group International notified the MDL of its filing; the news media became aware of this notification and reported that Washington Group International had filed because of asbestos liabilities.

Bibliography

"ABA Delegates Set to Vote on Claims Standard Amid Opposition," *Mealey's Litigation Report: Asbestos 2,* Vol. 18, No. 1, 2003.

"ABA Votes to Adopt Medical Standards, Set to Lobby for Legislation," *Mealey's Litigation Report: Asbestos 2,* Vol. 18, No. 2, 2003.

Abbott, G., and P. Mallette, "Complex/Mass Tort Litigation in State Courts in Mississippi," *Mississippi Law Journal,* Vol. 63, 1994, p. 363.

Agency for Toxic Substances and Disease Registry (ATSDR), *Toxicological Profile for Asbestos,* Washington, D.C.: United States Department of Health and Human Services, Public Health Service, September 2001.

Albin, M., C. Magnani, S. Krstev, E. Rapiti, and I. Shefer, "Asbestos and Cancer: An Overview of Current Trends in Europe," *Environmental Health Perspectives,* Vol. 107 (Supplement), 1999, pp. 2289–2298.

Algero, M. G., "In Defense of Forum Shopping: A Realistic Look at Selecting a Venue," *Nebraska Law Review,* Vol. 78, 1999, p. 79.

Alleman, J., and B. Mossman, "Asbestos Revisited," *Scientific American,* July 1997, pp. 70–75.

Altonji, G., K. Horvath, and E. Simpson, *Asbestos Claims Surge Set to Dampen Earnings for Commercial Insurers,* Special Report, Oldwick, N.J.: A.M. Best Company, Inc., May 7, 2001.

American Thoracic Society, "The Diagnosis of Nonmalignant Diseases Related to Asbestos: 1996 Update: Official Statement of the American Thoracic Society," *American Review of Respiratory Disease,* Vol. 134, 1996, pp. 363–368.

Anderson, H. A., L. P. Hanrahan, D. N. Higgins, and P. G. Sarow, "A Radiographic Survey of Public School Building Maintenance and Custodial Employees," *Environmental Research,* Vol. 59, No. 1, 1992, pp. 159–166.

Anderson, H. A., L. P. Hanrahan, J. Schirmer, D. Higgins, and P. Sarow, "Mesothelioma Among Employees with Likely Contact with In-Place Asbestos-Containing Building Materials," *Annals of the New York Academy of Sciences,* Vol. 643, 1991, pp. 550–571.

Andersson, G. B. J., and L. Cocchiarella, *Guides to the Evaluation of Permanent Impairment,* Fifth Ed., Chicago: American Medical Association, 2000.

Angelina, M., and J. Biggs, "Asbestos Claims: Is This the Beginning or the End?" Casualty Actuaries of the Mid-Atlantic, Annual Conference, Chicago, May 30, 2001.

Asbestos Panel Presentation, Annual High-Yield Conference, Merrill Lynch, presentations by Andrew Berry, Joseph Cox, Robert Drain, and Francine Rabinovitz, December 18, 2000.

Austern, D., "Memorandum to Manville Trust Claimants," Fairfax, Va.: Claims Resolution Management Corporation, June 21, 2001.

_____, "Memorandum to Attorneys Who File Manville Trust Claims," Fairfax, Va., Claims Resolution Management Corporation, July 5, 2001.

_____, "The Manville Trust Experience," Mealey's Asbestos Bankruptcy Conference 2001, Fairfax, Va., Claims Resolution Management Corporation, 2001.

_____, "Letter to Joseph F. Rice," Fairfax, Va.: Claims Resolution Management Corporation, August 20, 2002.

Banaei, A., A. Bertran, M. Goldberg, A. Gueguen, D. Luce, and S. Goldberg, "Future Trends in Mortality of French Men from Mesothelioma," *Occupational and Environmental Medicine,* Vol. 57, No. 7, 2000, pp. 488–494.

"Bankruptcy Judge Lifts Stay, Allows Coverage Litigation to Proceed in State Court," *Mealey's Asbestos Litigation Reporter 13,* Vol. 3, No. 8, 2004.

Baron, F., "An Asbestos Settlement with a Hidden Agenda," *Wall Street Journal,* May 6, 1993, p. A6.

Beers, M. H., and R. Berkow, eds., *The Merck Manual of Diagnosis and Therapy,* 17th ed., Whitehouse Station, N.J.: Merck Research Laboratories, Merck and Co., Inc., 1999.

Behrens, M., "Some Proposals for Courts Interested in Helping Sick Claimants and Solving Serious Problems in Asbestos Litigation," *Baylor Law Review,* Vol. 54, 2002, p. 331.

Berke, J., "Judge Won't Let Big Three Consolidate Lawsuits," *The Deal,* February 12, 2002.

Bernick, D. M., et al., *Road Map to B&W's Defenses to Asbestos Personal Injury Claims,* United States District Court for the Eastern District of Louisiana, October 18, 2001a.

_____, *Debtors' Consolidated Reply in Support of Their Motion for Entry of Case Management Order, Establishment of a Bar Date, Approval of the Claim Forms and Approval of the Notice Program,* United States Bankruptcy Court for the District of Delaware, November 9, 2001b.

Bhagavatula, R., "New Perspectives on Asbestos," presentation at the Casualty Loss Reserve Seminar, Casualty Actuarial Society, Arlington, Va., September 23, 2002.

Bhagavatula, R., R. Moody, and J. Russ, "Asbestos: A Moving Target," *Best's Review,* Vol. 102, No. 5, September 2001, pp. 85–90.

"Bill Seeking Medical Standards in Line with AMA Introduced," *Mealey's Litigation Report: Asbestos 1,* Vol. 18, No. 2, 2003.

Blot, W. J., and J. F. Fraumeni, Jr., "Cancer Among Shipyard Workers," in R. Peto and M. Schneiderman, eds., *Quantification of Occupational Cancer*, Banbury Report 9, Cold Spring Harbor, N.Y.: Cold Spring Harbor Laboratory, 1981, pp. 37–49.

Blot, W. J., and J. F. Fraumeni, Jr., "Cancers of the Lung and Pleura," in D. Schottenfeld and J. F. Fraumeni, eds., *Cancer Epidemiology and Prevention*, 2nd ed., New York: Oxford University Press, 1996, pp. 637–665.

Blot, W. J., J. M. Harrington, A. Toledo, R. Hover, C. W. Heath, Jr., and J. F. Fraumeni, Jr., "Lung Cancer After Employment in Shipyards During World War II, *New England Journal of Medicine*, Vol. 299, No. 12, 1978, pp. 620–624.

Blot, W. J., L. E. Morris, R. Stroube, I. Tagnon, and J. F. Fraumeni, Jr., "Lung and Laryngeal Cancers in Relation to Shipyard Employment in Coastal Virginia, *Journal of the National Cancer Institute*, Vol. 65, No. 3, 1980, pp. 571–575.

Bordens, Kenneth S., and Horowitz, Irwin A., "The Limits of Sampling and Consolidation in Mass Tort Trials: Justice Improved or Justice Altered?" *Law and Psychology Review*, Vol. 22, No. 1, Spring 1998.

Brodeur, Paul, *Outrageous Misconduct: The Asbestos Industry on Trial*, New York: Pantheon, 1985.

Brown, D. P., J. M. Dement, and A. Okun, "Mortality Patterns Among Female and Male Chrysotile Asbestos Textile Workers," *Journal of Occupational Medicine*, Vol. 36, No. 9, 1994, pp. 882–888.

Cabraser, E., "Life After Amchem: The Class Struggle Continues," *Loyola Law Review*, Vol. 31, 1998, pp. 373–394.

Camus, M., J. Siemiatycki, and B. Meek, "Nonoccupational Exposure to Chrysotile Asbestos and the Risk of Lung Cancer, *New England Journal of Medicine*, Vol. 338, No. 22, 1998, pp. 1565–1571.

Carroll, Stephen J., Deborah R. Hensler, Allan F. Abrahamse, Jennifer Gross, Michelle J. White, J. Scott Ashwood, and Elizabeth M. Sloss *Asbestos Litigation Costs and Compensation: An Interim Report*, Santa Monica, Calif.: RAND Corporation, DB-397-ICJ, September 2002.

Case, B. W., "Health Effects of Tremolite, Now and in the Future," *Annals of the New York Academy of Sciences*, Vol. 643, 1991, pp. 491–504.

_____, "Non-Occupational Exposure to Chrysotile Asbestos and the Risk of Lung Cancer," *New England Journal of Medicine*, Vol. 339, No. 14, 1998, p. 1001.

"Cases in Four West Virginia Counties Consolidated," *Mealey's Litigation Report: Asbestos 12*, Vol. 6, No. 16, 1991.

Castleman, Barry, *Asbestos: Medical and Legal Aspects*, 4th ed., Englewood Cliffs, N.J.: Aspen Law & Business, 1996.

Cauchon, D., "The Asbestos Epidemic: An Emerging Catastrophe," *USA Today*, Feb. 8, 1999, pp. 1–7.

Chambers, L., "Where Is the Asbestos Litigation Going?" *The Wall Street Forum: Asbestos,* New York: Mealey Publications, July 18, 2002.

Chin, A., and M. Peterson, *Deep Pockets, Empty Pockets: Who Wins in Cook County Jury Trials,* Santa Monica, Calif.: RAND Corporation, R–3249-ICJ, 1985.

Claims Resolution Management Corporation, *Manville Personal Injury Settlement Trust: Selected Operations Data for Presentation at Courts Hearing,* Fairfax, Va.: Claims Resolution Management Corporation, December 13, 2001.

Clark, D., "Life in Lawsuit Central: An Overview of the Unique Aspects of Mississippi's Civil Justice System," *Mississippi Law Journal,* Vol. 71, 2001, pp. 371–372.

Cole, G. M., "A Calculus Without Consent: Mass Tort Bankruptcies, Future Claimants, and the Problem of Third Party Non-Debtor 'Discharge,'" *Iowa Law Review*, Vol. 84, 1999, pp. 753–800.

Commonwealth of Massachusetts, Middlesex Superior Court, "Massachusetts State Court Asbestos Personal Injury Litigation Order," September 1986.

"Congoleum Files Prepackaged Chapter 11 Petition in New Jersey Bankruptcy Court," *Mealey's Asbestos Bankruptcy Report 2,* Vol. 3, No. 6, 2004.

Connelly, R. R., R. Spirtas, M. H. Myers, C. L. Percy, and J. F. Fraumeni, "Demographic Patterns for Mesothelioma in the United States," *Journal of the National Cancer Institute*, Vol. 78, 1987, No. 6, pp. 1053–1060.

"Consolidated Bankruptcy Judge Transfers Friction Cases to Delaware Court," *Mealey's Asbestos Bankruptcy Report 7,* Vol. 1, No. 5, 2001.

Cross, S., and J. Doucette, "Measurement of Asbestos Bodily Injury Liabilities," *Proceedings of the Casualty-Actuarial Society,* Vol. 84, 1997, pp. 187–300.

Cullen, M. R., "Chrysotile Asbestos: Enough Is Enough," *Lancet,* Vol. 351, 1998, pp. 1377–1378.

Daley, C., and J. Castle, *Distressed Digest: Special Asbestos Issue,* newsletter special edition, Lehman Brothers, November 28, 2000.

Dalton, A., "Asbestos Hazards: Past, Present, and Future," *Occupational Health Review,* 1995, pp. 34–36.

"Damages Awarded in West Virginia Second Phase," *Mealey's Litigation Report: Asbestos 15,* Vol. 5, No. 9, 1990.

"Debtor's Consolidated Reply in Support of Their Motion for Entry of Case Management Order, Establishment of a Bar Date, Approval of the Claim Forms and Approval of the Notice Program," *In re W.R. Grace Co.,* Ch. 11, Case No. 01-01139 (Bankr. D. Del. filed April 2, 2001).

"Delaware Bankruptcy Judge Appoints Mediator in Federal-Mogul Case," *Mealey's Asbestos Bankruptcy Report 14,* Vol. 1, No. 7, 2002.

Devesa, S. S., W. J. Blot, B. J. Stone, B. A. Miller, R. E. Tarone, and J. F. Fraumeni, Jr., "Recent Cancer Trends in the United States," *Journal of the National Cancer Institute*, Vol. 87, No. 3, 1995, pp. 175–182.

Diamond, S., M. Saks, and S. Landsman, "Juror Judgments About Liability and Damages: Sources of Variability and Ways to Increase Consistency," *DePaul Law Review*, Vol. 48, 1998, pp. 301–353.

Edley, C. F., Jr., and P. C. Weiler, "Asbestos: A Multi-Billion Dollar Crisis," *Harvard Journal on Legislation*, Vol. 30, Summer 1993, pp. 383–408.

Eisenberg, T., and L. M. LoPucki, "Shopping for Judges: An Empirical Analysis of Venue Choice in Large Chapter 11 Reorganizations," *Cornell Law Review*, Vol. 84, 1999, p. 967.

Enterline, P. E., "Proportion of Cancer Due to Exposure to Asbestos," in R. Peto and M. Schneiderman, eds., *Quantification of Occupational Cancer,* Banbury Report 9, Cold Spring Harbor, N.Y.: Cold Spring Harbor Laboratory, 1981, pp. 19–36.

Enterline, P. E., and V. L. Henderson, "Geographic Patterns for Pleural Mesothelioma Deaths in the United States, 1968–1981," *Journal of the National Cancer Institute*, Vol. 79, 1987, pp. 31–37.

Environmental Protection Agency (EPA), *Report on the Peer Consultation Workshop to Discuss a Proposed Protocol to Assess Asbestos-Related Risk,* May 2003 (http://www.epa.gov/superfund/programs/risk/asbestos/pdfs/asbestos_report.pdf; last accessed June 21, 2004).

Environmental Working Group, *Asbestos Litigation Reform Reconsidered,* March 17, 2004 (http://www.ewg.org/reports/asbestos/printerfriendly_PDF.php, last accessed July 1, 2004).

"The Fairness in Asbestos Reform Act—What Will It Do, Where Is It Now?" *Mealey's Litigation Report: Asbestos 28,* Vol. 19, No. 5, 2004.

Fazzari, S. M., R. G. Hubbard, and B. C. Petersen, "Financing Constraints and Corporate Investment," *Brookings Papers on Economic Activity,* No. 1, 1988.

"Federal Judge Denies Big 3 Automakers' Attempts to Have Cases Transferred," *Mealey's Asbestos Bankruptcy Report 3,* Vol. 1, No. 7, 2002.

Fitzpatrick, L., "The Center for Claims Resolution," *Law and Contemporary Problems*, Vol. 53, 1990, pp. 13–26.

"5,500 Mississippi Plaintiffs Settle with Phase I Defendants," *Mealey's Litigation Report: Asbestos 3,* Vol. 6, No. 10, 1991.

Fleming, G., "Is There a Future for Tort," *Louisiana Law Review,* Vol. 44, 1984, p. 1193.

"4th Circuit Rules that Ohio Plaintiffs Are Necessary to West Virginia State Action," *Mealey's Litigation Report: Asbestos 6,* Vol. 14, No. 13, 1999.

Franks, J., and W. Torous, "An Empirical Investigation of U.S. Firms in Reorganization," *Journal of Finance*, Vol. 44, 1989, pp. 747–769.

Fraumeni, J. F., Jr., and W. J. Blot, "Lung and Pleura," in D. Schottenfeld and J. F. Fraumeni, eds., *Cancer Epidemiology and Prevention,* Philadelphia: Saunders, 1982, pp. 564–582.

Freudenheim, M., "Appeals Court Orders Judge to Step Aside in Three Asbestos Cases," *New York Times,* May 18, 2004.

Galanter, M., "The Regulatory Function of the Civil Jury," in Robert Litan, ed., *Verdict: Assessing the Civil Jury System,* Washington, D.C.: Brookings Institution Press, 1993, pp. 61–102.

Gamble, J. F., "Asbestos and Colon Cancer: A Weight-of-the-Evidence Review," *Environmental Health Perspectives,* Vol. 102, No. 12, 1994, pp. 1038–1050.

Garber, S., "Product Liability, Punitive Damages, Business Decisions and Economic Outcomes," *Wisconsin Law Review,* Vol. 1998, 1998.

Glater, J., "For Armstrong, Bankruptcy Is Lesser of Two Evils," *New York Times,* Dec. 20, 2000, p. C4.

Green, M., *Bendectin and Birth Defects: The Challenges of Mass Toxic Substances Litigation,* Philadelphia: University of Pennsylvania Press, 1996.

"Halliburton, Equitas Reach $575 Million Deal," *Mealey's Asbestos Bankruptcy Report,* January 29, 2004.

Harrington, J. S., and N. D. McGlashan, "South African Asbestos Production, Exports, and Destinations, 1959–1993," *American Journal of Industrial Medicine,* Vol. 33, No. 4, 1998, pp. 321–326.

"Hatch Introduces $108 Billion Asbestos Trust Fund Legislation," *Mealey's Litigation Report: Asbestos 4,* Vol. 18, No. 9, 2003.

Hensler, D., "Fashioning a National Resolution of Asbestos Personal Injury Litigation: A Reply to Professor Brickman," *Cardozo Law Review,* Vol. 13, 1992, pp. 1967–1990.

_____, "A Glass Half Full, a Glass Half Empty: The Use of Alternative Dispute Resolution in Mass Personal Injury Litigation," *Texas Law Review,* Vol. 73, 1995, pp. 1587–1626.

_____, "The Real World of Tort Litigation," in Austin Sarat et al., eds., *Everyday Practices and Trouble Cases,* Evanston, Ill.: Northwestern University Press, 1998.

_____, "The Role of Multi-Districting in Mass Tort Litigation: An Empirical Investigation," *Seton Hall Law Review,* Vol. 31, No. 4, 2001a, pp. 883–906.

_____, "Revisiting the Monster: New Myths and Realities of Class Action and Other Large-Scale Litigation," *Duke Journal of Comparative and International Law,* Vol. 11, No. 2, 2001b, pp. 179–213.

_____, "As Time Goes By: Asbestos Litigation After Amchem and Ortiz," *Texas Law Review,* Vol. 80, No. 7, 2002, pp. 1899–1924.

Hensler, D., W. L. F. Felstiner, M. Selvin, and P. A. Ebener, *Asbestos in the Courts: The Challenge of Mass Toxic Tort Litigation*, Santa Monica, Calif.: RAND Corporation, R-3324-ICJ, 1985.

Hensler, D. M., S. Marquis, A. F. Abrahamse, S. H. Berry, P. A. Ebener, E. Lewis, E. A. Lind, R. J. MacCoun, W. G. Manning, J. A. Rogowski, and M. E. Vaiana, *Compensation for Accidental Injuries in the United States*, Santa Monica, Calif.: RAND Corporation, R-3999-HHS/ICJ, 1991.

Hensler, D., N. M. Pace, B. Dombey-Moore, E. Giddens, J. Gross, and E. Moller, *Class Action Dilemmas: Pursuing Public Goals for Private Gain*, Santa Monica, Calif.: RAND Corporation, MR-969-ICJ, 2000.

Hensler, D., and M. Peterson, "Understanding Mass Personal Injury Litigation: A Socio-Legal Analysis," *Brooklyn Law Review*, Vol. 59, 1993, pp. 961–1064.

Higginson, J., "Proportion of Cancers Due to Occupation," *Preventive Medicine,* Vol. 9, 1980, pp. 180–188.

"Hillsborough Holdings Reorganization Plan, Veil-Piercing Settlement Agreement Confirmed," *Mealey's Litigation Report: Asbestos*, Vol. 10, No. 4, March 17, 1994, p. 19.

Hodara, F. S., and R. J. Stark, "Protecting Distributions for Commercial Creditors in Asbestos-Related Chapter 11 Cases," *Journal of Bankruptcy Law and Practice*, Vol. 10, July/August 2001, pp. 3, 8.

Hodgson, J. T., J. Peto, J. R. Jones, and F. E. Matthews, "Mesothelioma Mortality in Britain: Patterns by Birth Cohort and Occupation," *Annals of Occupational Hygiene,* Vol. 41, Supplement 1, 1997, pp. 129–133.

Hogan, M. D., and D. G. Hoel, "Estimated Cancer Risk Associated with Occupational Asbestos Exposure," *Risk Analysis,* Vol. 1, No. 1, 1981, pp. 67–76.

Horowitz, I., and K. Bordens, "The Effects of Outlier Presence, Plaintiff Population Size, and Aggregation on Simulated Jury Decisions," *Law and Human Behavior,* Vol. 12, 1988, pp. 209–230.

_____, "An Experimental Investigation of Procedural Issues in Complex Tort Trials," *Law and Human Behavior,* Vol. 14, 1990, p. 269.

"Inactive Asbestos Dockets: Are They Easing the Flow of Litigation?" *Columns—Asbestos*, HarrisMartin Publishing, February 12, 2002.

Johnson, W., and E. Heler, "Costs of Asbestos-Associated Disease and Death," *Milbank Memorial Fund Quarterly,* Vol. 61, No. 2, 1983, pp. 177–194.

"Judge Hopes to Resolve 6,000 Cases in Consolidated Trial," *Mealey's Litigation Report: Asbestos 20*, Vol. 5, No. 23, 1991.

"Judge Wolin Appoints Consultants to Assist in Consolidated Proceedings," *Mealey's Asbestos Bankruptcy Report 2*, Vol. 1, No. 6, 2002.

"Jury Returns Mixed Verdict in Phase I of Consolidated Trial," *Mealey's Litigation Report: Asbestos 2*, Vol. 17, No. 23, 2003.

Kakalik, J., P. A. Ebener, W.L.F. Felstiner, G. W. Haggstrom, and M. G. Shanley, *Variation in Asbestos Litigation Compensation and Expenses*, Santa Monica, Calif.: RAND Corporation, R-3132-ICJ, 1984.

Kakalik, J., and N. Pace, *Costs and Compensation Paid in Tort Litigation*, Santa Monica, Calif.: RAND Corporation, R-3391-ICJ, 1986.

Kakalik, J., M. G. Shanley, W.L.F. Felstiner, and P. A. Ebener, *Costs of Asbestos Litigation*, Santa Monica, Calif.: RAND Corporation, R-3042-ICJ, 1983.

Keating, G., "Distributive and Corrective Justice in the Tort Law of Accidents," *Southern California Law Review*, Vol. 74, 2000, pp. 193–224.

Kilburn K. H., and R. Warshaw, "Pulmonary Functional Impairment Associated with Pleural Asbestos Disease," *Chest*, Vol. 98, No. 4, 1990, pp. 965–972.

Kjaergaard, J., and M. Andersson, "Incidence Rates of Malignant Mesothelioma in Denmark and Predicted Future Numbers of Cases Among Men," *Scandanavian Journal of Work and Environmental Health*, Vol. 26, No. 2, 2000, pp. 112–117.

Kritzer, H., "Lawyer Fees and Lawyer Behavior in Litigation: What Does the Empirical Literature Really Say?" *Texas Law Review*, Vol. 80, 2002, p. 1943.

Landrigan, P. J., "Asbestos: Still a Carcinogen," *New England Journal of Medicine*, Vol. 338, No. 22, 1998, pp. 1618–1619.

Levin, S. M., and I. J. Selikoff, "Radiological Abnormalities and Asbestos Exposure Among Custodians of the New York City Board of Education, *Annals of the New York Academy of Sciences*, Vol. 643, 1991, pp. 530–539.

Liddell, F.D.K., A. D. McDonald, and J. C. McDonald, "The 1891–1920 Birth Cohort of Quebec Chrysotile Miners and Millers: Development from 1904 and Mortality to 1992," *Annals of Occupational Hygiene*, Vol. 41, No. 1, 1997, pp. 13–36.

Lilienfeld, D. E., J. S. Mandel, P. Coin, and L. M. Schuman, "Projection of Asbestos-Related Diseases in the United States, 1985–2009," *British Journal of Industrial Medicine*, Vol. 45, 1988, pp. 283–291.

Luce, D., P. Brochard, P. Quenel, C. Salomon-Nekiriai, P. Goldberg, M. A. Billon-Galland, and M. Goldberg, "Malignant Pleural Mesothelioma Associated with Exposure to Tremolite," *Lancet*, Vol. 344, 1994, p. 1777.

Magnani, C., A. Agudo, C. A. Gonzalez, A. Andrion, A. Calleja, E. Chellini, P. Dalmasso, A. Escolar, S. Hernandez, C. Ivaldi, D. Mirabelli, J. Ramirez, D. Turuguet, M. Usel, and B. Terracini, "Multicentric Study on Malignant Pleural Mesothelioma and Non-Occupational Exposure to Asbestos," *British Journal of Cancer*, Vol. 83, No. 1, 2000, pp. 104–111.

Manton, K., "An Evaluation of Strategies for Forecasting the Implications of Occupational Exposure to Asbestos," unpublished report prepared under Contract No. 82-62 for the Congressional Research Service, Government Division, The Library of Congress, 1983.

Manville Personal Injury Settlement Trust, *Financial Statements and Report for the Period Ending September 30, 2000, In re Johns Manville,* reprinted in *Andrews Asbestos Litigation Reporter,* Document Section D, 2000.

Manville Personal Injury Settlement Trust, Claims Resolution Management Corporation, *Selected Operations Data for Presentation at Courts Hearing,* December 13, 2001.

McDonald, A. D., B. W. Case, A. Churg, A. Dufresne, G. W. Gibbs, P. Sebastien, and J. C. McDonald, "Mesothelioma in Quebec Chrysotile Miners and Millers: Epidemiology and Aetiology," *Annals of Occupational Hygiene,* Vol. 41, 1997, pp. 707–719.

McDonald, A. D., and J. C. McDonald, "Malignant Mesothelioma in North America," *Cancer,* Vol. 46, 1980, pp. 1650–1656.

McDonald, J. C., and A. D. McDonald, "Mesothelioma as an Index of Asbestos Impact," in R. Peto and M. Schneiderman, eds., *Quantification of Occupational Cancer,* Banbury Report 9, Cold Spring Harbor, N.Y.: Cold Spring Laboratory, 1981, pp. 73–85.

McGovern, F. E., "Toward a Functional Approach for Managing Complex Litigation," *University of Chicago Law Review,* Vol. 53, 1986, pp. 440–493.

_____, "Resolving Mature Mass Tort Litigation," *Boston University Law Review,* Vol. 69, 1989, pp. 659–694.

_____, "Symposium: National Mass Tort Conference: An Analysis of Mass Torts for Judges," *Texas Law Review,* Vol. 73, 1995.

_____, "Rethinking Cooperation Among Judges in Mass Tort Litigation," *UCLA Law Review,* Vol. 44, 1997, pp. 1851–1870.

_____, "The Tragedy of the Asbestos Commons," *Virginia Law Review,* Vol. 88, 2002, p. 1721.

"MetLife Settles 35,000 Cases for at Least $125 Million," *Mealey's Litigation Report: Asbestos 4,* Vol. 9, No. 10, 1994.

"Michigan High Court Hears Docket Arguments," *Mealey's Litigation Report: Asbestos 19,* Vol. 19, No. 1, 2004.

"Michigan Supreme Court to Consider Implementing Inactive Asbestos Docket," *Mealey's Asbestos Bankruptcy Report 13,* Vol. 3, No. 3, October 2003.

"Miss. Jury Returns $150 Verdict Against AC&S, Dresser Industries, 3M Corp.," *Mealey's Litigation Report: Asbestos 1,* Vol. 16, No. 19, 2001.

"Mississippi Jury Awards $48.5 Million in 12 Cases," *Andrews Asbestos Litigation Report 1,* Vol. 20, No. 12, 1998.

Mnookin, R. H., and L. Kornhauser, "Bargaining in the Shadow of the Law: The Case of Divorce," *Yale Law Review,* Vol. 88, 1979, pp. 950–957.

National Center for State Courts, *Examining the Work of State Courts, 2001,* Williamsburg, Va.: National Center for State Courts, 2001.

National Institute for Occupational Safety and Health (NIOSH), *Worker Health Chartbook, 2004,* prepublication copy, Department of Health and Human Services, Centers for

Disease Control and Prevention, DHHS (NIOSH) Publication No. 2004-146, 2004 (http://www.cdc.gov/niosh/docs/chartbook/pdfs/Chartbook_2004_Prepub.pdf; last accessed July 1, 2004).

Nicholson, W. J., G. Perkel, and I. J. Selikoff, "Cancer from Occupational Asbestos Exposure: Projections 1980–2000," in R. Peto and M. Schneiderman, eds., *Quantification of Occupational Cancer,* Banbury Report 9, Cold Spring Harbor, N.Y.: Cold Spring Laboratory, 1981, pp. 87–111.

_____, "Occupational Exposure to Asbestos: Population at Risk and Projected Mortality 1980–2030," *American Journal of Industrial Medicine*, Vol. 3, 1982, pp. 259–311.

"OCF Admits to Liability in Massive West Virginia Consolidation," *Mealey's Litigation Report: Asbestos 1,* Vol. 9, No. 6, 1994.

Ostrom, B., et al., "What Are Tort Awards Really Like? The Untold Story from the State Courts," *Law & Policy*, Vol. 14, 1992, pp. 77–106.

_____, "A Step Above Anecdote: A Profile of the Civil Jury in the 1990s," *Judicature*, Vol. 79, 1996, pp. 233–241.

"Owens Corning Files Motion Seeking Appointment of Mediator in Chapter 11 Case," *Mealey's Asbestos Bankruptcy Report 11,* Vol. 1, No. 11, 2002.

Parloff, R., "Welcome to the New Asbestos Scandal," *Fortune,* September 6, 2004, p. 186.

Peterson, J. T., S. D. Greenberg, and P. A. Buffler, "Non-Asbestos-Related Malignant Mesothelioma: A Review," *Cancer,* Vol. 54, 1984, pp. 951–960.

Peterson, M., "Giving Away Money: Comparative Comments on Claims Resolution Facilities," *Law and Contemporary Problems*, Vol. 53, 1990, pp. 113–136.

Peterson, M., and M. Selvin, "Mass Justice: "The Limited and Unlimited Power of Courts," *Law and Contemporary Problems*, Vol. 54, No. 3, 1991, pp. 227–247.

Peto, J., A. Decarli, C. La Vecchia, F. Levi, E. Negri, "The European Mesothelioma Epidemic," *British Journal of Cancer*, Vol. 79, 1999, pp. 666–672.

Peto, J., B. E. Henderson, and M. C. Pike, "Trends in Mesothelioma Incidence in the United States and the Forecast Epidemic Due to Asbestos Exposure During World War II," in R. Peto and M. Schneiderman, eds., *Quantification of Occupational Cancer,* Banbury Report 9, Cold Spring Harbor, N.Y.: Cold Spring Laboratory, 1981, pp. 51–72.

Peto, J., J. T. Hodgson, F. E. Matthews, and J. R. Jones, "Continuing Increase in Mesothelioma Mortality in Britain," *Lancet,* Vol. 345, No. 8949, 1995, pp. 535–539.

"Plaintiffs Question Allocation of Damages in $169 Million Mississippi Asbestos Settlement," *Mealey's Litigation Report: Asbestos 1,* Vol. 14, No. 24, 2000.

Plevin, M., R. Ebert, and L. Epley, "Pre-Packaged Asbestos Bankruptcies: A Flawed Solution," *South Texas Law Review,* Vol. 44, 2003, p. 883.

Plevin, M., and P. Kalish, "What's Behind the Recent Wave of Asbestos Bankruptcies?" *Mealey's Litigation Report: Asbestos*, April 2001.

Price, B., "Analysis of Current Trends in United States Mesothelioma," *American Journal of Epidemiology*, Vol. 145, No. 3, 1997, pp. 211–218.

Price, B., and A. Ware, "Mesothelioma Trends in the United States: An Update Based on Surveillance, Epidemiology and End Results Program Data for 1973 Through 2003," *American Journal of Epidemiology*, Vol. 159, No. 2, 2004, pp. 107–112.

"Rapid American Hit with 5.5 Punitive Multiplier," *Mealey's Litigation Report: Asbestos 4,* 1994.

Renner, R., "Asbestos in the Air," *Scientific American*, February 21, 2000.

Rheingold, P., *Mass Tort Litigation*, Deerfield, Ill.: Clark, Boardman, and Callaghan, 1996.

"Road Map to B&W's Defenses to Asbestos Personal-Injury Claims," *In re Babcock & Wilcox Co.,* 2001 U.S. Dist. LEXIS 16741 (E.D. La. 2001) (No. 00-0588), 2001.

Rothstein, P. F., "What Courts Can Do in the Face of the Never Ending Asbestos Crisis," *Mississippi Law Review*, Vol. 71, No. 1, Fall 2001, pp. 1–34.

Rourke, D. L., "1997 and 2000 Grace Asbestos PI Claims Sample Design, Methodology and Results," Appendix K, *Debtors' Consolidated Reply in Support of Their Motion for Entry of Case Management Order, Establishment of a Bar Date, Approval of the Claim Forms and Approval of the Notice Program,* United States Bankruptcy Court for the District of Delaware, November 9, 2001.

Saks, M., and P. Blanck, "Justice Improved: The Unrecognized Benefits of Aggregation and Sampling in the Trial of Mass Torts," *Stanford Law Review*, Vol. 44, 1992.

Schuck, P. H., *Agent Orange on Trial: Mass Toxic Disasters in the Courts,* Cambridge, Mass.: Belknap Press, 1987.

_____, "The Worst Should Go First: Deferral Registries in Asbestos Litigation," *Judicature*, Vol. 75, 1992, pp. 318–328.

Schwartz, G., "Mixed Theories of Tort Law: Affirming Both Deterrence and Corrective Justice," *Texas Law Review*, Vol. 75, 1997, pp. 1801–1834.

Selikoff, I. J., "Constraints in Estimating Occupational Contributions to Current Cancer Mortality in the United States," in R. Peto and M. Schneiderman, eds., *Quantification of Occupational Cancer,* Banbury Report 9, Cold Spring Harbor, N.Y.: Cold Spring Harbor Laboratory, 1981, pp. 19–36.

_____, *Disability Compensation for Asbestos-Associated Disease in the United States,* New York: Environmental Sciences Laboratory, Mount Sinai School of Medicine of the City University of New York, June 1982a.

_____, *Disability Compensation for Asbestos-Related Disease in the United States,* Washington, D.C.: U.S. Department of Labor, June 1982b.

_____, "Asbestos Disease—1990–2020: The Risks of Asbestos Risk Assessment," *Toxicology and Industrial Health*, Vol. 7, Nos. 5–6, 1991, pp. 117–127.

Selikoff, I., J. Churg, and E. Hammond, "The Occurrence of Asbestosis Among Insulation Workers in the United States, *Annals of the New York Academy of Sciences*, Vol. 132, 1965, pp. 139–155.

————, "Asbestos Exposure and Neoplasia," *Journal of the American Medical Association*, Vol. 188, 1964, pp. 22–26.

Selikoff, I. J., E. C. Hammond, and H. Seidman, "Mortality Experience of Insulation Workers in the United States and Canada, 1943–1976," *Annals of the New York Academy of Sciences*, Vol. 330, 1979, pp. 91–116.

Selikoff, I., and D. Lee, *Asbestos and Disease*, New York: Academic Press, 1978.

Selikoff, I. J., and H. Seidman, "Asbestos-Associated Deaths Among Insulation Workers in the United States and Canada, 1967–1987," *Annals of the New York Academy of Sciences*, Vol. 643, 1991, pp. 1–14.

Selvin, M., and L. Picus, *The Debate over Jury Performance: Observations from a Recent Asbestos Case*, Santa Monica, Calif.: RAND Corporation, R-3479-ICJ, 1987.

"Senate Judiciary Committee Issues Report on Trust Fund Legislation," *Mealey's Litigation Report: Asbestos 6*, Vol. 18, No. 13, 2003.

Shanley, M., and M. A. Peterson, *Comparative Justice: Civil Jury Verdicts in San Francisco and Cook Counties, 1959–1980*, Santa Monica, Calif.: RAND Corporation, R-3006-ICJ, 1983.

Siskind, F. B., "The Cost of Compensating Asbestos Victims Under the Occupational Disease Compensation Act of 1983," *Risk Analysis*, Vol. 7, No. 1, 1987, pp. 59–69.

Smith, M., "Resolving Asbestos Claims: The Manville Personal Injury Settlement Trust," *Law and Contemporary Problems*, Vol. 53, 1990, pp. 27–36.

Sobol, R., *Bending the Law: The Story of the Dalkon Shield Bankruptcy*, Chicago: University of Chicago Press, 1991.

Spirtas, R., E. F. Heineman, L. Bernstein, G. W. Beebe, R. J. Keehn, A. Stark, B. L. Harlow, and J. Benichou, "Malignant Mesothelioma: Attributable Risk of Asbestos Exposure," *Occupational and Environmental Medicine*, Vol. 51, 1994, pp. 804–811.

Stallard, E., "Product Liability Forecasting for Asbestos-Related Personal Injury Claims: A Multidisciplinary Approach," New York Academy of Sciences, 2001.

"Statistical Analysis of Multidistrict Litigation," Judicial Panel on Multidistrict Litigation, 2004 (www.jpml.uscourts.gov; last accessed March 2005).

Stayner, L. T., D. A. Dankovic, and R. A. Lemen, "Occupational Exposure to Chrysotile Asbestos and Cancer Risk: A Review of the Amphibole Hypothesis," *American Journal of Public Health*, Vol. 86, No. 2, 1996, pp. 179–186.

Stiglitz, J. E., J. M. Orszag, and P. R. Orszag, *The Impact of Asbestos Liabilities on Workers in Bankrupt Firms*, Washington, D.C.: SEBAGO Associates, December 2002.

Strickler, H. D., J. J. Goedert, S. S. Devesa, J. Lahey, J. F. Fraumeni, and P. S. Rosenberg, "Trends in U.S. Pleural Mesothelioma Incidence Rates Following Simian Virus 40

Contamination of Early Poliovirus Vaccines," *Journal of the National Cancer Institute,* Vol. 95, 2003, pp. 38–45.

Strickler, H. D., P. S. Rosenberg, S. S. Devesa, J. Hertel, J. F. Fraumeni, Jr., and J. J. Goedert, "Contamination of Poliovirus Vaccines with Simian Virus 40 (1955–1963) and Subsequent Cancer Rates," *Journal of the American Medical Association,* Vol. 279, No. 4, 1998, pp. 292–295.

Sugarman, S. D., "Doing Away with Tort Law," *California Law Review,* Vol. 73, 1985, p. 555.

Sunstein, C., D. Kahneman, and D. Schkade, "Assessing Punitive Damages (with Notes on Cognition and Valuation in Law)," *Yale Law Journal,* Vol. 107, 1998.

Symposium, "Mass Tortes: Serving Up Just Desserts," *Cornell University Law Review,* Vol. 80, 1995.

"Texas Legislature Passes Tort Reform Bill Limiting Successor Liability Damages," *Mealey's Litigation Report: Asbestos 9,* Vol. 18, No. 10, 2003.

"3rd Circuit Judge Orders 5 Bankruptcies to Be Consolidated in Del. Court," *Mealey's Asbestos Bankruptcy Report 2,* Vol. 1, No. 4, 2001.

"Tobacco Lawyers Want New Asbestos Trial Site," *[Mississippi] Clarion-Ledger,* March 17, 2001, p. 10A.

"Trade Association Asks Mississippi High Court to Reject Mass Joinder," *Mealey's Litigation Report: Asbestos 5,* Vol. 14, No. 14, 1999.

Trangsrud, R., "Mass Trials in Mass Tort Cases: A Dissent," *University of Illinois Law Review,* Vol. 1989, 1989.

"Trials: Damages Awarded in West Virginia Second Phase," *Mealey's Litigation Report: Asbestos 15,* Vol. 5, No. 9, 1990.

Tweedale, G., *Magic Mineral to Killer Dust: Turner and Newall and the Asbestos Hazard,* Oxford, UK: Oxford University Press, 2000.

Tyler, T., "A Psychological Perspective on the Settlement of Mass Tort Claims," *Law and Contemporary Problems,* Vol. 53, 1990, pp. 199–205.

"Union Carbide Left as Remaining Defendant in W.Va. Consolidated Trial," *Mealey's Litigation Report: Asbestos 1,* Vol. 17, No. 18, 2002.

"Union Carbide Liable for Thousands of Asbestos Claims, West Virginia Jury Finds," *Mealey's Litigation Report: Asbestos,* October 24, 2002.

"UNR Trust Lowers Payment Percentage in Light of Increased Asbestos Claims," *Mealey's Litigation Report: Asbestos,* Vol. 15, No. 21, December 1, 2000.

U.S. Department of the Census, *2000, Statistical Abstract of the United States: The National Data Book,* 120th ed., Washington, D.C.: U.S. Department of the Census, 2000.

U.S. Environmental Protection Agency, *EPA Asbestos Materials Ban: Clarification,* May 18, 1999.

"Utex Industries Files Prepackaged Bankruptcy Plan; Confirmation Order Issued," *Mealey's Asbestos Bankruptcy Report 2,* Vol. 4, No. 1, 2004.

Walker, A., J. E. Loughlin, E. R. Friedlander, K. J. Rothman, and N. A. Dreyer, "Projections of Asbestos-Related Disease 1980–2009," *Journal of Occupational Medicine*, Vol. 25, No. 5, 1983, pp. 409–425.

Weinstein, J., *Individual Justice In Mass Tort Litigation: The Effect of Class Actions, Consolidations and Other Multiparty Devices*, Evanston, Ill.: Northwestern University Press, 1995.

Weiss, L., "Bankruptcy Resolution: Direct Costs and Violation of Priority of Claims," *Journal of Financial Economics*, Vol. 27, 1990, pp. 285–314.

"Welding Rod, Wire, and Cable Defendants Held Liable in West Virginia Consolidation," *Mealey's Litigation Report: Asbestos 20,* Vol. 10, No. 16, 1995.

White, M., "Survey Evidence on Business Bankruptcy," in J. S. Bhandari and L. A. Weiss, eds., *Corporate Bankruptcy: Economic and Legal Perspective*, Cambridge University Press, 1996.

Willging, T., *Asbestos Case Management: Pretrial and Trial Procedures*, Washington, D.C.: Federal Judicial Center, 1985.

Yano, E., Z-M Wang, X-R Wang, M-Z Wang, and Y-J Lan, "Cancer Mortality Among Workers Exposed to Amphibole-Free Chrysotile Asbestos," *American Journal of Epidemiology*, Vol. 154, No. 6, 2001, pp. 538–543.